Survivor

Sam Pivnik
Survivor

Auschwitz, the Death March, and
My Fight for Freedom

St. Martin's Press ⚕ New York

www.stmartins.com

ISBN 978-1-250-02952-2 (hardcover)
ISBN 978-1-250-02953-9 (e-book)

St. Martin's Press books may be purchased for educational, business, or promotional use.
For information on bulk purchases, please contact Macmillan Corporate and Premium Sales
Department at 1-800-221-7945 extension 5442 or write specialmarkets@macmillan.com.

First published in Great Britain by Hodder & Stoughton, an Hachette UK company

First U.S. Edition: June 2013

10 9 8 7 6 5 4 3 2 1

'There is a straight line from "You have no right to live among us as Jews" to "You have no right to live among us" to "You have no right to live".'

Raul Hilberg

Acknowledgements

There are so many people I would like to thank for bringing my story to publication that it is really impossible to name them all, but some stand out and so to them I would like to give my special thanks: Philip Appleby, for his patience and unfailing support – this book would have been impossible without him; Andrew Lownie, my agent, for believing in this project; Rupert Lancaster, Kate Miles and all the team at Hodder and Stoughton; all of the researchers and writers who have worked with me over the years, in particular Danielle Fox and Adrian Weale; my friends and supporters Ray Appleby, David Breuer-Weil and Alan James; Judith Hassan and all the staff at the Hendon Holocaust Centre; Chris Brassett; Jill Pivnik, my sister-in-law and Mei Trow, my able ghost writer who has brought my memories to life. But most especially I should thank all who have not been with me since I was a boy; my mother and father, my brothers and sisters and all my friends from Bedzin. They gave me the strength to carry on.

Sam Pivnik

I would like to thank four people in particular for their help on this book. First and foremost – as always – my wife Carol, who has spent many hours typing the manuscript, even with a dislocated elbow; my son, Taliesin, who

– again, as always – was an indefatigable researcher, gentle critic and, on this occasion, back-up typist; Greta Hofmann, for her indispensable translation work from various German texts; and Bryan Jackson, for the use of his extensive Holocaust library.

M.J.T.

Picture Acknowledgements

Author's collection: 1, 2 above and centre, 3 above, 8 above, 9, 10, 11, 12, 13. Aish UK: 14 above, 15. akg-images: 4 above, 5 above, 8 centre. Getty Images: 3 below, 4 below, 6 below (photo David Clapp). Courtesy of Bernd Janssen: 13 below. ©Estate of Mieczysław Kościelniak: 7 above. Adrian Weale: 6 above and centre, 14 below, 16. Yad Vashem The Holocaust Martyrs' and Heroes' Remembrance Authority: 2 below, 3 centre, 5 below. United States Holocaust Memorial Museum, Washington DC: 7 below.

Every reasonable effort has been made to trace the copyright holders, but if there are any errors or omissions, Hodder & Stoughton will be pleased to insert the appropriate acknowledgement in any subsequent printings or editions.

Glossary of Terms

Aktions – The removal of Jews, Gypsies and other 'enemies' of the Third Reich to the concentration camps.

Aliyah Bet – The codename given to the illegal immigration of Jews to Palestine in the 1930s and 40s.

Appell – Roll-call at the camps.

Appellplatz – The square where prisoners would assemble for roll-call.

Arschlöcher – German insult; arsehole.

Asos – Short for 'antisocial ones' – a category of prisoners including the homeless, long-term unemployed, sex offenders etc.

Baumeisters – Civilian engineers (see also *Steigers*).

Bedzin – Author's home town.

Berchtesgaden – Hitler's Bavarian retreat.

Berufsverbrecher – Professional criminals who worked in the camps.

Blockältester – Block senior.

Blockschreiber – Roll-call clerk.

Blocksperre – Lock-down.

Byelorussia – Belarus.

Dreckjuden! – German insult; 'Dirt Jew!'

Edelweiss Piraten – Anti-Nazi movement in Germany.

Einsatzgruppe – German taskforce, execution squad.

Eretz Yisrael – The Biblical Land of Israel; Greater Israel.

Fall Weiss – The Nazi's strategic plan for invading Poland.

Familienlager – Family camp.

Gau – German district.

Gauleiter – District leader.

Gordonia – A Zionist youth movement.

Hachshara – Preparation for emigration to Palestine/Israel.

Häftlingskrankenbau – Prisoners' hospital.

Haganah – Jewish Defence Force; paramilitary organisation.

Hausfrau – Housewife.

Heder – Religious primary school.

Hefker – Jewish term for being free of responsibilities; from the legal term to denote an ownerless property.

Hitlerjugend – Hitler Youth.

Jedem das Seine – 'To each, his own' – motto on gates of Mauthausen camp.

Judenfieber – Typhus; lit. 'Jew fever'.

Judenrat – Jewish council.

Judenrein – Cleansed of Jews.

Kaddish – Jewish prayer for the dead.

Kapos – Camp foremen, recruited from the ranks of the prisoners.

Kappellmeister – Bandmaster.

Kindertransporte – The transport of children – either to safety, or to the death camps.

Knochenmühle – 'The bone-grinder' – nickname for Mauthausen camp.

Kojen – Three-tiered bunk.

Kommando – German term for unit.

Kriegsmarine – German Navy.

Lagerälteste – Camp seniors.

Lagerführer – Camp commandant.

Lagerschreiber – Camp clerk.

Lausbub – German insult; rascal.

Lebensraum – Literally, living space, Hitler's foreign policy for expanding the Reich.

Machal – The Hebrew acronym for 'Overseas Volunteers'; soldiers who fought for the new state of Israel.

Maurerschule – Builders' school.

Muselmänner – Muslims (col. for starving camp inmates).

Oberkapo – Chief *Kapo*.

Operation Barbarossa – Codename for German invasion of Russia.

Organisation – Slang for black market operations in the camps.

Piepels – Boys used for sex by camp guards and *Kapos*.

Premiumschein – Ticket for canteen.

Rampe Kommando – Platform detachment.

Rapportführer – Sergeant Major, commander of Block.

Raus! – Out!

Reichsfeldmarschall – German rank of Field Marshal.

Rottenführer – Nazi Party section leader.

Scheissjude – Racial insult (lit. 'shit-Jew').

Schiffchen – Soft side-cap.

Schnell! – Quickly!

Schutzhäftlinge – Political prisoners (lit. protective prisoners).

Shabbat – Jewish Sabbath.

Sheitel – Traditional black wig worn by Jewish women.

Shem Yisborach – Hebrew name for God.

Sicherheitsdienst – German security service.

Smetana – Sour cream.

Sonderausweis – Passes that stated you were essential to the war effort.

Sonderbehandlung – Special treatment.

Sonderkommando – Special units; inmates who were forced to operate the gas chambers and crematoria.

Stahlhelmes – Steel helmets.

Stalags – Prisoner-of-war camp.

Steigers – Civilian engineers (see also *Baumeisters*).

Stiebel – Jewish prayer room.

Stube – Side room.

Stubendienst – Camp orderlies.

Sturmabteilung – Brown Shirts.

Sturmbrigade Dirlewanger – Notorious SS military unit composed of German prisoners.

Totenkopf – Death's Head units of SS.

Treif – Non-kosher food.

Treuhänder – A trusty; trusted helper.

Umgeseidelt im Osten – Resettlement in the East.

Untermenschen – Literally, subhuman. A Nazi term for Jews.

Unteroffizier/Unterscharführer – Corporal (Army/SS).

Volksdeutsche – Poles of German origin.

Vorarbeiter – Foreman.

Wehrmacht – Germany's armed forces.

Winterhilfe – Contributions to help soldiers on the Eastern Front.

Yad Vashem – Holocaust History Museum in Jerusalem.

Yiddishkeit – Jewishness.

Zyklon B – Chemical compound used in the gas chambers.

Contents

PROLOGUE

Facing the Angel

There was no calendar in Auschwitz. No dates, no anniversaries, nothing to mark the passing of time. For the lucky ones, those of us who survived, night followed day and days became weeks. Not many of us outlived the passage of months. So I don't know exactly when I fell ill. It was probably December 1943, freezing as only the Polish winter can freeze. In my thin striped tunic and trousers I should have felt bitterly cold, but that particular morning I felt hot and sweaty.

We slept five to a *kojen*, a three-tiered bunk, crammed together on the hard, damp wooden boards and it took me a while to take stock – to realise that all that shared body heat should have faded now I was standing alone. My head throbbed and the glands in my neck were painful and inflamed. In the days before the war if you felt ill you went to the doctor. If you couldn't afford a doctor, you stayed in bed, wrapped up warm and took an aspirin. In Auschwitz there were no doctors like that. And the only hospital was a place of death – it was the HKB, the *Häftlingskrankenbau*, the prisoners' hospital, known to us as all as the waiting-room for the gas chamber. I buttoned up my jacket and tried not to shiver as the raging fever gave way to chills.

I barely remember my work on the Rampe that day. Presumably the trains rolled in as they always did, with the rattling of trucks and snort of the engines, the hissing escape of steam; then the sliding of bolts and the poor, damned souls emerging, blinking into the sky's brightness. I'd seen them so often before, I barely noticed them now. Toddlers clinging to their mothers, crying; women clutching their children; Orthodox elders trying to talk to the *Kommando*, asking for an explanation of the inexplicable; old people, wild-eyed and shaking, limping along the Rampe at the prods of the SS men.

I knew which of those to avoid, whose eyes not to meet, which snarling, snapping dog to be wary of. And I went about my business as I always did, dragging the stiff, shit-caked bodies out of the trucks, trying not to breathe in the stench. We laid them down on the concrete, far behind the lines of the living, who were already being marched away. To the right, life. To the left, the gas. No rhyme. No reason. Just the random flick of an immaculately gloved finger. Right. Left. Left. Right. Left. Left.

I remember staring along the Rampe that day. It looked like a battlefield, as it always did. The bodies were being carted away, making way for the piles of coats and bags, a girl's doll, somebody's glasses. Everybody had been told to leave their belongings where they were. They'd all be returned to them later, after the showers. After the de-lousing. After the Zyklon B.

It was starting to whirl in my brain, the shouts of the SS and the *Kapos* echoing and re-echoing. Everything suddenly seemed far, far away – the snorting train and the disappearing columns of new arrivals. Work sets you free. '*Raus, raus!*' '*Schnell!*' 'You fucking Jew scum.' Work sets you free . . .

*

When I woke up, with a start, I didn't know where I was. There was a greyness everywhere, smudged by barely moving patches of black. As I focused and my head cleared, I knew exactly where I was. This was the hospital block, the whitewashed walls an attempt at sterility. The black patches were patients, like me, still in the striped uniform of the prison inmates.

How many hours or days I was there, I don't know. I was just grateful for the bed, which felt soft and yielding after the weeks on the hard boards. The mattresses were paper filled with wood shavings, but not as rough at least as the usual sacking and straw. We still slept three to a bunk, all of us infection cases in together. The soup was just a little thicker and there was an extra crust of bread. Little things like that give you a renewed longing for life; for little things like that, some men would kill each other in the main camp. The fever came and went, with a throbbing head, a chronic aching in my arms and legs, a sense of crippling weakness. I was seventeen and I felt like an old man.

I had typhus, what they used to call all over Europe 'gaol fever' because it broke out so frequently in prisons. Entirely apt, then, that I should get it in Auschwitz-Birkenau – the ultimate prison. Except that here they called it *Judenfieber*, Jew Fever. If you look up the symptoms today, you'll find the type of the disease I had was *Rickettsia typhi*, most common where hygiene is poor and temperatures low. Temperatures ran to 106° Fahrenheit and give you a hacking cough – a cough I still have today. Without proper treatment, the death rate can be as high as 60%.

Back then, I didn't know any of this. Neither did I know that the raw onion they gave me to eat in place of medicine did me no good at all. All I knew was that I was desperately ill but the will to survive drove me on, made it possible for me to get out of my bunk bed and stand to attention with the other patients the day that Mengele came. I had seen him often of course on the Rampe, the polite, handsome, immaculately uniformed SS officer, glancing at the prisoners as they tumbled out of the trucks. A pointed finger. That was all it was, in those expensive grey doeskin gloves. A finger to the right was life; to the left was death. That was the way my family had gone, losers in the ghastly lottery the Nazis had set up.

He was wearing his white coat today, open over his tunic. There was a stethoscope around his neck. Around him clucked a number of orderlies, SS men with clipboards and lists: the ward round from Hell. By the time he reached my bed I was literally shaking with terror. We all knew that anyone unable to stand by their beds went straight to the gas. But this was a man who had spent the previous months making selections at a glance, deciding life or death with just a look. What was I? Five foot three, five foot four? I weighed less than I should have after the experiences of the ghetto and this camp; but the food I'd scrounged from the Rampe gave me more strength than most. I was trembling uncontrollably from head to foot, unable to stop shaking.

It took him seconds. The finger pointed to the left. The gas chamber. The crematorium. Oblivion. Did I think, in those terrible seconds, that I would see my family again? That all this misery would soon be over? Perhaps. But the overriding urge was to live; to see another dawn; eat one more crust of bread. I burst into tears, throwing myself at his feet, blurting out something about wanting to be shot, not gassed. I think I even kissed Mengele's boots, polished like mirrors as they always were.

The boots moved away. And to this day I don't know why. All the accounts of Mengele that I have ever read agree that he couldn't bear to be touched by a Jew. As a doctor he examined plenty of them, but that was on his own terms, for his own purposes. I had thrown myself on him and I could have faced an instant bullet for that. I never looked into his face, so to this day I don't know why he changed his mind. Did he recognise me from the Rampe? Did he relent because he realised in my gabbling that I spoke German? Was it actually Mengele himself or an underling who had motives I cannot guess at? All I know is that the ward round moved on, the boots clicking on the floor and the finger pointing elsewhere, at some other poor bastard. The Angel of Death had gone.

The orderlies started moving out the immobile, to prepare them to become immobile for ever. One of them, a rare kindly face among so much hostility, leaned over as he picked me up and said, 'Don't worry, Szlamek, you can stay here.' I collapsed into bed, crying all over again.

In the three or four days I spent in the hospital, I had time to think. I had come as close to death as anyone is ever likely to and moments – seconds – like that make you concentrate. I was seventeen. My family were gone. I was alone. But it hadn't always been like that. Once – and it was actually only four years ago – there had been a magic time when no one thought or spoke of death. It was a time of life. It was my childhood.

I

The Garden of Eden

I t's the little things I remember – the singing of the birds in the high woods; the taste of the blackberries, wild and sweet by the roadside; and over it all, under a sky that seemed forever blue, the heady scent of the pine trees. I remember the rutted roads and the smell and rattle of the bus that took us there – eighty kilometres through a magic land; the furthest I had travelled in my life.

It was summer, of course, when we went there – just a holiday like any other. But not like any other. Summers like that would not come again, except in my fondest dreams. Summers that should have faded from my memory but refused to fade. Memories that may just have kept me sane in the years that followed. And I can hear them now, the friends and family crowding round, laughing, nodding, the old men tugging their beards, the women hugging us and clucking round, preparing the food. 'Here are the relatives,' was the first shout we'd hear, 'from Bedzin!' And for those few weeks, Bedzin could have been on the far side of the moon.

I can see the tables now, groaning with the food of the countryside. Butter, rich and yellow; the *smetana* cream, sharp and pure and richer than anything you can buy today. Cheese that melted in the mouth but bit back; the cheese with holes (Emmenthal or Jarlsberg), the *schweitzer* cake. Bread that smelled of Heaven dipped in *smetana*; pastries you'd give your right arm for. We ran through the woods, my brothers and I, running off a meal like that – Nathan, nearly a man in that last summer; Majer and Wolf, trying to keep up. Josek was too little to join us; just a babe in arms and never far from my mother's side. We kicked a rag ball around in the long grass, rode the tough little ponies of the Polish plain, splashed each other and swam in the cool, brown water of the river, dappled with trailing willows.

In the mornings, as the sun climbed lazily into the blue, we would sit in my uncle's workshop at the front of the little yellow-painted house in the market square. He was a shoesmith and I can still smell the leather and hear the steady tap-tap of his awl as he crafted the boots that our people had made for generations. They were tall and elegant, in rich mahogany colours or glistening black, ordered by the army or sold on consignment to wealthy riders. Uncle had been a handsome young man – I remember the photographs – but now he was an elder of the town, with a beard to match. He had status; we boys knew that. But when he measured our feet among the leather scraps and the gleaming lasts, all that was forgotten and he'd tickle us and express amazement at how big our feet were.

Another of my uncles was a butcher and he had a fine horse that he used to pull his meat cart. Sometimes he'd let us ride the animal through the town square, with its huge synagogue that looked like a castle to me.

Beyond the square the bustle of the town reminded us of home, but it was *different*. They were our people, of our faith and our past, but they were also the inhabitants of a magic land. I had known them all, ever since I could remember, because we saw them every summer. I last saw them when I was eleven. And I never saw them again.

The Garden of Eden had a name – it was Wodzislaw, eighty kilometres from my home, lying between the rivers Oder and Vistula. The water us kids splashed in was one of the several tributaries that ran through Wodzislaw, probably the Lesnica or Zawadka, I can't remember now. The meteorological office will tell you that its rainiest month is July, but that's not how I remember it. The sun always shone – on the synagogue built there in 1826, on the Christian monastery founded by Duke Wladyslaw of Opole centuries before, even on the otherwise grim derricks of the coal mines.

People have a stereotypical image of Jews as city-dwellers, urbanites scurrying the streets in search of a buck. The most famous Jew in English literature is Shylock and he came from Venice, in Shakespeare's day the most thriving marketplace in the world (and that at a time when there weren't any Jews in England). But when I was growing up in Poland there were Jews in all walks of life – or at least there were, before those walks were closed to us. My mother's people in Wodzislaw were country people. One of my aunts was Lima Novarsky. Her first name means flower and she got on famously with her landlady, a Christian Pole. Another of my aunts kept a mill. Wodzislaw may have been granted the status of a city under the Magdeburg Laws of the Middle Ages, but it was really just a country town; all my Wodzislaw relatives kept animals – sheep, goats, chickens.

For three or four weeks every year we ran in the grass of this Eden, and for us, at the time, the greatest of all misfortunes was that at the end of the holiday we had to go home.

Home was Bedzin, a town on the banks of the Przemsza River that ran into the Vistula. Its first mention in the history books came a little before my time; in 1301 it was a fishing village and acquired its city status fifty-odd years later under the same Magdeburg Rights that elevated Wodzislaw. What dominated the old city's skyline was the castle of Kazimerz the Great. It started out as a wooden fortress on a hill but Kazimerz rebuilt it in stone, with a circular keep and walls four metres thick and twelve metres high. It was there, on the hill over the Przemsza, to guard the Polish border against the constant eastward sweep of the Silesians. In the Middle Ages, the town had fairs and was an important trading post in the south of Poland; so important that the Silesians and later the Swedes did their best to burn it to the ground.

But it was the other building on the Bedzin skyline that coloured my life more than I realised, a building that is not there today: the great synagogue. The first Jews are recorded in the village long before the synagogue. They were there in 1226, worked the land and paid taxes to the Christian Church. By the fourteenth century they had turned to trade and money-lending, of which the Church officially disapproved. Under King Wladislaw I, Jews were given rights and equal status with the Christians of Bedzin, but gradually a change took place. In the twelfth century the general message from Gentile governments was: 'You have no right to live among us as Jews'; by the sixteenth century, it was changing to: 'You have no right to live among us.' In 1538 Jews had to wear yellow hats as a mark of their 'difference'.

But the Jews prospered and the arrival of new economies in the nineteenth century saw the advent of coal mining and tin production. By then, Bedzin was Russian and the world had turned. Historians have described Poland as a 'political football', kicked around by stronger countries just as us lads kicked our rag ball in the alleyways of the town. The 1897 Russian census records that Bedzin had a 51% Jewish population; by 1921, in the years before I was born, this figure had risen to 62%.

There had been a synagogue on the hill below the castle since the seventeenth century, but the building I remember was built in 1881. There was another one and, in my grandfather's time, more than eighty prayer houses. I was born into a vibrant, if poor, Jewish community and the great synagogue, recently rebuilt in the year of my birth, was the only one in southern Poland designed and decorated by Jews. Chaim Hanft was the architect – I can still see the huge exit door with its gleaming brass. Mosze Apelboin painted the vast fresco that filled the east wall with colour; Szmul Cygler daubed his unmistakeable style to the west. It was folk art, the art of a people who had made Bedzin their own, and it portrayed the ancient history of those people – I remember the animals marching two by two into the Ark with Noah. As the writer Josef Harif put it, Bedzin was 'a characteristic Jewish city with characteristic Jews, Jews hammered on a steel foundation, born in sanctity to maintain their *Yiddishkeit* [Jewishness] until the time of the Messiah.'

Yet even in the decade of my birth, Bedzin was a town of contrasts. There were different sounds ringing in the streets, and not just from the ghost of the rabbi's assistant

Abram Kaplan, whose booming voice echoed down the alleyways around the great synagogue '*Sha! Sha!*' – 'Quiet! Quiet!' In the old town the dialect was harsh and guttural, like the German spoken in Vienna. In the newer areas that stretched along the river, newcomers spoke a softer Polish, Yiddish and Czech. It was a city of wealth – powerful business leaders like the Furstenberg family employed hundreds – and a city of the desperately poor, like the beggarwoman called Crazy Sara who froze to death in the streets in the grim ice of my second winter.

The non-Jews were Catholic Poles with their church on the hill and Silesian Germans, a reminder that Bedzin had, at various times in its past, belonged to Prussia, Tsarist Russia and the Austro-Hungarian empire of the Hapsburgs. At home we spoke Yiddish, Polish, German and even, although we found it funny and didn't really understand it, a little of the English my father had picked up in London.

Today you have to go on-line to see the places I remember. Kazimerz's castle is there still, as a ruin, but it was a ruin when I was a kid. I remember the old market square, with its cattle, its horses, its chickens and the coloured awnings of the stalls. When I was four they knocked down the nineteenth-century railway station and built a new one, all flat roofs and modern detailing, in the best tradition of the Art Deco movement that was sweeping all Europe. The Third of May Square had a huge Art Deco statue in the centre of its tree-lined circle, a naked woman reaching into the clouds. There were trams and buses, trucks and the occasional car to remind us all that the twentieth century was here. And alongside them plodded the little ponies shackled to their carts, reminding us of an older Bedzin, an older culture smiling at us from the safety of a thousand years.

But most of all, in the faded photographs and the flashes of my memory, what comes back is Number 77 Modzejowska Street and the courtyard there. This is where I came into this world on 1 September 1926. All my life – all everybody's life – is a series of chances, of maybes, of what ifs. One of these surrounded my birth – I could have been born in London and for me there would have been no Holocaust, no destruction, none of the horrors that sometimes still come to me in the night.

My father was Lejbus Pewnik and he was born in 1892. Poland then was Russian and under the Tsar Alexander III there had been pogroms against the Jews – systematic, if sporadic, attacks backed by the Tsar's government and carried out by the Cossacks and the police. My grandfather died of cholera around the turn of the century – the dates are vague in my mind now – and my father went West, to England. Exactly why is not clear, but it was probably to avoid conscription into the Tsar's army – the Russian steamroller that would later break down in the marshes of Tannenberg and Galicia.

My father's sister was already in London, a city that represented a freedom the Poles had never known, at least not in living memory. There was a Jewish 'ghetto' in Whitechapel and Spitalfields and journalists like S Gelberg and Jack London described life there in the early years of the last century – 'Kosher restaurants abound in it; kosher butcher shops are clustered in thick bunches in its most hopeless parts (seven of them at the junction of Middlesex Street and Wentworth Street) . . . "*Weiber! Weiber! Leimische Beigel!*" sing out the women . . . and long after the shadows have lengthened . . . they are still vouching their own lives or the kindness of *Shem Yisborach* [God] to Israel for the quality of their wares.'

But Whitechapel had become the most famous Jewish community in London only because of the crimes of Jack the Ripper in 1888. My father lived in the more affluent and less well-documented Stamford Hill. Today Stamford Hill has the largest Hasidic community in Europe, often called the 'square mile of piety' because of all the strict Orthodox Jews walking to and from their synagogues. One school in the area has recently refused to study Shakespeare because of his anti-Semitic views.

It wasn't quite like that in my father's time. Stamford Hill wasn't a ghetto like Whitechapel, and London was the largest, most cosmopolitan city in the world. He never quite fitted in; 'The pavements weren't kosher,' he used to say, and the whole family knew what he meant. The twist of fate – the what-might-have-been – happened again and my father got a letter from his mother, Ruchla-Lea. Her other son, my Uncle Moyshe – the tailor from Szopoenice, near Katowice – wasn't being any help and the old lady was finding it difficult to look after herself back in Bedzin. She asked my father to come home.

I'm not exactly sure when this was. If it was after the Great War, then Russia had become convulsed in her own internal revolution and the children of Bedzin no longer had to offer prayers for the Tsar. If it was before the Great War, the threat of conscription had gone and Bedzin was under German control between August 1914 and the signing of the Armistice.

There is a studio portrait of my father taken at about the time of his return to Poland. He is a good-looking man, perhaps early twenties, with a stiff, starched shirt collar and highly polished shoes. He looks quite serious, as befitted his status in the community by the time I was born, but there is just the hint of a smile playing around his lips. I sometimes think he would need all his sense of humour bringing me up. What is odd is his suit – the jacket, worn open to show his waistcoat and watch-chain – looks too big for him. This is odd because my father was a tailor – in fact, he was a member of the Master Tailors' Association. Perhaps it was just the fashion at the time.

My father married his first wife soon after he came back to Bedzin. Many years later there were rumours in the family that she had died giving birth to their daughter Hendla, but this wasn't true. They must have divorced because I remember the woman. We didn't have anything to do with her, but I knew who she was. It was one of those things that happen in devout Orthodox families. There was probably a scandal of some kind and no one spoke of her again. My grandmother Ruchla-Lea, who lived with us at 77 Modzejowska Street, was the source of these stories, but she told them quietly, furtively even, as bedtime stories by candlelight. Hendla lived with us – she would have been about five years older than me, I suppose – and her mother visited her own sister in our apartment block. Inevitably she'd talk to Hendla as well. I seem to remember she married a shopkeeper in a nearby town, but it's all rather a blur now, one of the many shadows of my past.

My mother was Fajgla, a kind woman who was always, as they say nowadays, there for me. She was a good mother; most Jewish mothers are. I didn't realise it at the time but I was probably her favourite. Or perhaps because of the kind of kid I became she had to spend more time and energy defending me – it sometimes seemed that way. She wore her *sheitel* sometimes, but she wasn't as deeply religious as my father. Nathan was the eldest, two years older than me. We had that love–hate relationship that brothers close in age often have. Our temperaments were totally different and we spent the rest of our lives fighting and quarrelling. Did I love him, underneath all that? Of course; he was my brother. And blood, in Jewish communities especially, is thicker than water.

If I am vague about my other siblings it's because I never had the chance to get to know them as people. Hendla was lovely, kind and intelligent. She was never a bossy big sister, perhaps because she knew that that wouldn't work. Chana was pretty too – I was six when she was born. My other brothers were Majer, three years my junior, Wolf, born in 1935, and Josek, born three years later. That was the family unit – grandmother Ruchla-Lea, father Lejbus, mother Fajgla and us kids.

I suppose you'd say the Pivniks were climbing the social ladder in the Thirties. We had a radio and took a regular newspaper. Father's was Yiddish; mother and Hendla read a Polish paper. My grandfathers on both sides had been pedlars, men who walked the roads for hours with a horse and cart and often little to show for their efforts. The one who didn't die of cholera drowned one dark night coming home from a farm. He took a short cut he thought he knew and fell into the river. He was fifty-three. But my father was a tailor, a member of a respectable profession, and that gave us artisan status. His workshop, full of bolts of cloth and spools of thread and those huge, heavy scissors you don't see much now, stood across the cobbled courtyard from our house at Number 77. He worked six days a week, making suits, shooting jackets and skirts. My Uncle Moyshe in Szopoenice, with his bushy eyebrows and twinkling eyes, specialised in uniforms for officials. In those days everybody in Poland wore a uniform – postmen, railwaymen, policemen, firemen. Even the odd NCO or officer from the nearby army barracks came in with a special order – parade uniforms, or full dress for the proudest army in Europe, with its history stretching back to Marshal Poniatowski and his Lancers of the Vistula.

I can still hear the hum of my father's shop. Mother, Hendla, Nathan and sometimes even I would work there when demand was heavy or father was away consulting the rabbi. We only had one machine; the other had to be sold to pay for the time I spent in a sanatorium with a bad chest. Nathan had a job of his own, but when he could, he'd rattle all over town on his smart racing bicycle, delivering my father's handiwork. And I can remember the flats where we lived and the courtyard around which a little community had developed long before I was born. The apartments were largely flat-roofed, in the French style, and ours had two good-sized rooms and a kitchen. I slept with Nathan in one bed and our parents shared their bed with the smaller boys. In the other room (actually the kitchen), Hendla and Chana shared with grandmother Ruchla. By the standards of today it was crowded and in a way, I suppose, it prepared us for what was to follow.

We may have been 'upwardly mobile', as they say now, but we could never have afforded to buy the apartment.

Father rented it from Mr Rojecki, a Gentile Pole who lived on the first floor over the archway that opened into the courtyard with his wife and bachelor brother. He had no children, but he did have two little dogs. I don't know what breed they were, but they always seemed to be cold, shivering in their short hair in the savage Polish winters.

Mr Rojecki was a very large man, it seemed to me as a child. He was a Catholic and a member, I realise now, of a right-wing political group in the town. Despite this, he was kind to all Jews and fiercely protective of his tenants round the courtyard. He encouraged Nathan and I in what became a passion for us both. In the loft above his flat was a pigeons' nest and Rojecki let us build a coop for them. There was something about pigeons – the softness of their feathers when you stroke them and the gentle cooing that brings a quiet comfort.

On the ground floor there was a grocery shop, I remember, and father used one of the windows to advertise his wares. Another shop in the courtyard sold canvas for sack-making and opposite was the horse-dealer Piekowski's premises. He sometimes supplied horses for the artillery based in the town and he also made steel hawsers for industry.

I suppose our courtyard was a thriving cottage industry, always busy, full of coal-bunkers and children. Everybody had kids, except Rojecki, and I played with them all – conkers and football, splashing in the puddles, sliding on the ice. Three or four houses down was a pub, where they served food, peas and beans, as well as beer. It was the sort of community where everybody knew everybody else, united in faith and the struggle to survive the harsh economics of the poverty-stricken Thirties. At the pub there was a slate, and regulars paid when they could; never on Saturdays.

Looking back, three things dominated my childhood in Bedzin. The first was family, which, like everybody else, I took for granted until it was too late to relish its importance. The second was religion and the third was education.

Before my time the last two had gone hand in hand. Alongside the great synagogue stood the great academy, the house of study built in 1859 where the devout would go every day to learn and pray. In the Jewish faith there are prayers for every minute of the day, based on the psalms of King David. When I came home from school, my father would say, 'Sit down. We'll say a prayer together.' In my grandfather's time, Reb Abram Litwik was the organiser of the tailors and he would recite psalms on their behalf in the academy – 'Happy are those who dwell in Your house . . .' He was always the last to leave.

In those days, every four-year-old boy studied in the *heder*, a sort of religious primary school in which they learned 'the book' – the teachings of the Talmud and the Torah. The learning was by rote and woe betide the boy who failed to learn. By my day, things had relaxed, partly because there were actually slightly fewer Jews in Bedzin by the Thirties and partly because of a charismatic teacher called Yoshua Rapaport. He came from Warsaw and was one of the most inspiring teachers of his generation. We take our teachers for granted, whatever our race, religion or generation. I never appreciated Mr Rapaport – he was Principal of my school and a lofty figure, someone I was even a little afraid of. He certainly didn't suffer fools gladly but he opened up education for all of us. A keen sportsman himself, he introduced games into the curriculum as well as setting up the first orchestra in the town.

The school I went to was what today you'd call a state primary. We sang songs in the morning and had hour-long lessons, broken up into subjects like Geography and Maths, metalwork and woodwork. The language was Polish and the teachers were Christian. Katschinska was the name of my teacher in Class Three, the last time I ever sat in a class-room. We all had to wear a uniform. It was dark blue with a green stripe down the trousers and little round, green-trimmed caps. The teachers would inspect us, believing, as former generations had, that cleanliness was next to godli-ness. They checked our ears, our necks and made sure that our white shirt collars were stiff and starched. And we were given slippers to wear indoors, because the school was new, with central heating and floors polished like glass. You couldn't risk outdoor boots on floors like that. I liked gardening best. No doubt the school gave it a grand name like horticulture, but it was gardening nonetheless. Each class had its own plot and we'd compete with each other, growing flowers, tomatoes and radishes. I liked the earth, the fresh air, the sun. I was less keen on blackboards and chalk, on 'Answer this; do that!' Of course, school was designed to make men of us, but – as it turned out – a completely different sort of institution, one unimaginable to Mr Rapaport and Miss Katschinska, would do that.

At lunchtime we'd all go home, to the courtyard at 77 in my case, perhaps taking the opportunity on the way for a little illicit football in the backstreets, what I now refer to as my 'social functions'. My father took a keen interest in my education, testing me on what I had learned, but his real interest lay in the afternoon lessons I went to. These were Hebrew and religious classes, held not in the school or the synagogue but in private houses. There were twenty-five boys to a class and the teacher and his helper would instruct us in the mysteries of our faith. Father would test me every Saturday and if I hesitated or didn't know, I'd feel the back of his hand or his belt.

I can see my father now – a careful, precise little man with a neatly trimmed beard. If he didn't kick a ball around with us or play conkers, that didn't mean he wasn't a good father. He was. Times have changed. 'Spare the rod and spoil the child' was the dictum of his generation all across Europe. And I can remember sitting on the floor in wonder as he told us the great stories of Noah and the Flood; of Joshua and Jericho and all the history that had been handed down to a proud people, those chosen by God. It was my mother and Hendla who actually helped me with my homework and the only books I remember at home were religious ones.

Time and again I come back to the sad conclusion that I was just a naughty boy. I'd go to the pictures – there were three cinemas in Bedzin – and I loved cowboy films and *Tarzan* with Johnny Weissmuller, yodelling his way through the jungle. That was fine – perfectly acceptable behaviour – but we'd also smash windows with our football and pinch fruit from Mr Rojecki. I can remember one lady with a large, funny hat. When you're a little boy and it is snowing and there is a lady with a funny hat . . . well, I'm sorry to say she became a target for our snowballs and I'm sorry for that now. I had a pair of steel-bladed skates and a group of us would chase carts (which wasn't much of a challenge) and trams (which was downright lethal – one of us boys lost an arm doing that). More than once we were chased by the police. Who knows, today I'd probably have an ASBO! Whenever I was caught, I'd feel my father's belt – it was the way it was. My mother would intervene, as mothers will, trying to soften the blows. If she could have taken them for me, I'm sure she would. Whenever there was an issue – my behaviour or anything else – my father would consult the book. He had a standing in our community; people in trouble would come to him and he'd talk to them, hour after hour in the workshop as he sat cross-legged, stitching away. If he couldn't provide an answer, if the book came up short, he'd go to see the rabbi or spend time in the *stiebel*, the prayer room.

There was a time – I must have been about eleven – when Hendla told us all that she wanted to go to Palestine. For centuries the Jews of the Diaspora had longed for their promised land – Canaan, that flowed, the Bible tells us, with milk and honey. That natural homeland was Palestine, then lived in by Arabs and administered by the British, still the most powerful empire-builders in the world. Young Jews and Jewesses wanted to go there to found a Jewish state and Bedzin, like all Jewish communities, had its social clubs and youth organisations, from all colours of the political rainbow and Hendla had joined one. It was called *Gordonia* and Nathan was a member too. They wore blue scarves with a distinctive ring, talked about Palestine and tried to learn Hebrew. There was supposed to be a period of preparation for a year before going to Palestine; this was called *Hachshara*. The actual emigration, which thousands of Jews had undergone by the 1930s, was *Aliyah*. But farming? In the desert? It made little sense to my parents who were probably afraid she'd get mixed up with Gentiles, eat *treif* (non-kosher food) and get herself pregnant. I didn't understand this – I'd never seen Hendla with a boy, perhaps because I was too young to join the youth club. The bottom line was that, mystery of mysteries, Hendla didn't play football; we just weren't on the same wavelength! Hendla never had the chance to go to Palestine, although father pestered the rabbi about it.

So this was my childhood. Bedzin had its problems, of course. If you read the local papers from the late Thirties, it's full of friction – punch-ups at the general assembly of the Talmud Torah; people calling each other 'scoundrels' and shaking their fists. There was even a fight in the precincts of the synagogue. The editorial conclusion in one edition reads 'Let us have peace in our city.'

But I was twelve; I knew nothing of this. To me, it was all about football and the garden plot and the horse-manure smell of the courtyard of Number 77 and Mr Rojecki's shivering little dogs and the cooing of the pigeons. Above all, it was all about that sacred ground of my mother's people at Wodzislaw – the pines, the river, the bread, the cheese. The Garden of Eden.

But somebody else had the idea of a Garden of Eden too. He was a Bavarian ex-corporal who had joined a right-wing organisation in Germany soon after the Great War. The only problem was that he wanted to set up his Garden of Eden in somebody else's country.

Mine.

2

The World Turned Upside Down

Idon't celebrate my birthday any more. I haven't for a long time. Not since 1 September 1939, because that was the day the Germans invaded Poland. I don't remember whether I got any presents – I suppose I must have done. Times were hard but mother was used to juggling the family finances and my parents would never have disappointed me. I remember it was a Friday, a warm day in late summer, the skies above Bedzin a cloudless blue. School had not yet opened for the autumn term – that would happen on Monday – so my friends and I were playing around in the street. Who was there? I don't remember precisely, but it was probably Yitzhak Wesleman, Jurek and the three Gutsek boys. Somebody probably had a football. Somebody always did; but somehow, this day was different.

It wasn't that I was thirteen – we didn't have the word or the concept of being a teenager then. Whatever it was had nothing to do with us and yet we got caught up in it. Something was happening down at the huge army barracks near the railway station. People were heading over there, scurrying along the pavements in twos and threes, talking in murmurs, their faces serious, their eyes bright. We followed them.

I had always liked watching the soldiers, before soldiers came to mean something else to me. Our local regiment was the 23rd Light Artillery, still, like most of the army in Poland in those days, horse drawn. Us boys would watch them parading in the square, their shiny boots clattering on the cobbles, their uniforms khaki-brown with green collar patches and gleaming buttons and badges. They clashed out of town on manoeuvres from time to time, the horses hauling the painted guns and the wheels rattling over the stones.

Today, though, it didn't seem the same. The spit and polish was gone and there was what looked to me, even as a thirteen-year-old, to be nothing but desperation and panic. We couldn't see much beyond the fringe of onlookers. We asked some adults what was happening; why all the fuss? We'd all seen soldiers pulling out on manoeuvres before. War games. It was what soldiers did. I can remember the answer to this day. One man turned to us, looking down from his years of grim experience. He told us that the Germans had invaded. We looked at each other, uncomprehending. He tried again, saying that the war has started. Nothing. He shrugged and gave up in disgust. No doubt he muttered the cliché of every generation about the youth of today.

I suppose we stayed there until late morning, watching the comings and goings, listening to the creak of leather, the snorts and whinnies of the horses and the rattle of metal, the shouted commands. A little before midday the enormous barrack gates were thrown back and the regiment marched out. There was no band, there were no flags. Some people in the small crowd cheered, clapped and waved. The soldiers looked grim, focused, staring straight ahead.

We watched the last limber turn the corner out of the square and went back to the football we'd been playing before all this distracted us. The noise dawned on us only slowly; a distant rumble like thunder in the far-off Carpathians was getting louder. Sometimes, above our shouts or the thud of our boots on the rag ball, there were distant bangs and booms. We'd heard nothing like this before, any of us. But now we knew the war was coming to Bedzin. And nothing would ever be the same again.

We didn't know it at the time, nor for many years to come, but the Germans had crossed the Polish border at 5.45 that morning as dawn was promising another bright day. The original date for the invasion was 25 August but they had postponed it until they were sure they were ready. Besides, they had to wait until 'we' attacked them. This was all a put-up job of course. At eight o'clock the day before, Polish troops had attacked a German radio station at Gleiwitz, not very far from Bedzin. Every Pole knew this was rubbish; most Germans believed it. In fact the Polish attackers were SS men in stolen uniforms and the whole fiasco was set up to make Poland look like the aggressor.

There was no declaration of war. Only civilised countries did that. The Germans called the invasion *Fall Weiss* – Case White – and they put fifty-three divisions into the field against us. At the time we had thirty infantry divisions with nine in reserve, eleven cavalry brigades and two motorised brigades, as well as smaller back-up units like the engineers. The Kraków Army had been created on 23 March as the main pivot of Polish defence. This was our nearest outfit, of which the Bedzin contingent was part. They had

five divisions, one mounted brigade, a mountain brigade
and one cavalry brigade. Their commander was Colonel
Wladyslaw Powierza serving under General Antoni Szylling
as divisional commander.

On that Friday at the start of what was to become known
as the September campaign, I knew nothing of this but it
would soon be all that adults talked about, leaving us to
pick up what we could. Armies, divisions, battalions, regi-
ments, cavalry, artillery – they were all just words; part of
a world I didn't understand. We were still kicking the ball
around by mid-afternoon when we heard it: the steady
drone of propeller aircraft coming from the west. We knew
the Polish Air Force had a fine reputation, but we'd never
seen a formation before. It took a while for your eyes to
focus, to take it all in. Then we saw the wave of camouflage-
painted fighter bombers, their fuselages flashing in the sun.
When they reached the castle, their formation split, aircraft
banking away to attack different parts of the town. Now
we could see the telltale black crosses on the pale blue of
their underwings. This, we would find out much later,
signalled the deadly new tactic of the Germans – *Blitzkrieg*,
the lightning war. They were hitting us from the air first.
The slaughter on the ground would follow. We had no idea
as the engines screamed overhead that the town of Wieluń
(around a hundred kilometres away as the crow flies) had
already been bombed. Three-quarters of the buildings
stood as blazing wreckage; twelve hundred people were
dead and most of those were civilians.

I can still remember the first resounding thump as the
bombs struck home, going for the railway station with its
flat roof and Art Deco facade; pounding the zinc and

copper works, destroying communications and the life-blood of Bedzin. It's funny – you don't just hear a bomb going off, you feel it. The shock wave was like being hit in the pit of the stomach. We played on, but with less certainty than before. Black smoke formed a backdrop to the turrets of Kazimerz's castle and the planes had gone as suddenly as they'd appeared. Eventually we all realised something terrible had happened and we thought of our families. There was only one place to be – home.

I dashed along Modzejowska and in under Mr Rojecki's archway. My mother and Hendla were already preparing the *Shabbat* meal for the evening, but there was no sign of my father. I knew where he'd be – he'd be at the syna-gogue or the *stiebel* with the other elders and the rabbi. *Someone* would have an answer to what was happening, the gulf of total war washing over us. I was gabbling away to them both about what I had seen. I probably exagger-ated it for effect, like thirteen-year-olds do. But my mother was saying nothing, just making small talk about the meal and *Shabbat*. I instinctively knew that my father wouldn't be bringing back some homeless person to join us at the table, as he often did. I suspect now that he had told her not to talk to us kids about the events of the day. Years later I learned that Britain and France were both on the point of declaring war on Germany, and that the British Prime Minister, Neville Chamberlain, had announced the war over the radio. The British may have evacuated their kids from the cities in expectation of *Blitzkrieg*, but we were actually seeing it and feeling it first-hand. The war was never 'phoney' for us.

From our windows, from the courtyard that led to

father's workshop, we could see the columns of smoke rising like chimneys straight up into the sunset that evening. We could smell the burning on the warm air – not the sweet burning wood of the Garden of Eden, but an acrid, pungent smell we didn't know. We gathered at the table as we always did and mother lit the candles, but there was no joy in our songs. The talk was stilted, strained. After dinner we all sat listening to father reading from the book, intoning the familiar words I had known all my life. But tonight was different. Tonight gave no real promise, I know now, of tomorrow.

Saturday 2 September. *Shabbat*. Another warm, sun-kissed day. We would usually have made our way to the synagogue with friends and neighbours to give our thanks to God. But we didn't go that day. And it would be twelve years before I would set foot in a synagogue again. The festivals ended. All the rituals of the Jewish year were abandoned or impossibly circumscribed. Nathan's Bar Mitzvah of two years earlier had been a full-blown ceremony. Mine was held in the kitchen of our home a few weeks after the invasion, with no Torah from the synagogue, no rabbi and no cakes and coffee. That day in September was the first, in a way, of my manhood. Yesterday I had played football and waved at the soldiers. Today I saw lines of refugees, those sad, homeless, faceless ones who would clog the roads of Europe for the next six years. It was like the Exodus the rabbi and my father talked about, but there were Gentiles in the crowd too, jostling their way eastward with the Jews, all running before the advance of the *Wehrmacht*. Every conceivable type of transport had been utilised – the wealthy had their cars; businessmen their trucks. Others were slapping the rumps of their carthorses, straining at the hames of wagons that held their lives. Suitcases, kitbags, beds and mattresses, the odd bird in a cage, a hip bath. There was no panic, not yet. Human beings are an optimistic lot, by and large. Something would turn up. God would make it all right. But nobody was staying long in Bedzin – it was too near the front line, and chances were tomorrow it would be the front line itself.

Rumours. For the next six years my life revolved around rumours. The Germans were bombing every town in their path and machine-gunning civilians left alive. Their Stukas were dive-bombing the streams of refugees moving east. But we were not to worry – the Polish army was pushing them back over the border. All would be well.

The truth, which no one in Bedzin knew on 2 September, was that units of General Reichenau's Tenth Army and General List's Fourteenth Army were converging on Kraków, batting aside any opposition they faced. General von Rundstedt's troops had already crossed the Warta River. His casualties were high – which is probably where the rumours about the Polish army pushing the Germans back came from – but his advance went on relentlessly to the east. So fast was this attack that units of our army could not liaise with each other and the reserves, around Tarnow, could not be brought quickly enough into the field.

I don't actually remember what I did that Saturday – or the Sunday, come to that. I suppose I played with my mates and we swapped rumours we'd heard on street corners and in our respective houses – except mine, where nothing was said. Some of the adults were clutching at the straws of Allied support. The British and the French, Polish radio said, had issued an ultimatum to Germany; either pull out of Poland or face a war on two fronts. That had to be good, the adults said; not even a madman like Adolf Hitler would risk a war like that.

I don't remember hearing any of the larger political stuff and my father never talked about it in front of us kids. It may be that Hendla knew, but she was a girl. She wasn't likely to understand what was going on, on those grounds alone!

Historians today can't decide just how mad Adolf Hitler was. Some of them point to his narcissism, his arrogance, his obsessive racism and his increasing megalomania. The Second World War, they say, was Hitler's war; you don't have to look any further than this comical little Bavarian corporal (who actually came from Austria) to explain the ghastly events of the 1940s. Others, from a different generation, look at external influences; they talk about the effects on Germany of losing the Great War; of the economic fallout from the Wall Street Crash that hit struggling Germany hardest of all. They talk about the injustices of the Treaty of Versailles which left a once proud nation humiliated and bereft.

I had no idea of what a 'greater Germany' was or of Hitler's concept of *Lebensraum* (living space) for his people. A believer as he was in geopolitics, he thought that anywhere with Germans living in it should be part of Germany. Have a look at my country's map overleaf as it was when I was thirteen. The Treaty of Versailles in 1919 had created the Polish Corridor, a strip of territory that led to the free port of Danzig on the Baltic Sea and was our only outlet for maritime trade. Hitler had said to

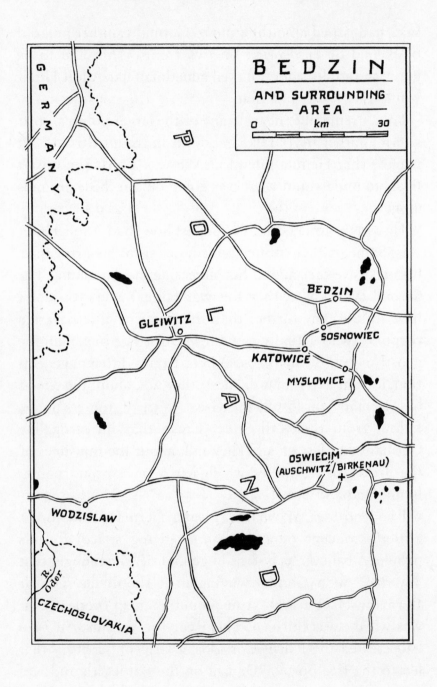

BEDZIN
AND SURROUNDING
AREA

0   km   30

GERMANY

POLAND

BEDZIN

GLEIWITZ

SOSNOWIEC

KATOWICE

MYSLOWICE

OSWIECIM
(AUSCHWITZ/BIRKENAU)

WODZISLAW

R. Oder

CZECHOSLOVAKIA

Colonel Josef Beck, the Polish foreign minister, 'Danzig is German, will always remain German and will sooner or later become part of Germany.' And to the east of Danzig lay East Prussia, part of the newly united Germany since 1871 and Hitler said it was not right that East Prussia was physically separated from the mother country by an alien power. The solution? Simple. Close the Corridor and incorporate East Prussia. Will the Poles object? Of course they will. Invade them and have done with it.

I knew none of this then, nor the hatred the man had in his heart for the Jewish people. All I knew was that all day Sunday and Monday the refugees continued to stream through, the carts, the dogs, the kids – and that it was chaos.

And of course, there was no school. Did I cheer and skip around? I don't remember. If I'd thought about it, I would have realised that the first of the constants in my life had already gone. School is one of the solidities, the certainties of childhood. It looms at least as large as family and faith. It's not only the place where you learn, it's the place where you learn to cope with the outside world. The Rapaport school never opened again while I was in Bedzin and my formal education came to an abrupt end.

It was Monday 4 September when they came. Among the most bizarre, yet persistent rumours was that the British and French armies were coming to rescue us. Nobody, least of all a thirteen-year-old kid, stopped to ask how this was possible. How had they got here and so quickly? The *actual* situation was that in Britain Neville Chamberlain made his famous announcement to his people at quarter-past eleven on the morning of the previous day. It was not until five o'clock in the afternoon that the French followed suit. In fact there would *never* be British or French troops in Poland, but no one knew that at the time.

To our north the Lodz Army had been beaten in a series of running fights; Reichenau had reached the Warta and List was marching on Kraków. By Monday he'd covered eighty kilometres. But rumour, not fact, was the currency in Bedzin in those September days. The British and the French were on their way. Relief. Euphoria. People were laughing, gabbling. Women and girls had collected the flowers of that hot, dry summer to throw at our saviours, to welcome the brave. We waited along the main street, nattering, excited; listening, shortly after midday, to the rumble of heavy vehicles roaring along the roads from the west. We heard cheering. People further down must be able to see them already, the flags of red, white and blue.

The first sight I had was of dark motorcycles with sidecars. Their riders wore low-rimmed *stahlhelmes* and grey-green uniforms with rifles slung over their backs. They were dirty from their hours on the road and the dust of summer lay like a film on their gauntlets and goggles. They were moving slowly, looking around them with wary eyes. Hard men and hard faces. Behind them came grey-painted trucks, all crashing gears and rattling tailgates. Each one bristled with soldiers armed to the teeth and scowling at us. Between the trucks came armoured cars, with cannon and machine-gun mountings – the face of total war.

The mood had changed. The flowers hung limply from the women's hands; the cheering had stopped. The chatter was stilled and the smiles were frozen on frightened faces.

I was standing near some Jewish refugees from Düsseldorf who had moved into our apartment building two years before to escape Nazi persecution as Hitler's racist net had tightened. I don't remember their name, but I remember the mother putting into words what we were all thinking – 'This isn't the French or the British. These are German soldiers.'

It was as if the sentence was the signal for the crowd to break up. People scattered, taking their flowers with them or throwing them with contempt on the cobbles. Home – that was everyone's aim. Get home, bolt the doors, cover the windows. Work out – somehow – what to do. I didn't go home. Just as I was fascinated by the bombers of two days earlier, I was mesmerised by the *Wehrmacht* and saw a sight I couldn't understand at the time and can't fully explain even today. In the vast cavalcade of troops pouring into the town was an open-backed truck driven by Germans but carrying men in Polish uniforms. They were laughing and joking among themselves as if riding in the enemy's vehicles was the most ordinary and natural thing in the world. I suppose I should have looked to see if they were armed or not because if they weren't, they may well have been prisoners of war. But if they were, why did they appear to be enjoying themselves? If they were Germans, why were they wearing Polish uniforms? People talked about this for days and we never found the answer. Most likely they were *Volksdeutsche*, Poles of German extraction happy to welcome the invaders with open arms. One of them was a short, stout man I remember, the *Kappellmeister* or band master of our local regiment with the three pips of a captain on his shoulder. He used to teach music to us kids in the Rapaport school from time to time. He never went off to fight, never left Bedzin as far as I recall. But like many of the events of the next six years, I still don't *know* quite what went on.

I went home to a kind of siege mentality. We were now in exactly the same predicament as the refugees we had seen passing through. Now it was *our* home ringed by Axis steel. But if we took to the road, loaded our belongings onto a cart – father's sewing machine, Nathan's Baloofka bike, my skates, all our worldly goods – where would we go? That Monday night we stayed indoors, occasionally venturing as far as the courtyard but not out into the street. There were trucks driving around as darkness gathered, loud-hailers barking in their distorted way that everyone must stay in their homes or be shot. We did as we were told, listening to the growl of the trucks and the sporadic crackle of rifle and pistol fire.

It's difficult to put into words after all this time, and everything that happened after, how I felt. I was scared, of course; who wouldn't be? I'd been brought up – we all had – to be loyal Poles; we'd said a prayer for the President every morning in school, just as my grandfather would probably have said one for the Russian Tsar. I didn't know then that the Polish government didn't care very much for Jews. Two years before the Germans arrived there had been anti-Semitic violence in some Polish towns, violence that had looked suspiciously like a pogrom. For the adults there was a sense of déjà vu about all this. Throughout time the Jews had been the victims of persecution. We had been kicked out of countless European countries, told to move on, find somewhere else – 'You have no right to live among us.'

If I was aware of anti-Semitism in my own life, it was only for a few days after the Christians had celebrated their Easter festival. I played with Gentiles as well as Jews at all other times of the year – Jurek and the Gutsek brothers among them – but at Easter there'd be fist fights as the Gentiles accused us of killing Jesus Christ. But there were always fist fights – over a football foul, a chance remark. If the war had not come when it did, doubtless we'd have been fighting over girls in the years ahead. It was all over and forgotten in a day. You carried your cuts and bruises with pride and then you forgot about it. The only trouble I heard about – and Nathan talked about it sometimes – were fights after football matches if the Gentile team lost. It was always started by outsiders. We had a good police chief who kept the lid on things like that. Until that September, the pogroms never came to Bedzin.

Would this be the same? And if not, could we Jews move on, as we'd always done, and find another safe haven? Where, in the end, could I find another Garden of Eden?

The next days are hazy in my mind. Elsewhere in Poland, I learned much later, the army was pushed ever further back, leaving us isolated and defenceless. On 6 September, List's Fourteenth Army took Kraków and the Polish government left Warsaw. Their army, exhausted, outnumbered and outfought nearly everywhere, was ordered back to a line along the rivers Vistula, Narew and San. Within a day they had to fall back to the Bug River.

Meanwhile, our own priority was to eat. We must have been allowed out to try to buy food but the curfew still held and there was no one except Germans on the streets after a certain hour. By seven o'clock we had to be indoors. We couldn't be seen on the streets again until eight in the morning. There'd been no fighting in Bedzin so in the town centre there were none of the ruined buildings or smashed walls that were to characterise so many of Europe's cities in these months. There were however soldiers everywhere, most of them in the grey-green of the *Wehrmacht* or wearing the chain around their necks to denote the military police. By the Saturday following the invasion – still no one mentioned the synagogue – I noticed the uniforms begin to change. Increasingly, we spotted the blue-green tunics of the civil police and soon men started arriving in light brown tunics with red, black and white swastika armbands – Nazi party bureaucrats who moved into the town hall and other civic buildings with filing cabinets, typewriters and paper-work. One of the many things I learned about the Nazis in the years ahead was their obsession with detail. Everything in triplicate, cross-referenced and filed. They were proud of their achievement. Most alarmingly, the Bedzin police were out on the streets too; they may have been *Volksdeutsche* or they may have just been jumping on the passing bandwagon of survival.

I also noticed the round-ups that began almost at once. Men were 'collected' by the soldiers, especially the Orthodox Jews with their black clothes, ringleted hair and long beards. They were herded together in squares and at street corners and marched out to the town's limits, to the bombed factories that we'd seen hit the week before. Their job was to find unexploded bombs because bombs could be 'recycled' for the war effort. They had no training and no safety equipment. They were human minesweepers and they were expendable. If a bomb went off and a couple of Jews were blown to pieces or suffered terrible injuries, so what?

I remember very clearly Friday 8 September. That was the day the *Einsatzgruppen* arrived. We had no name for them then and no idea what the precise mission was that they were undertaking. Most of them looked like policemen in a sort of combat uniform. Others had *Wehrmacht* uniforms but they were somehow different, with black epaulettes and collar flashes. They wore eagle badges on their sleeves and they turned up in the usual motley collection of motorcycles, trucks and jeeps. These were the execution squads, the men tasked by the Nazi high command with systematic attacks on my people. This particular unit I know now was commanded by SS-Obergruppenführer Udo von Woyrsch, a Silesian nobleman who had been a member of the Nazi party for years. The *gruppe* was about two thousand strong, made up of that peculiar combination which characterised these units. They were all members of the *Sicherheitsdienst*, the various police departments called Gestapo, *Kripo* and *Ordo*. They were ordered by Heinrich Himmler, head of the SS, to spread fear and terror throughout the Katowice area. They were the beginning of what the world has come to know as the Holocaust.

That afternoon I was indoors because it really wasn't safe to be anywhere else. From time to time we heard the crackle of shots ringing round the town's streets. And then, as the afternoon turned to evening, there was a smell of burning. It was different from the factories that had been blitzed the week before and I was keen to find out what was going on. My parents of course wouldn't have any of that. My days of kicking a ball around the streets in safety had gone. Mother kept her brood with her. But as dusk fell I crept out of the apartment and climbed onto the roof of a lean-to shed against a high wall. I could see the sky glowing red and the black smoke billowing into the purple of the oncoming night. It was the great synagogue, the symbol of my people and it was ablaze, the timbers cracking and collapsing on the ridge below the castle. And it was *Shabbat*, our special day.

I don't know how long I stayed there, on tiptoe, transfixed by the sight. There were no fire engines racing to put the blaze out and the fire was spreading to the buildings around the synagogue, all of them Jewish businesses, Jewish homes. Not until I heard Hendla shouting at me to get down could I pull myself away from that sight. The Pivniks were at home that weekend, huddled together as the world we knew was falling apart outside.

On Monday morning we summoned up the nerve to go out. We may well have had no food left by now so it was probably a matter of necessity. The sight we saw was almost unimaginable. All weekend the *Einsatzgruppen* had been carrying out their mission and the results were everywhere. There were bodies lying in the streets, sprawled in the agony of death, rivulets of their blood a rusty brown in the gutters. I had never seen a dead body before and these were people I knew – neighbours and family friends who days ago had been carrying out their work and going about their business without, I now realise, a real care in the world. Most of them were elderly Jews, easily identifiable by their devout traditional clothes and hats – the easiest targets for the rifle butts and bullets of the *Einsatzgruppen*. It would be a comfort to think that these men died quickly, but I don't think it was like that. They would have been taunted, humiliated and slapped around first, kicked to the ground and shot where they lay – the bruises on their blackening faces were testimony to that. And it wasn't only the old and the Orthodox who lay there. There were younger people too, of both sexes, and even kids of my age, caught in the murderous random firing of the Nazis that we had heard all weekend.

The most ghastly sight I remember was that of Jews hanging from the trees that grew in the square, black-coated men who looked like some ghastly parody of Christmas tree decorations. I remember how still they looked, their hands and feet dangling, their bodies at the mercy of the weather. I didn't count corpses and none of us looked too closely in case the *Einsatzgruppen* decided we should join them. Only God knows how many people died in Bedzin that weekend and it was not only Jews who died.

Some of the shootings must have been random. Someone running for cover between houses. Someone looking for family. Friends. Other murders were planned, deliberate. Bedzin, like every other Polish town, had its intellectuals, its nationalist groups, the right- and left-wingers who all knew clearly before September 1939 exactly in which direction Polish politics should go. We know now why these people were targeted. They were potential trouble and somebody in the community must have fingered them – how else would the *Einsatzgruppen* know on which doors to knock? They were hauled out of their houses, frogmarched to the edge of town and shot. That was the rumour, and after what I saw that Monday in the streets around Modzejowska I couldn't doubt it.

In seven days the world we knew and understood and loved had gone. I could read the bewilderment in my father's eyes. When trouble had loomed in the past he had always gone to the synagogue, to the rabbi, to talk to the other elders and ask God for guidance. Now the synagogue was a still-smouldering heap of rubble and many of the elders lay stiff and dead in the streets.

Historians still argue today over how many people died that weekend. Apart from those who may have burned to death in their own houses, the best estimate was about a hundred men, women and children; perhaps eighty of these were Jews. It seemed at the time to be far more to me – after all, wasn't just one too many?

But the Pivniks held together with a new-found stoicism. How much worse, we asked ourselves, could all this get?

3
Occupation

The Rapaport school had closed. The synagogue was a burnt out shell. My father was no longer a small businessman with pride in his tailoring skill and his status in the community. He was out of work like almost everybody else and he was a potential target for the uniformed thugs who roamed the streets.

We all had to adapt, to come to terms with a new way of life which, we didn't realise then, had swept the old one away for ever. Rumours reached us from the east, and the history books confirm it today, that the Russians invaded Poland on 17 September. We only had eighteen battalions along the River Bug because all our fighting units were in the west, trying to hold off the *Wehrmacht*. Poland was like a nut in the steel jaws of a nutcracker and the next day the President and the Commander-in-Chief were imprisoned. They left messages telling the troops to fight on.

The 23rd Light Artillery Unit had long gone and we never saw them again. We Jews were used to fighting back in our little scraps over football and Easter but this was different. We were civilians and hard though it was to follow, the rabbi's teachings had always been to turn the other cheek. Between them, Adolf Hitler and Josef Stalin, two men who dismissed the rabbis' teachings out of hand, condemned millions of my people to death.

Officially, although we never used the term, Bedzin became Bendsburg in the German *Gau* of Upper Silesia. The position of our Christian neighbours in the town was that they faced a stark choice. Those with German ancestry could sign papers to become *Volksdeutsche*, halfway to being an Aryan. The rest were told to leave, carrying their world on their backs or in their carts and prams and settle in the area the Germans called the General Government. Hans Frank, Hitler's lawyer, was put in charge. 'Poland shall be treated like a colony,' he announced over the radios, while the people of Bedzin still had radios. 'The Poles will become the slaves of the Greater German Empire.' His headquarters were in Kraków, but his tentacles reached out to all of us. Jews of course could not become German citizens but now we were liable to the Nuremberg Laws which had been operating against German Jews for four years.

Jews could not work in the professions. Rapaport and other Jewish teachers in the schools lost their positions. We could not, even if we'd wanted to, join the army, but in any case our army was on the point of collapse somewhere along the banks of the River Bug and nobody considered trying to join the *Wehrmacht*. As for university, forget it. Bright boys from my school had their education cut short – as did I – that September and Poland was to suffer for years from its lost generation of intellectuals.

Along with countless other small businessmen, my father became a wage slave – and the wages were pitiful – as German civilians came in and bought up Jewish businesses at knockdown prices. They brought in their own Aryan managers and if part of the Jewish workforce was retained, it was always with a lower status, no bonuses and the most basic wage. I remember standing in my father's workshop, perhaps in that October, as what had happened began to sink in. Uniformed officials had marched into the little courtyard where Nathan and I kicked a ball around. They had taken my father's scissors, thread, sewing machine and bales of cloth. And of course there were no tailoring orders any more. Most of the civilian officials were gone and though I never thought about it quite like this, some of Uncle Moyshe's army clients in nearby Szopoenice were probably dead.

It was six months before Alfred Rossner came to Bedzin and until then we got by as best we could. Rossner was an odd-looking man with missing teeth and a bad hip. No one knew it at the time but he was a haemophiliac and consequently lucky to be alive. He was what the Germans called a *Treuhänder*, a trusty, who managed two clothing factories and worked directly for the SS. One of his leading managers was Arje Ferleizer, a Jew who had once employed Rossner and who had got out of Germany in 1938 to escape persecution. It was rather ironic that he ended up in Bedzin.

Both Hendla and my father went to work in Rossner's 'shop' along with nearly 10,000 Jews he employed until 1943. We didn't appreciate the dangerous game Rossner was playing on our behalf. Unlike the more famous Oscar Schindler, Rossner was not an independent businessman but a manager on behalf of the SS and his options to help the Jews were limited. Even so, my father and Hendla were taken on as skilled workers and they were deemed indispensable to the German war effort. Accordingly they were given *Sonderausweis*, special blue card passes that kept them, at least in theory, safe from the random violence of the SS. We didn't know it at the time but these passes would help to keep us together as a family for just a little longer. And while Alfred Rossner greased Nazi palms, provided senior SS men with extra-special uniforms and kept their wives in the height of 1940s fashion, he was also keeping the Pivniks alive.

It wasn't so easy to find work for me. Father was a master tailor and Hendla, at eighteen, was already a skilled seamstress, but I was a young boy, with no real training at all. The basic sewing I could manage couldn't hold a candle to the skills most of Rossner's people possessed. Then I had a lucky break. I had always been fond of horses – we all were – and one animal I used to pat and stroke in his hames belonged to a Jewish delivery man named Dombek. I'd feed and groom the horse and work with him in his furniture delivery business, running errands, lifting, carrying. I don't remember what he paid me – it was probably peanuts – but it was my first wage and I was proud to be helping out at home.

All this changed early in 1940. By this time I had found work in a furniture factory belonging to a man named Killov and managed by Herr Haüber. These men were kind Germans too, but not in the same league as Rossner. The factory made furniture and wooden packing cases and the workforce was segregated, Jews and Gentiles. I was making the heavy beech-wood crates used for transporting and storing the 500-kilogram bombs that the Dorniers and Heinkels of the Luftwaffe were raining on towns and cities all over Europe. We had no idea as 1940 became 1941 what was happening in the rest of the world. By this time we'd lost our radios and mail was a thing of the past as far as we were concerned. My father asked me to mention that I had an elder brother available for work and since Dombek no longer had any help with his horses, it made sense that Nathan worked for him.

If anything, Nathan loved Dombek's horses more than I did and he ended up in charge of two of them, until the cart slipped on the hill to the station one day and went over his foot. Eventually he got a hernia and his work with Dombek was over.

My time in the factory was surreal. It felt like we were all part of a machine. Us Jews were paid less than the Gentiles, of course, and with their typical Teutonic obsession the Germans deducted tax and social security from our weekly wage packet. These deductions increased as the 'contributions' called *Winterhilfe* were levied, providing cash for warm clothing for the troops on the bitter, appalling Eastern Front.

A vital factor in my work at the Killov factory was the food, a constant which became more important as everything else began to fall apart. We had soup or stew at midday and a leisurely forty-five minutes in which to eat it. Being young – probably the youngest on Killov's roster – I caught the eye of Herr Haüber and he took a fatherly interest in me. He'd get me to run errands and in the early days before the orders from Berlin became ever harsher, I would walk his little daughter to school in the morning. Nathan did the same. This was the Furstenberger school, for Gentiles, which continued to function after the invasion. If ever I had to go to Haüber's home – I sometimes drove him there for lunch in his two-horse carriage – Frau Haüber would slip me extra food for the family. I'd like to say it was a pot of jam, a loaf of bread, sausage, tea, sugar, butter . . . but that was the stuff of the Garden of Eden and it was already becoming a distant memory. Even so, vegetables and potatoes were very welcome to a family like ours. Chana was still only seven and the boys Wolf and Josek younger still. Even Majer was only eleven and in a town where jobs were at a premium, he couldn't earn anything.

But the factory had its downside. Killov and Haüber might have been kind but their underlings were not. The official who clocked us in and out every day was a confirmed Nazi and regarded us with contempt. He was a vicious bastard with only one arm and there was always an anti-Semitic jibe, often followed by a clip round the ear if he was in that kind of mood. Nobody complained, nobody did anything, largely because the Poles had mainly become *Volksdeutsche*. In many ways this was the hardest thing to take during the Occupation – friends and neighbours now stared at us with ill-concealed hatred, glad they didn't have to work alongside us in the workshops. When the drip-drip of Himmler's rabid racial policy was reinforced by guns and dogs and the total application of martial law, it's surprising how quickly people changed.

Beyond the factory, life was getting harder by the day. Shops and businesses began to reopen in the weeks following the invasion but of course they were run by Germans or at least Polish *Volksdeutsche* and Jews were not allowed to use them. So, confined to certain areas of the town and able to buy from a limited range of premises, queues – *the* symbol of home life in wartime all over Europe – became the norm. Women and children in particular would stand for hours in the pouring rain or the biting wind just to get some bread. This was why the Killov soup was so vital – Nathan and I at least had one half-decent meal a day. I knew our parents went without, to make sure that the little ones had enough.

But queuing wasn't just an inconvenience caused by wartime shortages. We wore no yellow armbands in those days – that stigma would come later – and non-Orthodox Jews looked pretty much the same as everybody else. Polish kids – some of my friends among them – would scuttle along the lines, shouting '*Jude! Jude!*' and pointing to Jews in the crowd. They got extra butter and marmalade for this, like the pieces of silver in the Christian New Testament. The police – by this time entirely German – would haul the Jews out of line and slap them around, often leaving them and their blood on the snow.

There was something of a joke in Bedzin in the early days of Occupation: you either worked for Killov or Rossner or you were a member of the *Judenrat*, the Jewish Council – there wasn't anything else. Like all the other institutions of the Nazi state, it was a puppet creation. Its basic function was to maintain order in the Jewish community by informing on troublemakers and getting us all identified and registered. My father was not a member but several of his friends were and the *Judenrat* headquarters were just along from our house on Modzejowska Street, nearer to the marketplace. Outside the door was a notice-board with important messages in Yiddish, translating Nazi orders so that no one could be in any doubt as to what was happening. It may have been jackbooted Germans who took away my father's sewing machine but it was the *Judenrat* who told them where to look. Systematically the Jewish community in Bedzin was looted and the leaders of that community connived in that.

The leader of the councils in Eastern Silesia was Meniok Meryn, who acted as a go-between for the German *Gauleiter* and Molczacki, head of the Bedzin *Judenrat*. Some people regarded Meryn as a chancer and a collaborator; others believed that he slowed down the speed, at least, of Nazi persecution. Molczacki, it was rumoured, used to ferret through his employees' waste paper baskets looking for evidence against them. I was just a kid; what did I know?

The real extortion started in February 1940. In that month the Russians were fighting the Finns in the frozen north, using skis and snow-camouflage. We of course had no knowledge of any of this. Bedzin was one of the few places in Poland where the Nazis had not set up an actual ghetto, so you could say it was easier than it might have been for us. Even so, Bedzin represented a siege situation. No one was allowed to leave or enter the town without permission from the SS and the parameters of my life were more restricted still. I walked to the factory and I walked home. From time to time I'd go with Nathan and my grandmother to pick over the slag heaps on the edge of town looking for coal pieces good enough to burn. There were police and guards everywhere and you got the impression they were just itching for an excuse to pull those triggers.

In that February, the Nazis pressured the *Judenrat* into handing over more than 15 kilograms of gold and 60 of silver from the Jewish community. This was in recompense for some imaginary crime we'd committed. No doubt if pressed, they'd say we'd killed Christ or used the blood of Christian children in some ritual – this was before they stopped having to find reasons for such punishment at all. Council members went round the town, knocking on doors and shuttered windows, invading the sanctity of our homes, which was all we had left. I don't know if they managed to reach the demanded amount or how much was still squirrelled away under floorboards and in attics against the day – and surely it could come – when the Germans left. We all had to hand in any ski equipment we had (the Pivniks had none) presumably for the war against the Finns. Our radios had already gone for the most part, but anybody still in possession of one lost it now. Then they banned us from various streets and public areas, creating a sort of ghetto without a name. Nathan became a victim of this. Caught in a Nazi no-go area, trying to obtain bread illegally, he was frogmarched to the town gaol. I don't remember the formalities, whether he had to appear before a magistrate or an SS official. I do remember the unbearable tension at home when he'd gone and the helplessness my father felt when he couldn't do anything about it. Nathan was there for six weeks.

Yet, despite it all, somehow life went on. The factory was bearable – in fact I looked forward to going to work. And I could still manage to kick a football around occasionally, even if the number of friends I played with had dwindled. And I still had my pigeons, cooing unconcerned in Mr Rojecki's loft. For them, I remember thinking, there was no war, no clip around the ear, no tightrope to walk.

If I'd thought about it though, I would have realised that there wasn't as much food for them either.

Food was a major problem. Nathan and I were growing boys, so was Majer. Ten of us lived in the little house at Number 77 and only four of us brought in any money. My grandmother was too old and my mother had her hands full with the little ones (Josek was only three). There was a black market of sorts, people who knew people, and you'd occasionally see cash and food parcels changing hands furtively on shadowy street corners. And we still had some Polish friends.

We didn't know it then, but the Reich orders that were being drawn up in Berlin would come down hardest of all on Poland in the months ahead. If a Pole helped a Jew and gave them shelter by the time of the *Aktions*, the removal to the camps, that Pole and his entire family would be sentenced to death. It hadn't reached that point, of course, in 1940, but the Christians were still taking a risk. They'd slip us food when they could and this sometimes put the older Pivniks in an awkward position. One day I came home with a food parcel tucked under my jacket. It was a present from the mother of my friend Dudek and it was pork sausage. Now this didn't prove too much of a problem for me – in the years before the war I'd often eaten pork at Dudek's house – but to my father it was anathema. With all that had happened to Judaism in Bedzin – the burning of the synagogue, the closure of the schools, the hangings, burnings and shootings of Jews and the wholesale treachery of the *Judenrat* – there were still principles and my father could not deviate from the teachings that were part of his life. His initial reaction was to throw the sausage away. I don't remember a row between my parents, nor even a discussion. Perhaps father just looked into mother's eyes and what he saw there was enough. She was a good Jew too, but her children were hungry and for a mother that was the only priority. In the end, he left the house while we ate the pork, and from that point on, that was the unspoken agreement. We wouldn't eat pork in front of him and we wouldn't tell him if we ate it behind his back. It was one of the prices we all had to pay for being the targets of madmen.

In some ways, the Occupation hit my father hardest of all. He was a proud man, a traditionalist, and he was used to having the respect of the community. Now he had none. And it got worse when one day he came home, shaking and covered in blood. He'd gone out to try to buy bread and had been gone for some hours. We weren't concerned at first because that was how it was with queues. You just had to wait for as long as it took. This time a neighbour brought him home. He'd been denounced in the queue – the dreaded pointed finger which would become such a feature of my life from now on – and several policemen had had a go at him. He was badly shaken but the wounds on the inside must have been worse than those we could see. From then on, the only place he went was Rossner's factory. Hendla, Nathan and I stood in the queues. It was my mother who became the rock in our family, the one who kept us together. Looking into my father's face I could see that all the fight – all the life – had gone out of him.

The younger generation had more of a will to fight back – the exuberance and folly of youth, I suppose, and a sort of resistance movement developed in Bedzin in the spring of 1940. It came from the youth organisations I had been too young to join before the invasion and couldn't now because they were technically illegal. *Poale Zion, Dror, Gordonia, Hashomer Hatzair, Hanoar Hatzoni, Hashomer Hadati* – I remember their names still, as many young Germans would remember the anti-Nazi *Edelweiss Piraten* movement in Germany itself. Hendla in particular was heavily involved in *Gordonia*, although her dreams of going to Palestine seemed more remote than ever now. One of my cousins, Hirsh Wandasman, was involved still further and it was people like him the Nazis watched most carefully.

The way to do this was via informers and there were two of them in particular I had cause to remember. One of them was a publican called Kornfeld. He would have been in his thirties, I suppose, and before the queue incident confined my father to Number 77 and the Rossner factory, he and Nathan would occasionally go to the pub on Saturday afternoons (with Nathan strictly on the lemonade!). Kornfeld's brother-in-law was a little younger and worked as a shoemaker; his name was Machtinger.

I was coming home from work one evening when I saw Machtinger ahead of me, walking along Modzejowska. With him was a German police officer, a nasty bastard named Mitschker I'd come across before. The two of them were behaving, as the police would say today, suspiciously, checking to see no one saw them as they sneaked into the side door of the house of Piekowski, the horse dealer. As one of the richest men in Bedzin, Piekowski had been approached by the *Judenrat* to help with the extortion problem. He'd flatly refused, even though another horse dealer, Wechselmann, had given what he could.

What intrigued me about Machtinger and Mitschker was that they went into the ground-floor apartment of Piekowski's grand house. The Piekowskis lived on the first and second floors; their pretty blonde daughters lived in a separate flat on the ground floor. I waited for a minute or two – there was no sign of the Piekowski parents. Then I ducked through the bushes and round the back of the house, standing on tiptoe to peep through a gap in the curtains of the window that overlooked the garden.

I was fourteen by this time and even though what I saw wasn't much of a rite of passage, I was astonished nevertheless. There were beer bottles on the table, the room lit with lamps to compensate for the drawn curtains. The younger girl was about eighteen, not much older than me but a woman in every sense. She was stark naked, lying on the settee in a languid pose. The older one was reclining on a bed. She'd have been a few years older with a fuller figure and I stood transfixed. I'd often seen those girls around, of course, but never with their clothes off. Mitschker and Machtinger couldn't get into the action fast enough. They were both struggling with their shirts, throwing off their boots and wrenching their trousers down.

I suppose my tongue must have been hanging out but this was no ordinary peep show. I knew that these girls weren't enjoying themselves, even if the men were. They were going through the motions, their faces stony and passionless. This was blackmail of some sort, payment for an easy life and for the authorities to look the other way. I got scared and ran away.

Life is full of 'ifs' isn't it? If this wasn't wartime, if we weren't Occupied, if I hadn't known about the treachery of Mitschker and Machtinger, I'd probably have dashed around to Dudek and the others and enjoyed being centre of attention while I told them all what I'd seen, their eyes wide and their mouths open before the sniggering started. But this wasn't a story to spread. Its consequences were too drastic. Word got round nevertheless – and not from me. An SS man sleeping with a Jew was a shooting offence. And there was no honour among lowlife like that.

Mitschker had a scare – I don't know the details – but he dropped his two informers like hot cakes. Machtinger and Kornfeld were among the first to go once the deportations started. Piekowski, his wife and daughters followed later.

I couldn't at the time take in what was happening. Mine was a constantly shifting world in which policemen had sex with girls they should have been protecting and the *Judenrat*, our own people, were waiting for a chance to earn Brownie points, getting into bed in a different way with the SS.

It must have been in April 1941 that refugees began to stream into Bedzin. Others, they told us, were moving to nearby Sosnowiec. They weren't refugees in the same sense as the homeless people running away from the *Wehrmacht* in the autumn of 1939, but their homes had gone nonetheless. They came, in their carts and wagons, sledges and prams, carrying as many of their belongings as they could, from the town of Oswiecim, just over forty kilometres away. I'd never been to the place, but it was not unlike a small version of Bedzin with half its population Jewish. The photograph that somebody took at the time of the new arrivals confirms what I remember – by this time we all had to wear yellow armbands with a black Star of David. They had been moved out of their homes because the Germans were building a big new camp at the artillery barracks near their town and there was no room for them. We didn't realise then how many of them would be moving back there before too long.

It must have been about this time – and perhaps because of the new influx – that the noticeboard outside the *Judenrat* headquarters announced that every Jew must have his photograph taken. Throughout time people have been afraid of this sort of registration and classification. Primitive peoples in nineteenth-century empires were afraid of the camera because they believed it stole their souls. Excessive record-keeping, often a forerunner to increased taxation, was viewed with dread too. In England in 1086 when William the Conqueror's men asked people how many ploughs and cattle they had, they thought it was Judgement Day from God. The optimists among us thought we might be deported to Palestine and Hendla would have her wish after all. Pessimists predicted every hellhole they could think of, perhaps in the Far East. I know now that this was part of the Madagascar Plan, one of the many 'final solutions' the Nazis envisaged for us Jews.

The plan was hatched the previous year and there had indeed been a brief flirtation with Palestine among the Nazi high command, but it was considered unviable. Madagascar belonged to the French but France had been overrun by the *Wehrmacht*, except Vichy France in the south, which was collaborating with the Germans. The cash to send us all to the island off Africa would be found from confiscated Jewish property. Even at 228,000 square miles and the world's fourth largest island, Madagascar was too small to house all the Jews in Europe – not that our continued prosperity was of any concern to the Nazi high command. The problem arose because the British would not play ball with Hitler, and Britain, as even the Germans had to acknowledge, ruled the waves. Nevertheless, we all dutifully stood for our 'mug shots'. The one of my grandmother still survives – one of only two pictures I have of her; she was slowly going blind, even then.

We struggled on as best we could but the arrival of the Oswiecim Jews made resources more limited still and the black market worked overtime. Father, a broken man though he was becoming, still had the energy to smuggle scraps of cloth out of Rossner's uniform factory and he'd sit at home at Number 77, cross-legged on the floor with his needle and thread, making clothes for Gentiles in exchange for flour or some sausage.

But danger was never far away. Men and women in the factory sometimes lost fingers in the unguarded machinery. There were no safety regulations for Jewish workers. But one day things got too close for comfort. Our near neighbours were the Schwartzbergs; they lived three doors down from us and in the spring of 1941 Mr Schwartzberg and his eldest son were taken away by the Nazi police. I didn't see it but it was the talk of the street for days. Their crime? Schwartzberg senior had bought a cow from a Gentile farmer, slaughtered it and sold the beef. How flagrant could the man be, the Nazis would have asked themselves. Clearly, Schwartzberg had enough money to buy the animal in the first place, even though he should have handed any surplus to the *Judenrat*. He was also undermining the SS ration system which was at subsistence level. And he was raising two fingers at their authority. We heard after a few days that both Schwartzbergs had been shot.

Next came the Wechselmanns, another family we knew well. One of them had bought a sack of flour from a Gentile and all of them had eaten the bread it made. They hanged the Wechselmanns and I saw their bodies dangling from the trees that ringed the main cemetery. Again, as with the invasion, the purpose was deterrence. Cut out the black-marketeering or this – this frozen, grey corpse with the awkwardly jutting neck – will be you.

In the eighteen months of Nazi Occupation, I saw my parents ground down by the sheer strain of keeping the family going. I saw it in the streets too and in Killov's factory – young men grown old and grey with fear, with malnutrition, with exhaustion. I was working twelve-hour shifts as a boy of fourteen and struggling to find a crust of bread to eat. I didn't appreciate the fact that we were still together as a family, still hoping that official policy would change; that one day all Germans would be like Rossner and Killov. And what, after all, had we done? The Schwartzbergs and the Wechselmanns had broken the law, but it was an unreasonable law, an unjust law. And the rest of us? We were Jews and that was enough.

4
Day Turned to Night

I t's difficult to be accurate about the pace of change in Bedzin before they set up the ghetto. All I know is that it was downhill, a one-way process heading in the wrong direction.

On 22 June 1941 the Germans launched their Operation Barbarossa, the invasion of Russia. News of the whole thing reached us of course second-hand and days later, but the Russians seemed to have been totally unprepared for what happened. The statistics available today make grim reading – by midday on that first day, the Luftwaffe had knocked out nearly 1,200 Soviet planes and Army Group North, commanded by Reichsfeldmarschall Wilhelm Leeb, had advanced forty kilometres into Russian territory. The Army Group South which had been massing, unbeknownst to us, in the general area east of Bedzin, was doing less well, but was advancing nevertheless.

The knock-on effect for us was that deportations began in earnest. Young men in particular were targets, being rounded up and taken away to labour camps. The only safety net was being accepted as an essential war worker, what they called in other parts of Europe as having a 'reserved occupation'. My father and Hendla were all right because they worked on *Wehrmacht* uniforms in Rossner's factory. I was all right because I counted as a skilled labourer under Killov and Haüber. The problem was Nathan.

My big brother was nearly eighteen and well within the age when deportations were most likely. And at this point he still worked with Dombek, outside the factory complex proper, and was more exposed than the rest of us. The obvious solution was to get him inside, working with me, and by hook and by crook we did that and Nathan Pivnik became a joiner.

The timing had not been good, however. The *Judenrat*, ever more anxious to do the Nazis' bidding, were busy drawing up lists for deportation and would pin these to the dreaded noticeboard outside their offices in the old Furstenberger school. It was around this time – April 1942 – that Nathan was arrested. This was a ghastly experience for him, a seventeen-year-old boy with what he assumed was his whole life stretching before him. My father was at least allowed to visit him and take him food although there was precious little of that.

The deportations which now scarred our lives were part of the ongoing – and continually changing – Jewish policy of the Third Reich. We had no idea that new initiatives usually sprang from the unminuted and secret meetings that Hitler had with Himmler at Berchtesgaden or in Berlin. For the moment the Jewish solution was still a territorial one. Madagascar had failed, but there were other options. The euphemism 'resettlement in the East' began to be heard all over Europe. But we were in the East already, and for us the natural destination was the labour camp. By May or June 1942, we noticed another change. It wasn't just the young, active men who were appearing on the lists of the *Judenrat*, it was the old and the crippled, the people who needed all the help society could give them. Except that society wasn't giving them any help at all. Old ladies with their *sheitels*, their traditional black wigs; old men with no teeth and people with an artificial arm or leg; those confined to wheelchairs; the blind. They were expendable, all of them surplus to requirements in the brave new world Hitler and Himmler were cooking up between them.

And we began to notice an increased frequency in freight trains that rattled and rumbled through the junction near Modzejowska. Wooden boxcars with slats, the sort of thing you'd see every day if you lived near a railway, trucks taking cattle, pigs, sheep or poultry to slaughter. But these weren't quite the same. There were padlocks on the sliding doors and barbed wire around the air holes. On the roof sat SS men with rifles and yet more in the guards van. As a fifteen-year-old I didn't know what to make of this – they were probably transporting Russian prisoners-of-war to a labour camp further west. Then I saw the faces of the truck inmates – pale, drawn men of all ages with long, straggling beards and frightened eyes staring out of the shadows. I know now that they were Jews, my own people, singled out for special treatment, what the Germans called *Sonderbehandlung*, bound for the camps of Belsen, Treblinka and Sobibor.

More and more in the summer of 1942 there was talk of the camp at Oswiecim which the Germans called Auschwitz. It wasn't far away and people knew people who knew people. There was talk of a little white house where Jews were sent to be killed. But that was nonsense, surely. This was the 1940s, the twentieth century; things like that

had happened in the Dark Ages under madmen like Genghis
Khan and Timur I Leng. People who whispered these things
must be idiots.

12 August 1942. It was a sweltering day, the sky over
Bedzin a cloudless blue. This was the day of the *Aktion*,
the day the *Judenrat* had been threatening for months.
Every Jew in Bedzin and its outlying villages was to report
to one of the two football stadiums in the town and we
were to bring our papers. Jews had always had to be
prepared to show their papers but the war had brought a
new urgency to this. Every Jewish male now had 'Israel'
appended to his name; every female, 'Sara'. The Pivniks
made their way to Hakoah, the stadium on the edge of
town. I'd often been there before, cheering on the local
teams from the terraces, hoping to catch sight of my
schoolboy heroes, like Nunberg, the best goalie in Poland.
But the day of *Aktion* was different.

There must have been 20,000 of us crammed into that
football field, most people sitting in their family clusters,
talking in muttered asides, anxious, apprehensive. Mothers
tried to quieten their grizzling babies, tetchy and fretful in
the climbing heat. Small children, naturally wanting to run
around as they always did, were told to sit down and
behave. I noticed my mother keeping Josek close to her.
There were SS men patrolling the grounds, armed and
watchful, the odd dog straining at the leash and barking
at the nearest Jews.

Shortly before midday, an SS officer made an announcement over the tannoy system and the muttered hubbub
faded into silence. We were told a selection was to be made
– the first time I had come across the idea. We were all to

be divided into three groups. Essential workers, Group A, would stay here in Bedzin. Group B would be sent to the labour camps. Group C – and in German, it sounded even more sinister, would be *'umgeseidelt im Osten'* – resettled in the East.

If ever we believed in omens – and the Jews are prone to it – what happened next made the hairs on the back of my neck crawl. There was a rumble of thunder directly overhead and the sky crackled with lightning. In minutes, day had turned to night and the sky was black as pitch. The rain stung down on us, sending the little ones scurrying under their parents' coats for shelter. The ground we sat on became waterlogged and the rain seeped through to our skin. Nobody had come prepared for this, not even the SS and they got as wet as we did, shouting orders, marshalling us into lines, prodding us forward with their gun muzzles. Now the kids were crying in fear and little Wolf and Josek were near to tears themselves.

Jostling started in the crowd. The lines couldn't form properly, there wasn't the room. Those at the edge of the field began to look for ways out, digging under the chain-link fence under cover of the sheets of water and the press of people. I recognised some of their helpers as friends of Hendla and Nathan from *Gordonia*. The Zionist groups that learned Hebrew and longed for a kibbutz in Palestine had turned into partisans, an Underground pledged to resist this latest example of Nazi bureaucracy. They were hauling up the wire and helping people to scrabble through. As I turned round, I saw my brother Majer join them, wriggling his way through the undergrowth, his jacket, hands and face daubed with the mud that was suddenly everywhere. I didn't understand at the time why Majer went, but as the hours wore on, the situation became clear. And beyond the wire, the shooting started.

Still the thunder rolled and the faces of the terrified were lit by the lightning flashes. You could tell the rattle of rifle fire from the noise from the heavens and we all jumped every time we heard it. What if they were shooting at Majer? I had a lot of faith in my little brother; at twelve, he was strong and fast but no one can outrun a bullet. We saw through the mist of the rain the rifle butts and clubs of the SS fall again and again on saturated, desperate bodies struggling beyond the wire. The *Aktion* was judgement day and none of us would be quite the same after it.

It rained all night and all night we waited in the open, huddled together. I don't think anyone slept. We were cold now, chilled to the bone, exhausted and hungry. We hadn't eaten since breakfast the day before and the little ones were complaining, asking when they could go home and what was going to happen to us.

It was now that we thanked our lucky stars for Alfred Rossner's blue cards, proof that my father and Hendla were essential war workers. And now I understood why Majer left. My parents had sent him, hugely risky though it was. Nathan and I had similar documentation from Herr Killov so we were all going to stay put in the essential workers group A in Bedzin. The cards we were issued with during our long, terrible wait at the stadium gave permission for two people each to stay. That meant that my mother and the little ones could be included and would be safe. With Majer gone, however nerve-wracking a situation it was for my parents, the numbers added up. Almost. The exception was my grandmother, Ruchla-Lea, because we were a family of ten and were one card short. The last I saw of her was in that sodden, churned field with rows of exhausted Jews dependent on a piece of paper to determine their lives. She was eighty-two by now and far from well, frail and half blind. All my life I had known and loved her, her kindly twinkling eyes, her bony hands, her bedtime stories. She was part of my life and now she was ripped from us. There were sudden, tearful farewells, empty-sounding phrases. We said we'd see each other soon and my parents urged her to look after herself; then the frail old lady was shepherded away to stand with a huddle of other town elders, shivering with shock and fear. I never saw her again.

As we were leaving the stadium, numb and trembling, a strange thing happened. A neighbour of ours, a Christian Pole, took my father by the arm and offered to take little Josek away, to raise him as his own child. Agonising decisions like that take days, weeks, perhaps months, to make. My father, who had just lost his own mother, now stood to lose his youngest child too. In those whirlwind seconds he went with what must have been his gut reaction and said no. He wanted to keep what was left of our family together.

The *Judenrat* posted another list. Nathan's name was on it. My father pointed out in vain that Nathan was an essential war worker but he hadn't been in Killov's factory for long enough and was deemed expendable. The usually supportive Herr Haüber wasn't there at the time because he'd been sent away on service. The only other solution was to hide Nathan.

It seems extraordinary to me today that a teenage boy could hide in a town like Bedzin, where everybody watched everybody else and a network of spies was everywhere, reporting to the *Judenrat* or the German authorities. I never knew where he was and looking back, my father and mother probably engineered it that way – better I shouldn't know. The less I knew the less I could tell anyone who asked. I remember various members of the *Judenrat* hammering on our door at Number 77, while we could still call that place home, looking in cupboards and outbuildings without success. These were policemen, in uniform, with jackboots and what today we call 'attitude'. But they were also Jews and none of us could understand how they could hound us, looking for another Jew they had branded a criminal because he didn't want to leave his family. For most of the time, Nathan was in fact hiding in Killov's factory, sleeping in the hayloft above Dombek's horses.

Then came the day when our world fell apart. Since my father had been beaten up by the police and quite possibly before that, it was my mother who had become our anchor. She kept us fed, somehow; kept us dressed. And if she didn't laugh as much as she used to, she tried to keep us kids cheerful. One day – and the pain of it has blotted out exactly when – the *Judenrat* police arrived with a solution to the problem of Nathan. They would take my mother away and hold her, effectively as a hostage, against his return.

Now there was no one to look after the little ones; Majer was back with us of course, soon after the Hakoah selection, but Josek was still only five and the rest of us were handling the long factory shifts at Rossner's and Killov's.

So, faced with this, my father got a letter to Nathan. I never saw that letter so I don't know whether father told his eldest son to come home or whether he told him the news and left it up to his conscience. Either way, Nathan turned himself in. Even at this late stage, he tried to see Herr Haüber, but the man was still away. Desperate, he tried to see Haüber's cook, to get him to vouch for him. But everyone was aware of a renewed intensity in Nazi persecution, a lurch towards the genocide no one wanted to believe could happen, and the cook refused to see him. Hendla went with Nathan to the police station and she came back alone.

Then my mother came back and it must have been heart-breaking for her – for both my parents – to know they had secured her freedom at the price of her son. There have been so many farewells since that one and the years have dimmed it in my memory, so that I can no longer be sure exactly when or in what order these things happened. But one thing I do know for sure; I would be the only one to see Nathan again, to hold him, crying, in my arms. Except for one day, when he was given special permission to help us move into the Kamionka.

To the east of Bedzin was a hill called the Kamionka which had been used as a quarry since the nineteenth century. I knew the place well – it was a kids' paradise with alleyways that ran through a shanty town and little rickety homes built in the caves that had been gouged out of the chalky stone. When the quarries were abandoned, squatters had moved in, as they did on the edge of many industrial centres across Poland, and they'd built themselves a town. Over time, the wooden shacks had been replaced with brick but it was still very run down – very much an enclave that was on the wrong side of the tracks. Seven months after the *Aktion* at Hakoah, the Kamionka became our home.

Essentially, it was a straight swap. Poor Gentiles moved into Number 77 and we ended up in the Bedzin ghetto. If you read history books today you will find that they argue about what was behind Nazi Jewish policy in the Third Reich. Some have an intentionalist theory: the ghetto was a halfway house to extermination, the genocide that the Nazis planned all along. Others have a functionalist explanation: the Nazis had not really thought what they were going to do with the millions of Jews they found in Poland and now the millions more in Russia. Certainly, in terms of speed and timing, the creation of ghettoes was erratic and sporadic. And no two were alike. Warsaw had its thick walls, Lodz its barbed wire; at the Kamionka, there was nothing at all but markers in the ground – as if to say, *this is all of Poland you've got now, Jews; make the most of it.*

Why did they move us at all? After all, we'd struggled along somehow for nineteen months under Nazi control, living at Number 77 and doing the best we could. At the time we didn't understand it and anybody who asked probing questions of the *Judenrat* ran the risk of instant deportation, so you didn't ask. The explanation usually trotted out – where it was trotted out at all – was that ghettoes were there to limit the spread of disease, especially typhus, that was known in these years among Germans as *Judenfieber*, Jew fever. Another theory ran that they were glorified prison camps to keep us penned in while the Reich turned all its attention to beating the Russians on the Eastern Front.

We had heard rumours from Lodz in the north that they had a sealed ghetto from as early as April 1940 and there, as in Bedzin, the *Judenrat* became the administrative unit of government, still jumping around as their Nazi masters pulled their strings.

When the day of the move came, the Pivniks took what they could carry. Nathan had managed to borrow Dombek's horses and cart and we loaded everything on it before making our way to the Kamionka. And then Nathan had to say goodbye once more. It was yet another Exodus and it reminded me of the fleeing thousands I'd seen when the invasion started and again when the Jews of Oswiecim came to our town. Now we were part of it, a dispossessed people on the move. I would never live in our little court-yard in Modzejowska again.

The photo library of Yad Vashem in Jerusalem has photographs of the Kamionka, showing dilapidated shacks and mothers hanging clothes on washing lines, as they tried to keep as normal an appearance as possible. Alleyways and streets were full of furniture, rotten in the rain or brittle-dry in the sun, the bits and pieces of peoples' lives that could not fit in this exercise of Nazi 'downsizing'. All eight of us were crowded into a one-roomed house, but at least it was brick built.

The German police prowled the perimeter of the Kamionka night and day. Polish auxiliaries helped them; so did the fire brigade. I remember thinking that those men wore the uniforms my uncle Moyshe used to make for them in Szopienice, all a reminder of the catastrophe and the chaos of the last three years. And every day, the *Judenrat* police force also patrolled inside the ghetto. They wore white covers to their peaked caps and even though they were only allowed rubber clubs rather than weapons, the yellow stars on their tunics meant nothing. They were policemen, as corrupt and vengeful as any I'd known. But I'd been dodging people like that for years; I had nothing but contempt for them.

In the Kamionka, food shortages became severe. I don't know if anyone has analysed the figures for Bedzin, but in Warsaw the daily calorie intake for Jews was 300, at a time when for Poles it was 634 and for Germans 2,310. I only remember one shop in the ghetto, a general store that sold bread, vegetables and, very occasionally, scraps of meat. The queues to which we'd long grown accustomed continued, my mother and the little ones waiting patiently to hand over their ration coupons for whatever they could get.

And the rumours went on. The Germans had been stopped at the Russian city of Stalingrad. I don't remember hearing that things were going against them in North Africa too, where the British 8th Army had beaten Feldmarschall Erwin Rommel at El Alamein, but if I had, I don't suppose for a moment that I put two and two together. If the war wasn't going well for the Germans, that was bad news for us. Yes, we longed for liberation from all this; my father in particular just wanted to go back home and to his workshop at Number 77. But no one realised it would get worse before it got better.

The one touch of reality at the Kamionka, the sense of continuity, came from work. But even here there was a change. Before the ghetto we made our own way to the factories, albeit only along certain streets. Now we tramped in a column, watched and guarded – a people on the move every day. It was less than a kilometre to Killov's and the clocking in and the relatively good food kept us sane.

The cold came and the snow and still we had no word of my grandmother or of Nathan. The world turned, filled with rumour and counter rumour, filled with dread. You keep your nose clean, you keep your head down, you get on with your work. As the spring of 1943 gave way to summer, the tension was palpable. The deportations continued. The first ones were accompanied by the empty promises of the *Judenrat*: council members would be going with the groups that were rounded up; they would be accompanied by doctors. Their destinations? Labour camps, of course, to keep up the war effort, to serve the Reich. It wouldn't be long, the official line went, before Comrade Stalin would surrender and there would be peace. A Slav army, after all, was no match for the Master Race.

But no doctors went with the groups and the *Judenrat* members stayed behind in Bedzin. Even so, it was still relatively civilised; deportees took suitcases with them, food parcels for the journey. Sometimes it would have to be cattle-trucks used for transportation, but not always and anyway, that was a temporary, regrettable inconvenience. There was, after all, a war on.

One deportee was a Polish friend called Vladek. He used to come home once a month from a labour camp but he was very tight-lipped about what went on there. Before all this madness started he too had pigeons and we spent quite a bit of time together. He bought Nathan's bike with 100 kilos of potatoes – paper money was virtually worthless in the Kamionka.

It was while we were living in the ghetto that we heard news of Nathan. An old Polish friend of the family told us that he was working at the camp at Blechhammer in Slawiecice, a chemical plant, and he was well. Mother sent him some barley and some underwear but we had no idea whether he ever got them as he was not allowed to write.

We noticed – even possibly little Josek, who was six by now – that the visitors to the ghetto were becoming more frequent. And the visitors were SS men, grey-uniformed with their lightning-flash collar insignia and the grinning death's head above the peaks of their caps. They came with their own German police, the Gestapo, and the ghetto police ran at their heels with their vicious dogs, trying to look important. The barking and clatter of boots echoed around the Kamionka, ringing in our ears and reverberating around the hovels we called home. I remember hearing the thud and crash as they kicked down doors and shouted orders. There was no need now for the '*Ist ein Jude hier?*' that we'd heard before the ghetto. Everyone in the Kamionka was a Jew and the question was redundant. Now they were looking for certain Jews – the young and able or the surplus relatives of the young and able. It was time to go. And if anyone objected – and a few did – the answer was a bullet in the head. Those were the sounds of the ghetto – dogs barking, boots clashing, furniture going over. Then the short, sharp screams punctuated by the dull crack of a pistol or rifle. And stillness.

How long would it be, we all wondered, before they came for the Pivniks? By the long, hot summer of 1943 I was nearly seventeen, ideally eligible for deportation. What were our options? We could run, father emotionally drained and exhausted, three little children being shepherded through the alleyways by mother, Hendla and me. How far would we have got in the night, in the dark, against the dogs and guns of the ghetto guards?

The alternative was to hide and this we tried to do. Our house may only have had one room but it had a steeply pitched roof and there was an attic space which might *just* be big enough for us when the jackboots came to a halt outside our door. I was an experienced carpenter by now and my father and I built a wooden partition from scraps behind which we stashed food and water. We put a chamber pot and a bucket there too.

Things like this were happening all over the ghetto and it was part of the quiet resistance by Jews, a story which still waits to be told. Why didn't they fight back, the Holocaust deniers ask today; if things were so terrible, why didn't the Jews do something about it? The answer is that we did and it started in the Kamionka for the Jews of Bedzin. Scraps of information, pieces of timber and nails lifted from the factory, food that would keep in a small, cramped space in a hot summer. It's not the stuff of heroism which overgrown schoolboys like me still dreamed about, but it was resistance nonetheless. Rumours reached us about the ghetto rising in Warsaw in April. It gave us pride. It gave us hope.

On 19 April partisans inside Warsaw had snapped and hit back. Deportations there, we learned long afterwards, were on a far larger scale than those from Bedzin. In October 1940, nearly half a million Jews were crowded behind those seven-foot walls; two years later, only 70,000 were left. The Jewish partisans stole guns, slaughtered the

SS wherever they found them and lost their pursuers in the Warsaw sewers, with cholera, typhus and rats for company. Nearly a month later – and it was as well perhaps that we didn't know this at the time – the SS commander there boasted that 14,000 Jews had been killed since the rising began and a further 40,000 had been sent to Treblinka.

The end for us came on a hot, dry Saturday late in July. Beyond the Kamionka I remember seeing the harvest in full swing, men in shirtsleeves and vests swinging their scythes and sickles under the bristling guns of the SS. The sheaves of corn they collected stood like silent sentinels in the fields, as I remembered them in the Garden of Eden through all the summers of my childhood. I'd been working all day as usual, in the factory, barely able to remember now the rituals of *Shabbat* in peacetime. We ate supper and went to bed. I don't remember the conversation or anything else different about that day until the early hours of the morning.

I woke up with a start. Jackboots. Dogs. Shouts in German. Coming our way, up our alley, to our door. Father had time to pop his head out and ducked back inside again. Germans and far more than usual. He shepherded us up into the loft space, Mother and Hendla quieting the children who by now knew better than to ask anything but whispered questions. There was shooting and screaming as Father and I dragged the false partition into place and crouched there, hardly daring to breathe.

By turning my legs and leaning sideways, I could see our alley through a peep hole we'd made from a loose brick and beyond that to the ghetto square. Something was going on. This wasn't a conventional raid for deportation purposes. This was a gunfight. The people were fighting back. Police were running in all directions, firing indiscriminately, the flashes from their pistols illuminating the twisted little houses they ran between. The SS, lights reflecting off their insignia, were more organised, in control. I even saw members of the Hitler Youth, with their ridiculous shorts and scarves waving their little *Hitlerjugend* knives in the air and shouting some rabid Nazi slogan. They were boys of my age and younger and they wanted to kill us.

Perhaps Hendla had known something about this and had kept quiet. Perhaps she was not, as young people say today, 'in the loop'. The resistance leaders, I know now, were Baruch Giftek and Frumka Plotnika and the freedom fighters were all members of the *Gordonia* and the other Zionist groups. How they got hold of weapons I don't know, but this was not Warsaw. We had no sewers to hide in and perhaps our desperation was not so great. In the fighting of the next few days, over 400 partisans were killed, many of them just like us, civilians caught in crossfire. The German casualties? One.

All that terrible night we crouched in our homemade Hell and at dawn watched through the brick loophole as neighbours were frogmarched out of their hovels with whatever they could carry and kicked along the alleyways. What we were watching was the 'liquidation' of the ghetto, that appalling casual euphemism that actually means the deaths of thousands. I heard my father say in one of his grimmest moments, 'What's happened to the others will happen to us too,' and we prayed. We prayed every day in the Kamionka just as we had in our real home.

Sunday was 1 August. Christians call it Lammastide, the festival of the candles. Beyond the Kamionka, beyond Poland, the war went on. Behind our partition we sweltered and worried, filling the chamber pot, the bucket. The heat and the stench were unbearable but we daren't move. Random shooting throughout the day told us that the Nazis had not just melted away. They were doing what they did best, hunting Jews.

By the end of Monday we had run out of water and our food supplies were getting low. Whatever plan my father had to stockpile essentials had not counted on a siege of many days' duration. To sneak out and find fresh water would be to invite certain death. The dogs would smell us, the prowling SS men were alert to catch any sound. Tuesday was just as hot, just as unbearable. We sat, caked in our own sweat, our mouths bricky dry, ill with dehydration. I don't know who suggested it, but I remember my mother sprinkling a little of the sugar she still had into a cup. The cup was passed and we drank from it, gratefully. It was warm, but it was sweet and it was liquid. It was urine.

I would be seventeen in a month's time and I was crawling in a sweltering attic in semi darkness, drinking piss and listening to the sobs of my siblings while outside the Germans were still shooting my people.

The end of the ghetto. The end of all things?

5

Descent into Hell

Our little resistance effectively ended on Wednesday 6
August. The liquidation of the Bedzin ghetto had
lasted for four days. In the end, for us, the summer heat
was unbearable and we climbed out of our partitioned
hidey-hole and gave ourselves up to the inevitable.

I can only remember fragments of that day, like the
glimpses of a dream. It must have been mid-morning when,
stiff and aching with dry, cracked lips, we joined a moving
column that wound its way down the hill from the
Kamionka to the station. It was less than a mile, but it
was like running a gauntlet. We had been assembled in the
ghetto square, perhaps a thousand strong. It crossed my
mind that even this tiny group of Jews outnumbered the
SS men who were marshalling us. But there were old people
in the crowd, babies and little children. In my family, Majer
was fourteen but Chana was a year younger; Wolf was
only eight and little Josek six. We were weak with hunger;
unarmed. You can't fight back against grown men with
machine-guns, rifles and dogs with resources like that.

During the trudge down the hill, local Gentiles jeered at
us, mocking and laughing. One or two were crying, their
heads in their hands. It symbolised the schizophrenic attitude of Poland to its 'Jewish problem'. These people had
been our neighbours once, men who placed their tailoring

orders in my father's workshop; women who had talked babies with my mother; shopkeepers we used to buy from; lads who kicked a football around with me. Now they were helping themselves to our furniture and meagre belongings, like hyenas picking over a kill and taking away the choicest bits. And I recognised the local police too and the fire brigade, herding us along like cattle. The SS men I didn't know but they prodded us with their gun muzzles and rifle butts. The little ones clung tightly to mother or father, terrified of the snarling, snapping dogs.

I used to love to watch the trains snorting and wheezing as they pulled in and out of the new, flat-roofed Art Deco station. The place now looked like nothing on earth. There were no civilians, nobody going about their daily business. Just more SS men and police and dogs, all the paraphernalia of the Nazi state. There was no sense to any of this. No one told us where we were going, just yelling '*Lausbub!*' '*Scheissjude!*' and '*Arschlöcher*' at us. *Scheissjude*. Shit Jew. Centuries of pointless hatred wound up in one snarled, unimaginative insult. If anyone faltered or dragged their feet, the batons of the police came down, cracking heads or shoulders.

There were no trains. So we stood on the platform in silence. Anyone who spoke was dragged out of position and hit. Terrified mothers kept their babies close to them, whispering in their unknowing ears, holding them close to their breasts, the only security they could offer.

Those forty or so minutes on the platform crawled by like years. Then we heard the shrill whistle and saw the smoke of a locomotive in the distance, a black engine with five carriages. On the roof sat SS men, armed to the teeth.

They wore their *stahlhelmes* with their distinctive low brim and with motorcycle goggles attached to them. I couldn't understand how they could hold on while the train was moving, but perhaps they had some sort of harness up there.

If there was going to be trouble it would be now. There were not many men in our group. My father was in his early fifties – I saw that then as being ancient – and I was sixteen. What could we do? Rush the lines of the SS? Jump the tracks and run for it? Everybody had a family – wives, mothers, kids. Still, in the chaos of boarding *something* might have been tried. In the event, nothing was. Like sheep we waited while the SS checked that the cars were empty and then we moved forward to the yelled orders '*Einsteigen!*' Get in! Get in! It didn't take long. We didn't have much in the way of personal possessions when we went into the Kamionka; we had even less now. Some people had a single suitcase or a bundle tied with string. These were thrown in along with the people. If there was a delay, it was caused by the old struggling to climb the steps or the little ones unable to make it by themselves. We were pushed into the carriages, some people crushing their backsides on the hard-slatted wooden seats, others jammed against walls and windows standing up. Kicks, thumps from the batons – this was our farewell to Bedzin. We didn't know it then, but most of us were leaving our birthplace for the last time. Within days, the SS could claim with smugness and satisfaction that yet another Polish town was *Judenrein*, cleansed of Jews. Another job well done.

They locked the doors and the train moved off, rattling and clanking its way out of Bedzin station. I remember my mother checking, as she probably had a hundred times that morning, that we were all together. And I remember too what happened next. A rabbi in the carriage with us took out his prayer book; so did my father and the other Orthodox men and they began chanting the psalms of King David.

I was never a particularly religious man. Certainly as a callow sixteen year old, whose Bar Mitzvah had been held in secret in a kitchen, I couldn't share my father's convictions. I prayed every day with my father because that was expected of me. I looked at the men praying, their faces grey and frightened under their hats. But their eyes were bright with optimism as they took comfort from the words they were reciting. They *knew* that God would help us. Hadn't that been His promise all along? He would find a way, give us a sign.

But He didn't.

We passed the same factories and mines, in this industrialised part of Poland, that we'd all passed so often before. The silver birches shone like burnished metal in the noon sun, dappled by their whispering leaves, the whistle and rattle of the train the modern, machine-driven sound which was the backdrop to the deep, sad, echoing psalms in the carriages.

I suppose we'd been travelling about an hour when we felt the train slow and jolt into a siding. Crouching a little and peering out between the crammed shoulders of people around me, I could see rows of upright concrete posts, curving inwards at the top and rows of barbed wire strung between them. Beyond that were more rows, this time of low, single-storey huts. This was a camp, probably, we all told ourselves, one of the labour camps they'd been sending Bedziners to for months. There was a screech of brakes and the carriage doors were thrown open. '*Raus! Raus!*' I hadn't appreciated how guttural and heartless the German language sounded until I heard it on that platform. We scrabbled together our few belongings and stumbled down onto the concrete, blinking in the sunlight.

There was a wall of noise – a voice snarling orders over a loudspeaker system, guards in the uniform of the Waffen-SS pushing and prodding with their guns, big dogs on chain leashes growling and barking, their teeth bared, their hair standing on end. It was difficult to tell who was more rabid – the dogs or their handlers. But it was the other men who fascinated me. I'd seen the SS and their outfits before, but these people wore prison clothing, with vertical stripes of blue and dirty white that looked like pyjamas, and they were yelling at us too. They told us to leave our luggage, to put it there on the Rampe. We'd get it later, they said, and they told us to line up.

We were all numb with shock. What kind of camp was this? My father stood with his mouth open, frowning, trying to make some sort of sense of what was happening. Hendla clung to his right hand, Chana to his left. The boys clustered around my mother, as they had for the whole journey here. Only I was standing alone.

To one side of me, one of our old neighbours from the Kamionka was trying to get some answers, to inject some sanity into this chaos. He was talking to one of the men in striped trousers who had a scruffy black jacket over his tunic and a shapeless workman's cap on his head. From nowhere, he brought a thick wooden club down on the

My father's brother – Uncle Moyshe, the tailor from Szopoenice. He never knew his influence saved my life.

My father with his mother, Ruchla-lea.

edzin, the town of my birth, howing the Great Synagogue entre) and the old Kazimerz astle, which still stands.

My beautiful sister Chana, who went straight to the gas at Birkenau 6 August 1943.

The Gordonia Youth Group in 1938, which grew into a Resistance organisation. My older sister Hendla is sitting in the second row, second from the left.

Alfred Rossner's tailoring shop. My father and Hendla worked for Rossner after the Germans came in 1942.

My grandmother, Ruchla-lea, as she looked the last time I saw her when day turned to night at the Hakoah Stadium.

Jews arriving in Bedzin in 1941 from Oswiecim, where the Nazis were building Auschwitz-Birkenau.

Jews moving out of their homes in Bedzin to the Kamionka ghetto.

Jews arriving at Auschwitz-Birkenau. They had been in the cattle trucks for days.

The 'lookalike' of the Rampe Kommando. The boy on the far left has often been cited as me, but I had left Birkenau by the time this picture was taken.

Selection at Birkenau. The women, children and elderly selected for death are on the left and the healthy, selected for work and perhaps survival, on the right.

'Life unworthy of life'. Women, children and old people walking to their deaths in the gas chambers. They had no idea.

Block IIa – the quarantine section of Birkenau, my home for ten days.

The primitive toilet facilities in the quarantine block. Here, Yitzak shat his diamonds.

Bed in Birkenau – five to a bunk and a rough straw mattress.

Death in Birkenau – quick and effective. The artist
Mieczysław Kościelniak depicts something I saw many times.

In the company of Cain – the SS of Birkenau enjoying a little R&R.
Front row, left to right: Karl Höcker, Otto Moll, Rudolf Höss, Richard Baer,
Josef Kramer, Franz Hössler and Josef Mengele.

Me, shortly after liberation in Neustadt May 1945. There are no surviving photos of me before this.

The *Cap Arcona* in her prime as a luxury cruise ship.

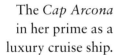

The *Cap Arcona* as she looked when she was bombed by the RAF, 3 May 1945.

questioner's head, shouting at him to shut up and do as he was told. And then, as if to emphasise that might is right, he gave him a thump with the stick, calling him, between blows, a filthy fucking Jew. The man from the Kamionka wasn't asking questions any more. He was lying on the platform, bleeding and gasping in shock.

I felt my shoulder jolted and another man in stripes yelled over my head to leave the luggage and get in line. Then as he looked down and saw me he whispered something I didn't understand – 'Tell them you're eighteen . . .' – and he was gone through the crowd, shouting his orders again.

What kind of place was this where men were clubbed senseless for asking polite questions? Where madmen in pyjamas told you in secret to lie about your age?

Lines were forming, after a fashion. In Bedzin we'd been forming lines for three years, queuing for bread; but this was different. We weren't soldiers; we knew nothing about drill. And the SS were obsessed with things like this. Regimentation. Instant obedience. Mindless subservience. The heel-clicking militarism of the old Prussia given a sinister, appalling purpose by a savage adherence to the sick mentality of the Third Reich. We huddled together about ten metres from the train, still snorting and belching smoke in the siding. Anybody still stumbling about, shocked, dazed, unable to move quickly enough, was being hit with sticks and rifle butts or bitten by the snarling dogs, their ivory teeth sinking through cloth and flesh.

An SS man was walking the platform, keeping up a shouted commentary to get families together in one place. Others were stopping at various points along the line, singling out individuals, asking how old they were, how many children they had, and they were winkled out of line.

Eventually two groups had formed, still in columns but something had happened. I didn't know it then but I had witnessed my second selection, the casual decision as to who should live and who should die in accordance with whatever insanity was currently coming out of Berlin. The first selection had been in the stadium back in Bedzin but there was something altogether more sinister – more final – about this one. My column was full of families, the old with their haunted, grey faces; the children with their tear-stained cheeks; parents with panic written all over them, trembling in the summer sun. The other column was all men, from their teens to their fifties, some of them glaring anxiously across to where we stood.

Along the platform a knot of SS men stood together, chatting, almost unaware of the rough-handling that had just happened. Beyond them, their engines running and the exhaust fumes rippling the ground, stood grey-painted trucks and a military ambulance. There were more snarled orders. The column of men moved off, past the knot of SS. I heard my mother's voice whispering Yiddish in my ear, 'Szlamek, save yourself,' and she gave me a hard shove in the direction of the men's line. I hadn't always obeyed my mother, the woman who had given me life and had held us together for the last three years. I stared at her, not knowing what to say. What could I have said? 'See you later?' 'See you tomorrow?' 'I'll be back in time for supper.' 'Back for *Shabbat*.' I looked at her, at all my family, for the last time. Father, whose world had fallen apart so long ago, whose God had forgotten him; mother, my anchor who would have forgiven me anything; Hendla, who had dreamed of Palestine; Majer, Chana, Wolf, Josek. My family. My blood. Dumbly, unable to grasp exactly what was happening, I joined the marching line.

We were walking past the knot of SS and I particularly noticed the officer who was with them. I am a tailor's son and I know a beautiful, hand-stitched uniform when I see one. He was dapper, good-looking, with dark hair, and when he smiled there was a gap between his front teeth. His boots were like mirrors in the summer sun and in his right hand he carried a pair of grey doeskin gloves. I remember this especially because he was looking each one of us up and down, flicking the gloves to left or right. I never saw him speak, but the flick was a command in itself. SS men alongside him hauled men out of line; left, left; right; left.

Those to the left were being sent back, marshalled in a tight U-turn along the platform to join the women, children, the families and the old. I'm not the tallest man in the world. When I was sixteen I suppose I stood about five foot three and probably looked strong. I'd been hiding in a stinking ghetto attic for four days, a stranger to soap or a comb, and I hadn't eaten or drunk very much, but I was wearing my factory overalls and stout boots. I remembered the striped lunatic on the platform, 'Tell them you're eighteen.' It began to make a kind of sense. I hoped the officer would flick his gloves to the left – that I'd be sent back to my family again and be able to hug them all. But he flicked to the right. He didn't ask my age or what work experience I had or where I was from. And I still didn't know that this was another selection and the officer didn't speak to me because he was Aryan, a member of the Master Race and I was a Jew, *Untermenschen*, sub-human. Nothing else mattered.

We were shunted to one side, to stand and watch as the family column went through the same procedure. I tried to see my family, but I was at the back of our column and I couldn't. As they passed the SS officer, the gloves flicked again left and right and a few people were separated out. Some of them were young women, and I wondered if Hendla was among them, wrenched from her family as I had been minutes before. But I couldn't see her. One or two men were singled out too and I couldn't understand why. They joined the bulk of the procession making its way towards the waiting trucks.

We saw the striped prisoners helping them at the tail-boards, passing babies and toddlers up to mothers and fathers, supporting the old and crippled. Still I couldn't see the Pivniks, though I believed I'd see them all later. The trucks cranked into action and snaked away in the afternoon, the ambulance bringing up the rear of the convoy.

After the initial panic and chaos of the arrival at the platform, a sense of calm had descended. Hell became Purgatory. The murmurs of the families had died away with the drone of the trucks' engines, but now, Hell came back. More orders. '*Schnell! Schnell!*' and we were being herded along in the wake of the trucks, our shuffling turning into a march and the march into a run as the SS and the striped men took up the pace. Anyone who couldn't keep up was pummelled to the ground or kicked where he lay.

We stood, panting and wheezing on that still hot August

day outside a bleak-looking barracks. Through the main door was a huge bare room which was used as a warehouse. We were told to strip and leave our clothes in neat piles. The striped men gave us bits of string to tie our boots or shoes together. Anyone who didn't move fast enough, anyone fumbling with his buttons, would feel a club across his shoulders or round his head as the striped men walked among us, barking their orders in German. It was obvious to me at once that these were not SS but trusties of some sort, chosen men who, while not Aryan or even *Volksdeutsche* themselves, would nevertheless comply with SS regulations. And many of them seemed to be enjoying themselves, seeing us humiliated and afraid.

They shouted at us to give up our gold and dollars and called us 'fucking Yids'. They knew we had them, they said, and we were to hand them over. It was all ancient nonsense, whipped up by the Nazi propaganda machine. Jews are obsessed with money. Jews are rich – they hoard gold. The trusties were shaking out trouser pockets, jackets, forcing open clenched fists looking for anything they could find. They pocketed coins and notes, tucked away cigarettes and rings. Prayer books were tossed onto the floor.

Once we were all stark naked, shivering for all the heat of the day, they gave us scraps of hard white soap and took us through into the next room. This one was as big and empty as the one we'd just left but it smelt damp and the floor was wet and slippery. Shower heads jutted from iron pipes overhead and we heard a trusty shout, 'Make sure you have a thorough wash.' The door slammed shut and we heard it lock. We'd all heard stories about showers in the camps and about what the SS made their soap from and for one long, ghastly moment, I started to believe it. Then the showers started – ice cold water that took my breath away and then turned warmer. After those stinking, sweltering days in the liquidation of the ghetto, it was a little bit of Heaven in this Hell.

No sooner had the water started to warm up, it was switched off with a loud clanking through the pipes. A door at the far side of the room was hauled open and we were moved on again, still naked and soaking wet. Here the trusties carried mechanical clippers of the type I'd seen used to shear sheep in the Garden of Eden and they started work on us. I can hear the whine of those contraptions to this day and I remember the pain of the process. They sat us down on hard wooden chairs and ran the clippers in swift swathes over our heads, like mowing a lawn. The agitating teeth ripped out hair and left cuts, deep and painful.

I don't think I had any chest hair so I was spared that, but the clippers ripped under my arms and around my balls. Anyone who screamed or cried out could expect a sharp tap with a club. I looked around at the others once the procedure was over. They had taken away our identities. Bald as babies, with cuts and scrapes all over us, we now all looked the same – Szlamek Pivnik, the schoolboy who had become a furniture maker was now an anonymous member of the *Untermenschen*. No clothes, no personal possessions, no hair and no hope.

Again a door opened. If I wasn't so terrified and demoralised I'd have been impressed by the cold efficiency of the place. Dehumanisation in less than two hours. In the next room were trestle tables with a trusty sitting behind each one. But before we reached them, we had a final indignity to undergo. A trusty grabbed my chin, forcing open my jaw and he peered inside my mouth. This wasn't amateur dentistry. The man was looking for valuables. Then I was jolted forwards and my feet kicked apart. I've never felt pain like it, doubled over as the trusty shoved some sort of prod up my arse. Nothing valuable there either. Shocked and bleeding I stood in line until it was my turn to go forward to the trestle table.

I'd been here before, witnessing the SS obsession with paperwork. I'd seen it at the Hakoah football stadium on the day the skies darkened so I knew what to expect. The trusty asked me my name. I told him it was Szlamek Pivnik. He asked me my date of birth. For a second I remembered it again, the whispered line of the trusty on the Rampe, 'Tell them you're eighteen.' In the end I told him the truth '1 September 1926.' He asked my place of birth and I told him, Bedzin.

I was still answering these questions when I felt a sharp pain in my left forearm. A trusty had written a number on my still damp skin in ink and started to scratch over it with a large needle mounted on a block of wood. Instinctively I pulled away, but he grabbed my wrist, slammed my arm down on the table and told me to stop fucking around. He growled in a German accent I hadn't heard before that he was tattooing my number. Tattooing is anathema to the Jews. I wondered briefly whether my father was undergoing this terrible indignity in another room. I kept still. Better to bear this pain than worse that would follow if I made a fuss.

The trusty looked me in the face, reading there all the

pain and the fear and the loss. He asked me who I had come with; was it my parents? The accent was still strange, but the voice soft. It was the only soft voice, other than my mother's, that I'd heard all day. I opened my mouth to speak but could make no sound.

He nodded, telling me I mustn't worry about it now. He finished his tattooing, and said, 'They're probably already in Heaven.'

Then they'd finished with me and I stumbled out through yet another doorway, numb with the shock of what I'd just heard. I looked down at the numbers on my arm, glittering with blood. It read 135913. I was an animal, stamped with an indelible number like sheep on their way to the slaughter. If I'd been able to read what the trusty had written on his lined foolscap sheet I might have been less impressed with Nazi efficiency. He'd got my personal details right, and the date – 6 August 1943 – but there was no mention of Bedzin. The official record reads: 'From the Sosnowiec ghetto.' In the scheme of things, you couldn't exactly call it the final indignity.

The next room was another clothing store. This one served to continue the essential anonymity of the camp. A trusty threw me a bundle of clothes and told me to put them on. Everything was striped – a shirt, a jacket, a pair of trousers, a cap. There was no underwear and the pair of wooden clogs was several sizes too big. In fact, nothing fitted at all and the cloth was rough and coarse, smelling disgusting. It was the ultimate in hand-me-downs. I didn't know it at the time but I was wearing a dead man's clothes. There was no belt. After all, we might use this to hang ourselves, so just to move about I had to hold my trousers up with one or two hands, depending on the circumstances.

It was well and truly dark by the time this whole induction was over and perhaps two hundred of us were lined up, in rows of five, to be marched into the camp proper. The SS were back in the equation now, leading us, along with the trusties, through a corridor of barbed wire through compounds of low wooden huts. We trudged for perhaps 300 metres, then came to a gate guarded by SS men. It was dragged open and through we went, our clogs clattering in the gathering dusk on a rough, stony track past yet more compounds surrounded by wire and electrified fences. Now we were speeded up. The march turned into a run and the shouts and the thuds of the trusties' clubs were the music of our advance. Two hundred metres more and we were at another gate. This was opened for us too and we were hurried past a long row of stable-like huts until they halted us outside one of them. Number 10 was painted neatly on the door. We would soon learn this was Block IIa, the Quarantine Block.

A trusty stood on the step in front of us. He wore a yellow armband with the letters KAPO in black stencilled on it and he called us to order. It wasn't the nicest welcome I've ever had. He called us fucking Jew scum and told us there was to be no talking. We were to get into bunks and sleep five to a bunk and that should keep us warm enough. We would get food and bedding in the morning, he told us. Then he ordered us to stay quiet and stay put. He paused so that what he had to say next had maximum effect, 'Cause any trouble and you're as good as dead.'

That did the trick. No one spoke as we went into the

near-darkness of Block 10. I squeezed in alongside four others, strangers. I'd never slept anywhere before other than with my family. Even on holiday in the Garden of Eden, we had all been together. Nobody undressed or even took off their clogs. My arm, my groin and my head stung with the treatment I'd received. My stomach growled and hurt – I hadn't eaten for three days and the only drink I'd had was my own sugared piss. The bunks were dusty and rickety, every slight movement causing the timber to creak and groan on the uneven earth floor. I wanted to cry myself to sleep but I was too scared even to do that. Instead, I lay in the darkness, listening to the breathing and snoring of the others, shaking uncontrollably.

Nothing could have prepared me for what happened during that long, dreadful night. I felt a rhythmic rubbing from behind and half turned to see a face leering in the darkness. He was a man in his forties who I remembered from the Kamionka. I didn't know his name and had never spoken to him and here he was, taking advantage of this bizarre night to bugger me. I couldn't believe that anyone could think of this after all we'd been through, but he clearly had other ideas and I felt my arse suddenly wet. I daren't cry out, for fear of the *Kapo*'s club or a bullet from the SS.

I closed my eyes and all night long the words of the tattooing trusty came tumbling into my head: 'Your family . . . they're already in Heaven . . .'

6

The Razor's Edge

That night felt like the longest of my life. Did I sleep at all? I don't think so. Sleep was a luxury in the camps. We didn't dream; only free people do that. I lay there, listening to the groaning, sobbing and praying. Did I hear the *Kaddish*, the Jewish prayer for the dead? I was too busy praying there'd be no more attention from the man who had abused me, but he lay like the dead too. The smell was awful. For all it was a hot August, the place was rank with mildew as well as the stench of bodies that had been trapped for too long in the ghettoes. The older men were whispering, words I couldn't catch. But I had no one to talk to and I daren't ask questions because I wasn't sure I could bear the answers.

It was probably dawn when the door of Block Ten crashed back and the warm sun streamed in, illuminating the dust in the air. A trusty blocked out the sun for a moment. I could see he was wearing a cap and had a jacket over his striped uniform. The orders were in German and the accent, I learned later, was Hamburg. He ordered us to get of our fucking beds and called us lazy bastards. We had to get out and move ourselves.

I all but fell out of my top bunk and the next thing I felt was a clenched fist to the side of my head. I jolted backwards, my vision blurred and crackling. Then I felt a boot up my backside; a trusty was telling me to get a fucking move on.

He crossed back to the door. He'd probably cuffed a few of the others, but I thought then that he'd singled me out. He bellowed at us to get lined up. We stumbled into the open air, glad to breathe it in after the congestion of the night. I suppose there were forty or fifty of us, standing in a ragged line outside our hut and the one next door. I would later learn to avoid eye contact with anybody, keep my head down and do as I was told, but this was my first day in whatever camp this was and I was still too shocked not to react to what was happening around me.

The trusty with the handy fist and boot was walking along the line counting us and he called across to another man holding a ledger. The Teutonic obsession with counting and record-keeping – we'd seen it in Bedzin, before the ghetto and after it, but here it ran riot, a bureaucrat's paradise.

There was a weird silence. Thinking back, the whole of the previous day had been noise – the screamed orders of the SS, the barking dogs, even the psalms on the rattling train and the moans in the block-house. Now you could have heard a pin drop.

'You filthy fucking Jew bastard!' There it was again, the heavy Hamburg accent. I heard his boots crunch on the ground and saw him cross to a man a few places down the line from me. He wasn't much older than I was, but looked deathly pale under the brown scars of his haircut. I saw the trusty swing up his club and bring it down with a sickening crunch on the pale prisoner's head. He sank to his knees with an incoherent grunting, his arms flailing uselessly above his head as he tried to ease his pain.

'You filthy, dirty bastard. You've shit yourself.'

The trusty's face said it all. He couldn't believe what he

94

was seeing – and smelling. He brought the club down again, if anything harder this time. And again. Each time the cudgel struck home, there was a cracking of bone and spurts of blood arced through the air. I couldn't look but I couldn't look away. The prisoner pitched forward, flat on his face, and I hoped that was that. It wasn't. The trusty paused, took a couple of steps back and then kicked the head of the man he'd just poleaxed. There was another crunch, like sticks being broken. I could see his bloody teeth on the ground at the opposite end from the pool of liquid shit.

I looked at the trusty. There was no emotion in his face, no pleasure, no pride. And certainly no regret. An SS man was walking in our direction and I felt sure he'd intervene, take the man's club away, bawl him out and get the injured man to a hospital. But he just glanced vaguely in our direction and walked on.

The trusty was still calling his victim a fucking dirty pig and was still aiming kicks at the fallen man's head, neck, body. It didn't matter to him where those boots landed and by that time I don't suppose it mattered to the prisoner either. His whole head was a mess of blood and he didn't seem to be breathing.

The trusty stood in front of us now, hands on his hips, club smeared with blood and brains and told us our futures, such as they were. In this block, he told us, we had to stay clean. He added, of course, that we were fucking Yids. He paused, his hard eyes scanning our lines, learning our faces, watching for signs of fight or disobedience. 'Listen to me,' he said, probably the most unnecessary three words I've ever heard, because listening was exactly what we were all doing. He told us his name was Rudi and that he was the

Aerial photograph of Auschwitz-Birkenau, 13 September 1944. My family and I arrived at Birkenau before the railway lines were extended through the main gate. I was then separated from my family and, after being shaved and tattooed, placed into block 10 which was in the quarantine area.

Blockältester, the Block Senior. We were to do what he told us straight away or we'd get what the prisoner had got. He then asked, for good measure, if we understood.

Yes, there was a lot to understand. A lot to learn. If you didn't, you died. This was Auschwitz-Birkenau, the most deadly extermination camp the Nazis could devise. And no birds sang here. It had grown, I learned in the weeks ahead, from a small concentration camp – Auschwitz I – adapted from a Polish army barracks. As the decisions from Berlin on Jewish policy became ever more insane, its status changed. It became a killing camp and the methods used required larger premises, to house the prisoners like us and to provide the gas chambers and their attendant crematoria. If you read about the Holocaust today, you'll read about the creators of it – Adolf Hitler himself; Heinrich Himmler, Reichsführer-SS with his racial obsessions; Reinhard Heydrich, 'the blond beast' who was his Number Two; Rudolf Höss, our own commandant at KL Auschwitz-Birkenau. I never met these men, never saw them, not even Höss as far as I can remember. For me, the creators of the Holocaust were Rudi and all the other *Blockältestes* and *Kapos* like him. They were a breed apart.

At Auschwitz the SS ran the place, a job specifically given to the *Totenkopf*, Death's Head units, at the outbreak of war. They made the overall decisions and held ultimate power but the day-to-day business was handled by the *Lagerälteste*, the camp seniors; *Blockälteste* like Rudi; *Stubendienst*, the barrack orderlies, and *Kapos*, more or less foremen or overseers of the barracks. There were *Lagerschreiber* and *Blockschreiber* who kept written records. Many of these men had been drafted in when the camp had opened three years earlier, several hundred of them from other concentration camps, to act as heavies and strong-arm men. They were habitual criminals, hardened thugs the Third Reich could use to good effect and they wore green triangles on their uniforms – Rudi was one of these. These *Berufsverbrecher*, professional criminals, worked hand in glove with the SS.

Men who wore black triangles were the *Asos*, the antisocial ones. It struck me as ironic that this term could be better applied to the BVs in their atrocious treatment of us. This was a very wide group, alcoholics, degenerates and the long-term unemployed; people that nice Germans didn't want cluttering up their streets.

The red triangle denoted a political prisoner. In the prison record, they are called *Schutzhäftlinge*, protective prisoners. Most of them were Polish Gentiles, there because they'd joined partisan groups against the Reich or been rounded up in various *Aktions*. A few were ethnic Germans, who had been members of opposition groups to the Nazis before the war.

At the bottom of the heap in terms of discipline were the *Kapos*, with their distinctive arm badges. Many of these men were Jews, mostly from Germany or Western Europe, and they were recruited from the long-term prisoners. One thing they all had in common was their viciousness. Our education from them consisted of blows and harder blows if we moved too slowly or got something wrong. Most of them were just creatures of the SS, anxious to prove how useful they were to the regime. In Auschwitz, as in all concentration camps, the natural order of things was reversed. In the unnatural, topsy-turvy world of genocide, the riff-raff were in charge; the lunatics were running the asylum.

I didn't know any of this that morning as I watched a man being beaten to death because he had dysentery. It was 7 August 1943. Five years ago I'd have been splashing through the river in the Garden of Eden with my family. But I could not think of my family now. And yet I could think of nothing else.

'Please sir . . .' There was a hand in the air, a prisoner asking a question. That was as far as he got. Rudi's club thudded across his face.

The *Blockältester* told him that he didn't need to fucking talk and called him scum. We were going to the shitters to empty our bowels and get washed. We were not to fucking hang around and we were to make sure we were fucking cleaned up. And we had to follow him.

Rudi was strong. He had good quality boots with studs and a belt to hold his trousers up. He got better food than nearly everybody else and this was my fourth day with no food at all. We did our best, shuffling after him in loose, ill-gripping clogs and holding our trousers up at the waist. The rough wood was cutting my feet – I'd said goodbye to my socks the day before but the last thing I thought of was slowing down to rub the chafing. Rudi yelled that he'd told us to get a move on, as he jogged alongside us, swinging his club. It was the merest chance who he hit and he'd change sides so most of us got a taste of his club and his temper. The crack as the wood met bone was palpable and anybody who went down was kicked until he got up or couldn't move at all.

The camp latrine was a work of art. It was a long hut, not unlike Block Ten we'd just left. What light there was came through small windows in the roof space and between the uprights that supported the roof were long cement slabs with holes in them. I'd never seen anything like it. Even in the Kamionka we had our own toilet that only the Pivniks used. Here there was no privacy at all. On Rudi's command we all dropped our trousers and jostled each other for one of the holes. They were choked with shit and the smell was revolting. Everything just dropped down into a trench under the slab and there was no toilet paper or anything else to clean yourself with. Since I hadn't eaten for days, nothing came out, so I hauled up my trousers again and waited.

Then Rudi hustled us into the Wash Barrack next door. Again it was a hut, again badly lit. There were troughs full of dirty, cold water that made the warm showers of yesterday seem like heaven. Rudi shouted that we were to wash ourselves or he'd beat the shit out of us instead. And again, he felt he had to ask us if we understood.

No doubt this was Rudi's idea of fatherly concern – making sure we understood what was expected of us. There was no soap, no towel, just the water. I rubbed it over my face, hands and body.

Rudi roared at us to get back outside and on to Block Ten. The pace was exhausting, which of course was what it was intended to be. The gruelling runs, the vicious beatings, the casual violence, was supposed to break us. I would soon learn that this Quarantine Block was actually for the purposes of going through an initiation, a test of physical and mental stamina to see what we were made of.

The irony was that we were just flesh and blood, but nobody was interested in that. The last in line outside got more thumps and kicks from the *Blockältester* and the run back started. It followed exactly the same pattern as before but when we got back to our hut there were two *Kapos* there in their yellow armbands. They were standing by a pile of hessian sacks and a pile of dirty straw. There was also a large trestle table with bread on it and a bucket of black, steaming liquid.

Blockälteste Rudi was still in charge. He told us to take a sack and stuff it with straw. That was our bedding. We stood in line, watching what the man ahead was doing, avoiding anything that led to a clip from Rudi or the *Kapos*. I caught my sack, rough and smelling of stables. I scooped up armfuls of straw and knelt there, stuffing the sack before disappearing into Block Ten to find my bunk and put it there. I briefly remembered my attacker of the night before, but there was no sign of him. Then it was out into the sunshine again, to the accompanying rhythm of Rudi's barked orders. Again in line, standing as straight as we could and staring at the food. As we marched past the table, a *Kapo* gave me a chipped enamel bowl, a slice of hard, stale bread about four centimetres thick, a slice of salami perhaps half a centimetre thick and a sliver of margarine. I had no idea then that the rest of the rations, along with milk and sugar, had long been hived off by the *Kapos* who worked the kitchens. What was left wouldn't have kept a dog alive.

One of the *Kapos* told us to guard our bowls with our lives. If we lost ours, we wouldn't get another one. As we passed the bucket of black liquid, a *Kapo* slapped a ladle into my bowl. They called it coffee, but it was ersatz stuff made from roasted barley and it tasted bitter and burnt. The SS wouldn't have touched it. Rudi ordered us inside to eat. I hadn't realised until I drank the coffee how cracked and dry my lips were. My tongue was swollen and furred with the lack of liquid but the coffee helped and I was able to chew. God knows what kind of bread this was or what was in the sausage, but it was literally a life-saver to me then. It was gone in seconds. I was still a growing boy at sixteen and wasn't likely to grow much more if this was the meagre amount we were going to get.

I was still wondering when the next meal would come when we were ordered outside again, lined up in fives. I looked furtively around the lines. Almost everybody was older and bigger than me and I thanked whatever God I still believed in that my mother had pushed me into that line back on the platform and that nobody – yet – had winkled me out.

There was a *Kapo* in front of us who asked whether any of us were tailors. No one moved. He asked whether any of us could sew. He clearly wasn't looking for much in the way of expertise. A hundred thoughts flashed through my brain. My father was a tailor, so was my uncle. I could handle a needle and thread and could probably pick up working a treadle machine fairly quickly. But this, I already knew, was Auschwitz-Birkenau. They killed people here. A few hands rose timidly. Mine didn't.

The *Kapo* threw them scraps of yellow material and barked an order as the volunteers shuffled forward, telling them they would sew these on to each man's jacket. The bits of fabric were cut into the six-sided Star of David and the colour the Gentiles had made us wear at intervals since the sixteenth century. Auschwitz might have been Hell on Earth, but there was a nod here to history, to the continuation of hate.

The *Blockältester* told us that when the badge was sewn

on, we were to write our number on it, nice and clear, so it was easy to read. As always, the question: 'Understand?'

We understood. There would be no more names at Auschwitz. No touch of humanity. I was just a Jew with a number. And if that was supposed to make me feel somehow unique, it didn't.

Then we were back in the Block and the *Kapos* had gone and the *Blockältester* was looking for someone else to beat to death. In the gloom of Block Ten's interior, we started the odd furtive conversation, each of us learning the old prisoner's trick of whispering out of the corner of the mouth. Under the scalped heads and the cuts I recognised men from Bedzin, men from the Kamionka. They weren't friends exactly – no one had true friends in Auschwitz – but at least they weren't total strangers either. Maybe, I thought to myself, with food in my stomach and sitting on a straw-filled sack, it won't be so bad after all. My attacker was still nowhere in sight and I never saw him again. For weeks, maybe months, I jumped out of my skin if anyone came too close behind me but eventually I learned to forget.

I don't remember how long it took to sew the stars onto fifty jackets and for us to write our numbers under the star in indelible ink, but once it was done we were outside again, lined up in the usual fives.

That was when I first saw him: the man who haunts my nightmares to this day. He was above average height, I remember, stockily built with the close-cropped hair the Aryans approved of. He was maybe mid-thirties and wore a soft side-cap, the type the SS called a *schiffchen*, with its eagle and skull badge. On the right collar of his grey-green Waffen-SS uniform was another skull, another symbol of death, just in case you'd missed the one on his cap, and to the left, a single star. I didn't know it at the time but this was the rank badge of an *Unterscharführer*, a corporal. If he'd been a real soldier in the *Wehrmacht*, he'd have been an *Unteroffizier*, but this was the SS: they had ranks, rules and an attitude of their own. His name was Karel Kurpanik.

It would be a while before I got the measure of the SS guards at Auschwitz-Birkenau and it's only now, reading about it all later, that I realise the sort of men they were. Sadists and bastards – yes, that goes without saying – but it was infinitely more complex than that. Most of them were too old for front-line service and younger ones often tended to have been wounded and had been invalided out of the fighting units. A lot of them were *Volksdeutsche* and found themselves in a curious limbo. Even if they'd volunteered, the *Wehrmacht* didn't want them because they were not Aryan. Ironically, bearing in mind how racially obsessed the SS were, they had no such qualms and took these men on for the ever-growing number of concentration and slave labour camps.

Kurpanik was one of these. He was a Silesian from Bytom, in the Katowice area, just about as anti-Semitic and anti-Polish as it was possible to be. He had joined the Waffen-SS whose creed, I learned years later, was that each man 'must be a fighter for fighting's sake; he must be unquestionably obedient and become emotionally hard; he must have contempt for all racial inferiors and for those who do not belong to the Order . . . he must think nothing impossible.'

Kurpanik was a natural for Auschwitz and he was posted to the guard regiment. By the time I got to the camp, he was a *Rapportführer*, in charge of the Quarantine Block, with its own peculiar brand of tortures; but he cut his teeth supervising an early gas chamber. If you could stand that at all, you quickly became convinced that life meant nothing.

We stood in our fives while Kurpanik prowled the area watching the work of the *Kapos* and chatting occasionally to Blockältester Rudi. We were standing in a long, narrow compound, the ground dusty that August, churned by clogs and boots. By the autumn it would turn into a quagmire. One of the *Kapos* pointed to the far end. It must have been 400 metres away, with the concrete posts curving above the perimeter fence and the murderous barbed wire gleaming in the sun. To the one side was an open area with a road running through it and a far more solid fence, marking the perimeter. Along it were sentry posts and guard towers where helmeted men lounged alongside their machine-guns. In the first hours at Birkenau I allowed myself the luxury of looking through both rows of wire, beyond the electrification that ringed Hell, to the countryside beyond. This was part of the 'area of interest' as the SS called it, denuded of trees that could give shelter to escapees and dotted with single-storey storage buildings. If that was freedom, I thought, how do you get there? And how long would it be before a machine-gunner saw you? Seconds probably.

The *Kapo* was pointing to two huge heaps of stones, gleaming white in the morning sun. He told us that the work was to make the ground level throughout the compound, by filling the holes with stones, so he wouldn't fall over and break his neck. Another selection. The pointed finger. 'You, you, you . . .' I don't know how many he counted. The chosen stepped forward and were told to take a wheelbarrow or a shovel. He ordered them to take the tools to the stores and load the barrows.

They shambled off and visibly jumped as he yelled at them not to walk, but to run. And he was lashing out with his fists and boots, slapping men around the head and kicking their legs. If it wasn't so grim it would have been funny – shaven-headed men in striped pyjamas, clattering on badly fitting clogs and trying to hold up their beltless trousers while at the same time carrying shovels or handling wheelbarrows. Just for the sheer bloody hell of it.

Now the rest of us joined in. The *Kapo* showed us how to twist our jackets to make an improvised apron. In this we would carry the stones wherever they were needed – once again at a run, once again with the *Kapo* chasing us and lashing out at the stragglers. At the stone piles we waited in line while the barrows were loaded, then the shovellers dropped the stones into our aprons. We ran back, backs breaking, legs giving way, desperate not to drop our loads for fear of the beating we'd get. And all this with clogs that didn't fit and trousers that didn't stay up.

As I ran backwards and forwards I realised that I was the youngest and fittest there. The older men were floundering, stones slipping, trousers falling, clogs cutting into their ankles. None of this made any sense. We'd have done the job better if they'd left us alone. It wasn't rocket science as they say today – they'd have had a workforce capable of doing the job for days and doing it well. It eventually dawned on me that I'd missed the point. This had nothing to do with filling pot-holes or levelling ground; it had everything to do with establishing Aryan superiority and humiliating the slave labour at their disposal. They didn't care whether we lived or died and all morning they proved this point over and over again. Clubs, boots, fists – the insane, casual brutality was yet another kind of selection.

Some of the men who took beatings weren't getting up. Job done as far as the *Kapos* and Kurpanik were concerned. I noticed that the man from Bytom was enjoying himself enormously – anybody who got a baton in the face from him wasn't going to recover. Nobody's wounds were being tended. If a prisoner bled to death, so what? If his cuts became infected and gangrenous, who cares? There were, after all, neat ways of coping with the problem.

I don't know how many hours we sweated under that summer sun. We ran backwards and forwards, slipping and staggering under the weight of the rocks. My back and arms ached. My lungs felt like broken bellows as I wheezed and gasped my way along the wire. Then a whistle sounded and we were told to stop. We'd had no food since the dismal breakfast hours earlier and there was none now. Men sank to the ground and we gulped gratefully at the water they gave us.

It was during this half-hour break that a new humiliation was devised – singing. The *Kapos* walked among us, picking individuals to sing some song from their past. Anything – as long as we put our all into it. Mumbling wouldn't do; it had to be at full pelt, at the tops of our voices. I don't remember what I sang – probably something I'd learned in the soft, warm atmosphere of the Rapaport school, with its blue and green uniforms, so different from my stripes, and the polished floors, such a world away from the hard, rutted pot-holes of the Quarantine Block at Auschwitz-Birkenau. Some of the older men found this difficult. The more traditional of them only sang psalms in the synagogue and *Shabbat*. I could see the smouldering hatred in their eyes as the *Kapos* jeered and pointed, landing the odd clout with a club if they didn't like what they heard.

Back at work again, I had a lucky break. A *Kapo* swapped me with one of the shovellers from the rock-pile, so I wasn't staggering up and down anymore. It was still hard, driving the shovel into the unyielding pile, filling the barrows and unloading into the men's aprons. You try to twist, find a different position, change your angle, *anything* to stop the pain in your spine. What I couldn't do was stop, not if I wanted to keep my skull in one piece. I suppose it was handy that I'd worked for old Dombek in Killov's factory. I could lift and carry better than most and it occurred to me that some of the men around me, dropping things and keeling over, had been accountants and bank managers. They must have been completely out of their depth.

Time. You don't know how you miss it until it's taken away from you. At school, we lived by the bell. At home, there was the ritual of meal-time, even in the Kamionka. At the factory we'd clocked in and clocked out. At Auschwitz there were no clocks and we worked until we were told to stop or until we dropped.

So I'm guessing when I say we worked until about six in the evening, a twelve-hour day with thirty minutes rest, little water and no food. Welcome to Auschwitz. I didn't yet know about the wrought iron words above the main gate of Auschwitz I, the bitterly ironic slogan they'd imported from KL Dachau – *Arbeit Macht Frei*: work makes you free. If I had, I wouldn't have felt particularly free that evening as we took our tools back and lined up again in fives outside Block

Ten. Here we were at another ritual unique to camps like this one – the *Appell*, the evening roll-call.

I remember standing there, my body caked with cold sweat and chalk dust as the SS carried out the head count. A formality, surely? The work of minutes. No, that wasn't the point. The point was that everybody, even the dead, had to be accounted for. And if the count took an hour, two, all night, so be it. In time we got used to it. Used to seeing the corpses lying on the ground at the end of the lines, as if dead men could answer a roll-call. Men you'd seen carrying rocks hours earlier, struggling with shovels at the rock-pile, lay pale and bloody on the still uneven ground, their heads shattered and their bodies kicked to a pulp. You might have seen this happen, but you couldn't stop it; you couldn't even pause. A man dies in front of you – step round him. A neighbour from the Kamionka sinks to his knees with exhaustion – ignore him because he's going to die and if you help him, you'll die too. This was the law of Auschwitz-Birkenau. It was unspoken and universal and it was the law of the jungle.

Unterscharführer Kurpanik had an important role to play. Surely, even us Jews could recognise that. He was accountable to the camp commandant for the exact numbers in the Quarantine Block. In all other respects he was a law unto himself. And the same ritual happened the next morning and every morning. If anyone had had the temerity to die in the night, to slip away in agony and despair crammed with the still-living in his bunk, he must still be there in the morning, lying on the ground of the *Appell*, his name in the ledger of the damned.

After the roll-call, we lined up again outside our hut for

the evening meal, enamel bowls at the ready. The official menus at Auschwitz-Birkenau, some of which have survived, talk of soup with meat four times a week and with vegetables on the other three days. I don't remember ever seeing any meat and the vegetables were turnips and potatoes – the food the Gentiles in Bedzin and Wodzislaw fed to their pigs. Occasionally, it would be varied with cabbage, swede or sugar beet, but the end product was the same – a thin, grey slurry that tasted revolting. Even on that first day, however, we slurped it gratefully, ravenous after our day's exertions. There was no bread to eat with it and of course no spoons – metal objects could be sharpened into weapons, the last thing the *Kapos* or the SS wanted. I learned, like the others, to save part of the breakfast bread ration to eat with the soup in the evening.

I waited in line, hauled up my sleeve to show my number to the *Kapo* and he slopped the soup into my bowl. And that was another lesson I learned quickly. If you work hard, if you'd done the *Kapos* a favour or if they liked you, you might get a thick piece of vegetable from the bottom of the pot. If you'd pissed them off, forget it. You were scum and that's exactly what you got.

What this actually was, was slow starvation. Next time you see liberation photographs of the camps taken by disbelieving British, Russian and American soldiers and the Red Cross, look at the state of the survivors. They look like walking skeletons, the living dead; many of them were so far gone they didn't make it even after liberation and their photographs are all that we have of them. We called such living corpses *Muselmänner*, Muslims, and to this day I don't know why. Perhaps newsreels in cinemas before the war showed starving people in India, I don't know. If you became a *Müsselmann*, you'd probably die, but on the way to that state of emaciation, you'd meet another selection. Weak from hunger, you'd make mistakes in your work, slow down, get ill. Any of these things were crimes in Auschwitz-Birkenau, and they guaranteed a beating to death, a bullet in the head or a long walk to the gas chambers. Somebody else would carry you to the crematorium.

After the soup, the latrine and the wash room. I don't know if I actually shit this time – I probably did because you quickly trained your bowels to behave. There was no getting up in the middle of the night to answer the call of nature, unless you wanted to go on your bunk and the consequences of that didn't bear thinking about.

Each of us had our own little bundle which we stashed with our straw mattresses on the bunks. Our shoes were here at night-time, our clothes if we dared remove them and our food bowls. We didn't have anything else. The bundles became our pillows and we daren't leave any part of them lying about or they'd be stolen. No shoes meant running barefoot over the broken ground with sharp stones slicing your soles. No bowl meant no food. Reporting anything missing meant a beating. The stuff was your responsibility; the loss of it was your fault. I never saw a Bedzin man steal anything, but we all knew that we would steal, if push came to shove, because that was the nature of the camp – the law of the jungle, remember?

New arrivals had turned up at Block Ten during the afternoon as they had at the other barracks. These men were strangers, Polish Jews certainly, but not from Bedzin. It was the continuation of a rolling programme. We had replaced an earlier consignment and as men died or fell by the wayside, others replaced them. There was the usual shouting of the *Kapos*, the kicks and cuffs, the new men terrified into silence, wondering what kind of Hell they'd stumbled into. Not all of them would see the next day. For me, this second night would be different. Yes, I was still terrified; yes, I was still depressed. But the pervert who had attacked me the night before had gone. I'd never been so tired in my life and as my head hit my food bowl, I fell asleep.

Morning in Auschwitz-Birkenau: the dawn chorus of barked orders, guttural German and the crashing back of the barrack door. I was desperate to get to the latrine. The lack of food for those days followed by the hard bread, ghastly soup and dirty water were taking their toll. I just made it in time and was sitting on the latrine when I noticed a middle-aged man a few holes along literally poking in his own shit. I vaguely remembered him from the Kamionka and knew his name was Yitzak. He was glaring wildly around him in all directions as he rummaged about. Several people saw it but most looked away. Men went mad in Auschwitz. It was their way of coping; the mind closing down completely against what was happening. Paddling his fingers in his turds might just have been Yitzak's own hellish way out.

But that wasn't it. Not this time. Not with this man. He seemed to find something and scuttled off to the wash room. I followed and saw Yitzak washing his hands keeping his right fist tightly clenched. I kept him in sight as he made his way back to Block Ten and was horrified to see Blockältester Rudi leaning against the timbers.

He beckoned Yitzak over and I expected the club and the boot and another Bedzin resident would be on his way to meet his God. Instead the two men began talking earnestly, in whispers I couldn't hear and I thought it best to get into the hut to get ready for the day's work.

In the few moments we had before breakfast, Yitzak came in and was full of himself. He'd swallowed three or four small diamonds, family heirlooms, during the clearance of the Kamionka. With so little to eat, only one had come out so far, and he'd found it that morning. I don't know what Yitzak did in Bedzin before this madness but he was crafty and streetwise. If you've got nothing, as with the rest of us, you've got no negotiating power. A diamond wouldn't buy a Jew his freedom but it might get him some preferential treatment. Yitzak told us, in staccato whispers, that someone had shopped him to Blockältester Rudi but he'd been able to do a deal. In our ignorance, we had no idea what that meant.

Astonishingly, the roll-call was a full house; no one had died during the night. This seemed normal to us then, but we soon came to realise how unusual it was. As we lined up, bowls ready for breakfast, I saw Yitzak get an extra slice of bread and a double helping of margarine and sausage. The *Kapos* were past masters at lining their own pockets. The bread ration was supposed to be one loaf to every four prisoners, but the *Kapos* cut it into five and kept the middle piece for themselves. This they could eat or sell as they liked. At Auschwitz-Birkenau, we killed each other by percentages.

Over the next few days I grew to hate the shit-man Yitzak. His diamond had not only bought him extra food, it excused him from work duties too. While the rest of us were loading rocks and staggering with our full aprons feeling the clubs and kicks of the *Kapos*, Yitzak was lying on his back in Block Ten, scratching his balls and staring at the ceiling. He probably thought he was set for life. But he was wrong.

I don't know how many jewels a man can swallow and stay alive. In Yitzak's case it was three or four – a very finite future, that. The stones were probably worth a small fortune but in Auschwitz-Birkenau such value was meaningless. Morons like the *Kapos* traded them on the camp's black market for vodka, wine or cigarettes; *organising*, it was called. I sometimes wonder if anybody who knew their real worth ever got hold of them. In a corner of Block Ten was a *stube*, a side room where the *Kapos* drank and slept in relative luxury. No doubt that's where they planned what to do with Yitzak. A couple of days after he'd shit his last stone, Kurpanik killed him. I didn't see it myself but the rumour got round very quickly and it made sense. What delight it would have given that psychopath to beat the shit out of a Jew who was altogether too smug to be kept alive.

It's amazing to me now how quickly the routine of the Quarantine Block became a way of life. We were in fact living on a razor's edge all the time because every day our ranks got fewer and every roll-call was a selection that could mean death. I'd been there for about a week, I suppose, when again, during the morning call, they asked for tailors to work in the shop in the main camp making and repairing uniforms for the Waffen-SS. This time I seriously considered it. The back-breaking, exhausting ritual of the rock-carrying was taking its toll, even for a fit lad like me, just weeks short of my seventeenth birthday. Some, it had already killed. Tailoring would mean sitting down all day, under a roof and operating a machine, something I could probably do in my sleep. But something told me not to put my hand up. Life in the workshops was no life at all. No rumours from elsewhere. No opportunity to operate the black market. Just a slow, living death through starvation. And I could just imagine how little a slip you'd have to make to get the usual treatment from the *Kapos*. How many stitches did you need to drop before they dropped you?

It must have been my tenth day in the Quarantine Block, though to be honest I was finding it difficult to keep count. It was the middle of August and that morning the *Blockschreiber*, the clerk, called out eight or ten numbers. One of them was mine. Another selection. No rhyme. No reason. And certainly no explanation. I looked around. There was no one to say goodbye to. It's a hard thing to write now, but we weren't comrades. We were all going through the same Hell and you'd think that would bind us together, give us a 'them and us' mentality, but it wasn't like that. Fear drove wedges between us and it was every man for himself. The familiar faces from Bedzin were already fewer now, ten days in, and I was standing with strangers, my bowl in hand and a crust of bread in my pocket, saved from breakfast.

Then we were on the run again. Only the dying walked in Auschwitz; the rest of us moved at whatever speed the *Kapo* dictated. He ran us out beyond the perimeter fence, between the rows of vicious barbs and the hum of electric wire. For the first time I saw the rest of the camp, prisoners in stripes toiling away at whatever pointless task the *Kapos* had decided they should. Armed SS men prowled the outer perimeter, eyes like hawks, fingers resting expectantly on triggers. The camp seemed endless, blocks with rows and rows of barracks like Number Ten stretching away into the haze of August; KL Auschwitz-Birkenau like a dark stain on the golden harvest fields of Poland.

We must have jogged for ten minutes. And for each of us that little, dirty chipped bowl was like the Holy Grail of the Christians. I saw it as a symbol of hope, something which, once you'd found it, you must hang onto at all costs because, if they were running us to the gas chamber, surely we wouldn't be taking our bowls with us? We turned sharp left into a compound exactly the same as the one we'd just left and our names and our numbers were written down in yet another ledger by yet another *Blockschreiber* in yet another block.

I didn't realise it at the time but I had passed a kind of initiation test. I'd gone into the Quarantine Block a hope-lessly naïve kid, my family ripped from me and my dignity removed. I had slept with dying men, eaten with them, worked with them, shit with them. I looked at the new *Kapos* here in this section of the camp. What little tricks did they have up their sleeves, I wondered, before they decided it was my turn to die?

7
The Rampe

The day dawned like any other – shouting *Kapos*, latrine visit, wash house, roll-call, bread, sausage and 'coffee'. They weren't going to kill us, not today. Because the day, from this point on, was different. There was no running with heavy loads, no being driven with clubs and boots. The *Kapos* organised us into details and I was to join the *Rampe Kommando*, the platform detachment. It meant nothing to me then, but as time went on I remembered the striped-uniformed lunatic who whispered to me on the day I arrived, 'Tell them you're eighteen.' I looked down at the blue and white stripes, the battered clogs, my cracked, sore hands. If I'd had a mirror I'd probably have burst into tears – I had become that lunatic.

It was a railway siding, just like any other all over Europe, but this was Auschwitz-Birkenau, so it was different. Because the Pivniks had arrived nearly two weeks ago in a passenger train, that's what I expected to see, but the first locomotive to arrive was pulling cattle-trucks and I remembered I had seen them shunting through Bedzin before they liquidated the ghetto. And I remembered the frightened eyes staring out from the darkness between the slats. Did sheep look like that, I wondered, on their way to the slaughter?

We stood in rows behind the SS men with their guns and

dogs while the trains pulled into position and waited. There was no move to unlock the doors and let the 'passengers' out. The SS were going about their business, checking that everything was ready. Calmness, order, even a kind of peace. I remembered the sudden quiet that had descended when we arrived and I realised now what that was all about. There *must* be order, there *must* be calm. The people on that train were desperate, terrified, suffering from thirst and hunger. God alone knew how long they'd been on the rails. The last thing the SS wanted was a running fight on their hands.

There was an eerie silence, punctuated now and again by the snort of the locomotive or the bark of a dog. The cattle-trucks themselves were totally silent, with the odd glimpse of a frightened face peering out behind the barbed wire that criss-crossed the slats. I got to learn as the weeks went by that these were the vital ventilation holes that meant life or death for the occupants. I couldn't yet catch the smell inside the trucks themselves.

There was no whistle, no shouted order that I can remember, but by long-learned practice the SS guards moved closer to the trucks, their dogs snapping and snarling, barking over and over again. Intimidation, that was the name of the game. In the years ahead I would often be asked why these new arrivals didn't fight back, take their chances. There were supposed to be eighty of them per truck, but there were often more. Collectively they outnumbered the SS on the Rampe. I understand it did happen sometimes, but not while I was there. Most of the occupants of the trucks were the old, the sick, women and children. Some of them were already dying. No one had the physical or emotional strength to take on an army of SS men with dogs, guns and cudgels. This was a front line of a very different kind.

The padlocks were undone, the doors hauled back with loud bangs and rattles. People spilled out onto the platform, blinking in the morning sun. They were disorientated, having been in semi-darkness for however long. I couldn't take my eyes from theirs – large, popping eyes trying to acclimatise, brains trying to take in what was happening and where they were. And the cacophony of Hell started up as I'd remembered it, the snarled orders in guttural German: '*Raus! Raus!* Get off the fucking train, *Scheissjuden!* Move it, *Dreckjuden!* Shit-Jew! Dirt Jew! Keep it quiet you Jewish scum! Get over here, line up!'

Over the weeks ahead I saw countless train-loads arrive. The occupants of the trucks were mostly Jews, but they came from everywhere and it occurred to me that they couldn't understand what was being said to them. None of them could have missed the essential message however, because it couldn't be clearer. Orders here came with a stick. The new arrivals were always dirty and scruffy, wherever they had once called home. The men had several days' stubble on their faces, the women with wild hair, and no trace of make-up. French and Dutch Jews tended to be well-dressed; men in long overcoats and Homburgs, women in sharp-shouldered dresses, fashionable in the 1940s. The Greeks were particularly fashionable in the lightweight clothes of their homeland, which would have killed them in the average Polish winter, camp or no camp. Most bizarre of all were the Carpathian Jews from Romania, their wild mountains written all over them in animal skins and fur jackets; Dracula's children.

The yelling and the dogs and the swift clouts from clubs would quickly have their effects no matter where the travellers came from. The dogs carried on barking and terrified children could not be quieted, despite the best efforts of their parents. Imagine Waterloo station at rush hour, but with the sound turned right down. The prisoners huddled together in the centre of the Rampe, herded there by the dogs. When the SS barked an order, the whole crowd rippled in response, like a sharp wind through a cornfield in the Garden of Eden so long ago.

Whatever selection processes these newcomers had been through just to get here, *this* was the one that mattered most. I don't think it was that first day on the Rampe that I *knew* what had happened to my own family, but every day confirmed its likelihood. A point of a finger, to left or to right, the random decision of a madman; an SS officer playing judge, jury and executioner; the godless playing God – it was as simple and irrevocable as that.

I knew the drill by now, the strong and the young, men or women, were selected to live. They would go through what I had – the pointless Quarantine process in Block IIa or its female equivalent. Some of them would die of exhaustion, malnutrition, disease. Others would go down under the boots and cudgels of the *Kapos*. The rest . . . the rest would be escorted in their last walk by men like me, in striped uniforms, waiting to carry out their orders. They were a special unit taking an entire people to the gates of death.

That first morning on the Rampe followed a pattern I would get used to. Once the prisoners were cowed and quiet, the mood of the guards changed. They were working now, carrying out their duties with that Teutonic efficiency for which the Nazis were famous. This was actually brilliant psychology. It was a version of the good cop/bad cop interrogation techniques so beloved of TV shows and detective novels. A brute had just yelled at them, hit them with his club, let his dog bite them. Now a gentleman came forward, almost apologetic for what had happened.

Chief among these gentlemen was the officer with the grey doeskin gloves I had seen when I arrived, with his immaculate uniform, kind face and the gap in his front teeth. He often wore his white coat over his tunic of a captain of the Waffen-SS and there were many there who took comfort from that coat. Every doctor throughout Europe, even a Nazi, had taken the Hippocratic oath – 'First, do no harm.' Even now, even after the ghastly train ride and the ordeal of disembarkation, even now, all would be well. There was a doctor in charge. He was SS Hauptsturmführer Josef Mengele and he became notorious in these years as the Angel of Death. A dedicated doctor, he was fascinated by twins, and unbeknownst to us at the time, he used his enormous, even limitless power to experiment on them in the camp hospital. He was also a dedicated Nazi so the people parading before him on the Rampe were simply guinea pigs or laboratory rats. They were not human beings at all.

In all the time I worked on the Rampe I never heard Mengele raise his voice or be anything other than utterly charming. His keen eyes missed nothing. Other SS men might have to ask, 'How old are you? Are you well? What is your profession?' but all I ever heard Mengele say was 'Are there any twins here?' or occasionally 'Are these your children?' He never spoke to me or even, as far as I know, registered me at all, but perhaps I was wrong.

Our job was to collect the belongings that had been dumped on the Rampe. The new arrivals were told to leave their bags there; that they would get them back later and we'd pile up suitcases neatly. It wasn't part of our responsibility to mix with the prisoners – in fact, we weren't supposed to talk to them at all – but I ended doing exactly what that 'lunatic' had tried to do for me when I got here from the Kamionka. I targeted the younger ones, kids my age or younger, but in their teens – 'Tell them you're eighteen.' 'Tell them you've got a trade.' 'You're strong, you can carry bricks.' There wasn't time to be more inventive and the risks were too high. Most of the time they just looked at me, uncomprehending, my fierce whispers making no sense at all.

Once the selections had been made and the lines sorted, I'd find myself, in unguarded moments, staring after the straggling line of kids and women, walking the way my family had walked. I could see them in my imagination, my father holding hands with Hendla and Chana, my mother with the boys around her. I had never actually seen this, but I saw so many family groups like it, it had to have been this way.

Some were loaded into trucks, as my family had been. Others, when the numbers were too great, walked through the site of Birkenau III, still under construction. The more curious, the less cowed, would have asked questions. 'Where are we going?' 'What's going to happen to us?' The more naïve would have asked, 'When can we see our menfolk? What about our luggage?' They were going into a building, a large underground room to be deloused with disinfectant.

I don't suppose anyone asked what the disinfectant was called, but it was Zyklon B, in a canister like a coffee tin, containing pellets of hydrocyanic acid. You couldn't be too careful in camps like this, with so many people coming in daily from the ghettoes; disease was rampant so delousing was essential. Lice carried typhus and typhus was often deadly. What the SS guards didn't tell their would-be questioners was that Zyklon B was *always* deadly.

Some *must* have understood what was really happening. There had been rumours about Auschwitz and camps like it for years, even though the scale of the killings had only escalated over the last eighteen months. Most human beings, faced with a walk to their deaths, just can't take it in, can't believe what is about to happen. Mothers with children were always pointed to the left-hand column and they walked on, hand in hand, better to die together than be parted. Some mothers made a split-second decision to save their child, passing a whining, crying toddler to a relative in some vague, hopeless hope they'd be reunited later. Others did as my mother did and pushed their child into the right-hand column. Work sets you free and the young and the able-bodied could work – 'Tell them you're eighteen. Tell them you're eighteen.'

Sometimes on the Rampe I saw the opposite situation. A family was broken up, left and right but an occasional man or woman from the right would cross to the left, take up the hand of a little one, put an arm round an old relative, walk with their heads high. They were the real heroes of Auschwitz-Birkenau. As for the SS, they shrugged and let them go. It was only the crossings from left to right they put a stop to.

There was one situation where we weren't required on the Rampe and the SS did the job themselves. This was one night in April when the *Kindertransporten* arrived. We could hear the whistle and hiss of the locomotives from our block and everything that followed. The SS declared a *Blocksperre*, a lock-down, and the bolts were slid and padlocked on every hut in the men's camp. At seventeen I was still a kid myself, and didn't understand what it meant to be a father, but most of the men who still lived at Auschwitz-Birkenau were older than me and fathers themselves. There was no need for selection on the Rampe in those still watches of the night. Children were just mouths to feed, encumbrances, nuisances. *Every* child on these transports was marshalled to the left and all we could do was lie in our cramped bunks listening to the unearthly screaming of the children walking to their deaths. Years later I would learn that these were Jewish children from an orphanage at Izieu in France, torn from the safety of their institution by SS officer Klaus Barbie who was in charge of the Gestapo in nearby Lyons. All forty-two of them died that night along with the five adults accompanying them. I don't remember if I'd heard of the other kind of *Kindertransporte*, the sort that got very young Jews out of harm's way to neutral countries or to Britain. The only kind I knew was a one-way ticket to oblivion.

In the morning, we'd go through the usual motions and then out onto the Rampe to collect the debris of the night's arrivals. On the way there, we saw the bodies of the children, laid out naked and cold in the morning. More fuel for the fires. Through our tears we picked up the little coats, the shoes, the toys, trousers and dresses. Some had the child's name written neatly inside them – Miriam, Isaac, Solomon, Bathsheva – lovingly written by a mother who had only wanted what was best for her child. We scraped up the battlefield remnants, stacking them all into neat piles. Neat and tidy, just the way the SS liked it.

From the Rampe, everybody in the left-hand column was led like the Pied Piper of Hamelin's children into the huge room and told to undress. Eight hundred of them at a time, humiliated, frightened. Old ladies who had never taken their clothes off in front of anybody, not even their husbands. Teenage girls, self-conscious about their newly developing bodies. None of this mattered to the SS. These brief lives were about to end anyway. Anyone who sensed something was wrong, who was about to make a fuss, was taken out of the equation, out of the unrobing room, and a bullet would blast into his or her head.

When all 800 were inside, split roughly in halves between two chambers, the SS men slammed the doors shut and bolted them. A grill was slid back in the ceiling and the pellets of Zyklon B were thrown in. What happened next was a simple chemical equation; Zyklon B + Oxygen = Cyanide Gas. It also equals death. Those nearest the holes in the ceilings died first and every day of my life since then I have hoped that my family were nearest. If you were very young, or very old, or you gulped in the atmosphere in a desperate, convulsive attempt to stay alive, you died quickly. If you were further away from the holes or strong or young, you died slowly, but after twenty minutes it was all over. At various pressure times, when the cattle-trucks came in thick and fast, the doors would be opened after ten minutes.

I don't want to think too much about that scene, when

the *Sonderkommando* – more special units – slid open the heavy doors and began hauling the bodies out. Most of the corpses had crowded nearest the door scrabbling at the jamb in their desperation to get out. Some were still standing, others sitting or curled up, trampled by the others. They were all covered in blood and shit and piss and had all turned bright pink.

The *Sonderkommando* shaved off the women's hair and that of any men who still wore their hair in Jewish ringlets. Gold was ripped from their teeth. Any jewellery still on fingers was taken. Everything had a street value. Then the defiled, gassed remnants of people were dragged to the crematoria where they were burned. I know now that eight days before I arrived at Auschwitz a letter from the camp authorities to Administrative Group C of the Economic-Administrative office of the SS in Berlin gave the capacities of those crematoria. In any 24-hour period, Crematorium I could 'accommodate' 340 corpses; II could handle 1,440; III 1,440; IV 768; V 768 – a sickening total of 4,756 corpses in one day.

I lived with this knowledge – or some of it – during my time on the Rampe. Sometimes the thought of it became too much for me and I sank to a level of despair I can't describe. But always there was the notion of survival, the will to go on, day by day, coping with whatever the Nazi bastards threw at me.

What they threw at me on the Rampe was ghastly enough. You could say it was nothing compared with the duties of the *Sonderkommando* and I'd agree with that, but the *Sonderkommando* were replaced every few months and certainly after each big 'consignment' was processed.

The unwilling perpetrators became the victims; those doling out special treatment were at the receiving end of it themselves. In a sick sort of way, there were jobs for life at Auschwitz, but that could mean only a few days.

Some of the cattle-trucks had been on the rails for days and the state of them at the siding in Auschwitz-Birkenau was ghastly. The people themselves were so crammed in that they had no room to relieve themselves. The lavatory was a bucket in one corner if they were lucky and most of them, even the tolerably well-dressed, arrived caked in shit and piss, horribly embarrassed about the whole experience. The stench in those trucks when they'd gone was indescribable. I'd try to hold my breath as I went in with the others, hauling out luggage – a battered suitcase, a child's teddy-bear, spectacles, false teeth.

In the summer, with no water on board the trains, people died of suffocation and dehydration – I knew what it was like to go without water. In the winter, they just froze to death, despite the numbers of bodies in the trucks. I dragged their bodies out with the others of the *Rampe Kommando*, dead heads lolling back, or limbs stiff with rigor mortis. We stacked them neatly on the Rampe alongside their luggage, then loaded them onto handcarts that were rattled off to the crematoria by yet another special unit. From these crematoria black smoke belched constantly and the night sky glowed.

I'm not proud of my work on the Rampe. I became, along with everyone else, a human vulture. The floor of a cattle-truck suddenly empty after days can be a treasure trove. Notes, coins, rings, brooches, dropped in the shit by people who no longer knew or cared what they'd brought with them. We were all between the devil and the deep. If we took such items and were seen to have taken them, we'd join the next group on the trucks or the walk to the crematoria gates. But if we didn't, we'd die anyway because we were slowly starving to death. All around me were *Muselmänner* who were days or hours away from the gas, their buttocks flabby, their ribs visible through their skin, their eyes sunken and their will to fight on, gone.

Our job was to load anything left on the concrete or in the cattle-trucks onto hand carts that were then taken to one of the sorting warehouses like the one we all called Kanada. Any food we found – cheese, bread, sausage – we ate where we stood, crouching over in the process of picking up luggage and stuffing it in our mouths. As long as it didn't interfere with our work, the *Kapos* and the SS let it go on. I don't remember exactly when it was because the days blurred and times of year no longer add up in any memory, but on one particular day I saw the sun shine on something on my cart. You get used to fast, furtive movements in a situation when your life depends on them and the shiny thing was in my pocket in a second. It was a bracelet, maybe a present from a husband to his wife, boyfriend to girlfriend, father to daughter, I don't know. I only knew it had a street value.

Normally I'd have passed this to a *Vorarbeiter*, a foreman who would in turn pass it to a *Kapo*. Prisoners like me didn't have the clout to make deals – I still remembered Yitzak and his diamonds – so I decided to keep it. This must have been one of the most stupid decisions I've ever made in my life. Stealing from the Rampe was a death sentence and even if I got away with that, any trust I'd managed to build up with the *Kapo* would be gone and the end result would be the same.

As time went on that bracelet became an albatross around my neck. I had the presence of mind to hide it away from my bunk, stuffed behind a loose plank behind the wall. It didn't occur to me that the men on the nearest bunk would get the blame if it was found and I was still agonising over what to do with the thing when there was a commotion one morning in the barracks. Someone had found the bracelet. There were over 400 of us living in that Block and most of those worked on the Rampe so the chance of it coming back to bite me was fairly remote. The *Kapo* was furious and selected three or four of us at random to deliver beatings. If I'd have been braver I'd have owned up, taken the thrashing that someone else got. I'm sure my father would have expected that; my old headmaster, Mr Rapaport, certainly would. But this was Auschwitz-Birkenau; the rules were different. And you never put your hand up for anything.

I presume the *Kapo* traded the bracelet for vodka or cigarettes. He couldn't go to the SS as its very presence in our Block would rebound on him. It was a lesson I took to heart however: Szlamek, don't be too bloody clever.

This *organisation*, trading what you had, was a way of life in the camps. If you had nothing to trade, if you couldn't steal the odd scrap from the Rampe and if you were young and pretty, you could trade your body. Some of the *Kapos* and *Blockälteste* had been imprisoned by the Nazis for sex crimes in the first place. We of course had no links with the women's camp at all, so in the savage, all-male preserve of the men's quarters, many of the *Kapos* took out their sexual frustrations on their *piepels*, bum boys who were too young and weak to fight them off. There was no point in complaining about this. Reporting a *Kapo* or anyone else to the SS invited death. And most people preferred sexual abuse – it is not, whatever cliché they used in my grandfather's day, a fate worse than death. The saddest thing about this was that once a boy had lost his appeal or a particular *Kapo* got bored with him, he would disappear, gone to those gates, floating, like a memory, with the smoke of the chimneys.

Survival was all about food. I'd long ago ignored my father's aversion to pork and very occasionally it came my way in Auschwitz-Birkenau, but only in the form of skin or fat thrown into the monotonous soup to give the illusion of flavour. I remember once we had a surprise for supper – pickled mussels from Holland. I've no idea how this manna fell into our lap having been sieved through the corruption of the kitchen *Kapos*, but we got them. Seafood was a luxury to anyone in Central and Eastern Europe even before the war and shellfish was not kosher, so it raised a dilemma. It's a testimony to the faith of my people that even with everything we faced, as we were slowly starving to death, the old standards stood; the anathema remained.

One of my Block mates grunted as he saw what had landed in his bowl, that he wasn't eating that; he didn't eat worms. This was not a problem for Western Jews – the French, Belgians and Dutch who had arrived by now were tucking in with a will. One of them told me how good they were and that I ought to eat them. If I didn't, he would. Gingerly I scooped a mussel onto my bread and tried it. He was absolutely right and I wolfed the lot, wiping my bowl to get all the juices.

It's odd, but after all this time I can't remember what Block I lived in while working on the Rampe. I remember we had to pass through the main gate to reach it. I do remember our *Blockschrieber*, a Viennese Jew and that my *Blockältester* was Maurice, a nice man among so many who weren't. The *Kapos* who watched us on the Rampe changed with the shifts but they were normally Manfred or Hans. Manfred was a professional criminal, wearing his distinctive green triangle. He was built like a brick privy and got nasty if anybody crossed him, but his bark was worse than his bite and he certainly never hit me. Hans wore a black triangle and for all I knew could have been a murderer. He was a snappy dresser as far as any prisoner could be in Auschwitz-Birkenau and usually wore riding boots like the SS officers.

And, to my horror, Unterscharführer Kurpanik joined us on the Rampe too. Just because he could.

All my life up to this point I hadn't travelled very far. With the exception of the annual family holiday eighty kilometres away in the Garden of Eden, I had always lived in Bedzin. Even Auschwitz-Birkenau was a short train ride away. Now I was coming into contact with people from all over Europe and it was a real eye-opener. I remember the Greek Jews in particular. Their country had been overrun in the summer of 1941 and several of them were billeted with us on the *Rampe Kommando*, having survived the selections. It wasn't hard to see why they had – some of them had been professional wrestlers before the war and they had muscles to prove it. You can read the statistics today – between March and August 1943, 48,633 Jews were deported from Thessalonika and only 11,747 survived selection. A particular group, mostly Germans, Austrians and Czechs, stood out because of their good clothes. Some of the men I remember wore German medals pinned to their jackets from the First World War – how ironic was that? They'd bled on the Eastern Front for Germany and now the Germans were going to kill them. The SS ripped these medals from their clothing and threw them on the ground, telling them they weren't worthy to wear badges of honour like that. Life unworthy of life. They had come from Terezin in Czechoslovakia, the camp the Nazis called KL Theresienstadt, about thirty-five kilometres from Prague. This was a model camp with a humane reputation, set up by the Deputy SS Reichsführer Heydrich for 'special' prisoners, men with exceptional war records or Jews married to Aryans before the Nuremberg Laws made this impossible. By late 1943 Theresienstadt was just another transit camp, a holding facility before the cattle-trucks were loaded up for Auschwitz.

Even so, no selection was used on the Theresienstadt Jews. Instead they were all taken to the *Familienlager*, the Family Camp. This stood in section BIIb of Auschwitz-Birkenau, next to the Quarantine Block I knew only too well. I suppose there were those who hated the Theresienstadt Jews. Almost all of us on the *Rampe Kommando* had lost family – loved ones who failed the selections and had gone to the gas chambers. Yet here were families kept not only alive, but together. I often wonder whether this wasn't one of the more sophisticated tortures dreamed up by the SS. They even set up a Kindergarten, a nursery school, for the littlest ones and the older ones actually produced a camp newspaper and put on puppet shows. We knew nothing of this, but the rumours of better food rations in the Family Camp and the lack of hard, physical work grated on the rest of us. It was all about propaganda, of course. We didn't know it at the time but as 1943 became 1944 the war was going badly for the Reich. Perhaps they were hedging their bets, even as early as this; perhaps they wanted to impress the occasional Red Cross deputation that came to the camp. Look, the SS would say, this is the 'terrible' KL Auschwitz-Birkenau, where children sing songs in classrooms painted with fairytale scenes and everybody wears their own clothes and are well fed; tell the rest of the world about *that*.

But this special treatment didn't last for long. The Family Camp was in the next section to ours, beyond the wire and I often saw how the camp women were abused by the *Kapos* and *Blockälteste*. They would single out the prettiest and shove them against a barracks wall before pulling up their shifts and raping them.

Another group I remember who came in one afternoon were several dozen young men, Polish Gentiles. The whispers spread quickly. They were partisans, enemy fighters against the Reich. We all knew how empty that word was. The Orthodox Jews of Bedzin who had been machine-gunned and pistol-whipped by the *Einsatzgruppen* had been labelled 'partisans' – it was just more propaganda to give the world some vague justification for Nazi atrocities; many of the 'partisans' who had died were women and children. These newcomers were not registered as we had been – there was no shaving or tattooing for them – instead they were rounded up in a corner of the quarantine area and made to wait. For us it was another lock-down, the barracks padlocked but I saw what was happening before we were all inside. A team of *Kapos*, under orders from the SS, crowded round them and started to beat them with shovels, pick-handles and clubs. They threw them against the wire, where the sudden crackle, blue flashes and smell of burning clothes and flesh announced another electrocution. Once a man was clubbed to the ground, a *Kapo* would lay a shovel shaft across his throat and stand on both ends of it, crushing his windpipe. These partisans were not ghetto Jews, *Muselmänner* with no fight left in them. There must have been a mini battle which is presumably why we were locked down. A full-scale riot was not something the SS wanted. In the morning, the evidence was plain enough. Between the barrack huts in the quarantine compound lay a large heap of bodies, piled on one another, broken heads and ripped clothes. I couldn't see much damage to the *Kapos*, but I wouldn't expect to, *they* were the ones with the weapons. And no doubt if things had got out of hand, the guns of the SS would have come to their rescue.

These appalling rituals took place more than once and the only survivor of them that I am aware of was Antoni Czortek, known as Kajtek. He was already a boxing legend throughout Poland before the war, a medal-winning champion who had fought at the 1936 Olympics in Berlin. The SS kept him alive for their own entertainment. He was a bantamweight but they pitted him against much heavier men no less than fifteen times. No doubt this was another chance for a little wager among the SS who watched the bouts, cheering and whistling for their man. Kajtek himself was like a gladiator in Ancient Rome. Every fight was literally to the death in the sense that if he lost, the SS promised to shoot him.

After the constant torture of the Quarantine Block initiation, life on the Rampe had its compensations. It was a little like Killov's factory back in Bedzin – we sometimes had Sunday afternoons off. The trains rolled in regularly but there were lulls. It was almost eerily quiet in the camp during the day. At various times we could hear the strains of the camp orchestra wafting on the breeze. Needless to say, it was always German music. It took time to round up people from the ghettoes, still more time to train them to Auschwitz-Birkenau. During the gaps, on the slacker occasions, the *Kapos* would organise football matches or boxing and wrestling bouts which we were allowed to watch. The Greek wrestlers of course were the stars here and the SS and *Kapos* got quite excited about it all. Money was clearly changing hands among them, betting on the outcome of the bouts.

On one of the 'games' days, there was a flurry of excitement, a breath of pre-war freedom I could not quite believe. One of the other Bedzin Jews whispered to me, 'Guess what? Nunberg is here!'

My memory of this footballing hero was very clear. I'd often watched him playing in the Hakoah stadium back home and I was a real fan. He was probably the best goalie in Silesia and the best in Poland. Tall, blond and muscular, he could easily have passed for an Aryan, although he was Jewish and had worked before the war for one of the rich industrialists, perhaps Furstenberg in Bedzin, with as much time off as he needed for training. In the chaos of the ghettoes and its liquidation, I have no idea what happened to Nunberg. He couldn't have come on the train with me or I'd have been aware of him in the Quarantine Block. Yet, this Sunday, the legend that was Nunberg was going to strut his stuff, Jews vs. Gentiles.

The SS turned up in force on the *Appellplatz*, laid out as a temporary football pitch. There were jeers and anti-Semitic taunts and my mind wandered back to my childhood when we'd end up cracking heads with the Gentile lads back home. This of course was a vicious parody of that, a flash of my past through the dark mirror of the Holocaust. I remember standing on the sidelines staring at the apparition in the Jewish goal. Gone was the laughing six-footer that had been Nunberg and in his place was a shambling, shuffling *Muselmänn*, his eyes staring and sunken in his grey, drawn face. He looked confused, not able to follow the play and barely able to catch the ball. I don't remember the score but I can make a pretty good guess as to which side won. A few days later we heard that Nunberg had gone to the gas chamber. There would be no more autographs from him.

I must have been working on the Rampe for about five weeks when I was approached by a political prisoner. He was not from my hut or even my Block and he too was called Manfred. You rarely got surnames at Auschwitz-Birkenau, unless they belonged to the SS, in which case they were always prefixed by a rank. This man had heard my name on the *Appellplatz* or perhaps seen it written down in some ledger, because he asked me if I knew Moyshe Pivnik, the tailor from Szopoenice. To this day, I don't know why I said what I did, but there was something about this Manfred I knew I could trust and that the link with Uncle Moyshe was somehow important.

I lied and told him Moyshe was my father. He said he knew him, long ago, before the war. This enigmatic link stayed with me for days but I couldn't work out its signifi-cance. Manfred was a Gentile, a Christian *Blockältester* and I had no reason to trust him at all; but somehow I did. It wasn't exactly friends in high places, but having a *Blockältester* on my side was a strange comfort to me.

Throughout my time in Auschwitz-Birkenau I tried – we all did – to retain what dignity I could. This was reflected in a mania, prevalent among the SS and the *Kapos*, for cleanliness. They even had an orderly in each hut respon-sible for such things. The SS were terrified of typhus and spotted fever and endless scrubbing, shaving and delousing were deemed to be the way to keep them at bay. The image of constantly filthy concentration camps with *Muselmänner* wallowing in their own piss and shit comes partly from the experience of the shocked Allied troops who liberated the camps in 1945, by which time the SS had gone and the *Kapos* were busy making themselves equally scarce or reinventing their former roles.

The Auschwitz-Birkenau site was low-lying and marshy, so the outside areas were often wet and muddy in the autumn and winter. The huts however were different. We scrubbed woodwork and folded blankets when we got them. For all we were 744 to a barrack, we did the best we could to keep clean. From time to time we were allowed the luxury of a hot shower. Every time I handled the bars of hard, white soap, I wondered what it was made from.

Historians today have decided that the making of soap from human corpses is just so much anti-Nazi propaganda. I hope they're right.

Other attempts to retain dignity included an underground resistance movement in the camp. I wasn't part of it myself, but I heard rumours. Some of this, perhaps most of it, came from the Gentile Poles in the camp from its earlier days before I arrived, but there were plenty of examples of individuals going it alone, refusing to go quietly. Late in October 1943 there was a lock-down because an SS man had been killed. A train-load of Jews had been brought in from KL Bergen-Belsen and the majority were taken to Crematoria II and III. In the women's line a scuffle broke out. The version I heard, unlikely as it sounded, was that there were wealthy Jews from the west who had bribed the SS with the considerable resources still at their disposal with some vague notion of being allowed to slip quietly to Switzerland. The SS of course took the money and put its former owners on the trains to Auschwitz-Birkenau. One woman, realising as many did, what was going to happen, put on a strip-show for the benefit of the watching SS. She had been a dancer before all this madness and a couple of men, Unterscharführer Josef Schillinger and Rottenführer Wilhelm Emmerich, were captivated by her gyrations for long enough for her to grab Schillinger's pistol from the holster at his waist and shoot both men several times. She then ducked back into the crowd of half-undressed women and a brawl ensued during which the SS had the devil's own job to get their wounded comrades and the *Sonderkommando* out.

They gassed those already in the chamber immediately

and machine-gunned the rest. I never found out the name of this girl, but she became a heroine to all of us, especially because, for a while, the rumour ran that it was Karel Kurpanik who had been shot. Schillinger bled to death on the way to the hospital and Emmerich hobbled for the rest of his life.

Rebellion was in the air that autumn. Not long after the Schillinger incident, a French Jew named Ulick, who was a *Kapo*, bribed an SS guard with jewellery to get him out beyond the outer wire. We heard nothing for two days and nights and the whole time we were locked in our huts, having to shit in the corner. After two days they brought him back – I don't know how easily a Frenchman could blend in in occupied Poland – and he was interrogated as only the SS knew how.

At the next roll-call Ulick was the centre of attention. I don't remember the threatening speech that was made as we waited, shivering, in our lines. I don't even remember who made it. All I remember was Ulick's bruised and bloated face as he was made to kneel in front of us. An SS man put a bullet in the back of his head and he flopped forward, blood spraying from his skull. That wasn't the last we saw of Ulick. The SS strung him up above the *Appellplatz* for days as a warning to the rest of us.

For a long time I thought there was a surreal photographic record of my time on the Rampe. In one of several photographs taken during the camp's existence showing the arrival of prisoners at Auschwitz-Birkenau is one with SS officers in the foreground and the cattle-trucks idling in the siding behind the bewildered crowd of new arrivals. There are a few men in striped uniforms – the *Rampe*

Kommando. And on the extreme left is a boy, in profile, waiting to go to work after the selections had been made. Some friends contacted me some years ago and told me they felt sure the boy was me. He looks too blond perhaps – my hair was always dark – but with the shaved head it's difficult to tell. But the boy can't be me. The photo is part of an album found in a cupboard belonging to the SS at KL Dora-Mittelbau after the liberation. How it got there, I don't know, because it was definitely taken at Auschwitz-Birkenau and by coincidence, the woman who found it was an Auschwitz survivor too. She was a Hungarian Jew called Lili Jacob but she did not arrive on the Rampe until May 1944 and the photograph is a record of her family's arrival. I had left Auschwitz-Birkenau by then but I often wonder who the boy was, the lookalike from the *Rampe Kommando*. I hope he made it.

And of course there were so many times when I nearly didn't make it myself. Never more so than that December of 1943. It was then that I went down with typhus, Jew fever, and it astonishes me now that it took that long. The overcrowding was appalling. I've seen an inventory from January of that year that records twenty-one blocks as living quarters. Block Two, which was typical, had 234 beds and 702 mattresses – fine, you might think; except that there were 1,193 prisoners in that Block. Not that I ever had the idea or the opportunity of measuring it, but we each had 1.7 cubic metres of space. Wet straw, rotten boards, rats, all part of the lifestyle for us *Untermenschen*.

So I collapsed on the Rampe, along with so many others who did the same through shock, exhaustion, heart attacks or because they'd been laid out by the short temper of the

SS men. So they took me to the waiting room for the gas chamber. So I faced the Angel of Death. And you know already how that turned out.

As I rested in my hospital bed, heart beating, cheeks wet with tears, I believed in miracles. The Angel of Death had let me live. Only in the cold rationalism of that night did I wonder if Blockältester Manfred may have been my miracle. He could cut no ice with the SS, especially someone as focused and driven as Mengele, but he certainly had clout with hospital orderlies. All it would take was a nod of the head, a name scribbled out of a ledger, some *organisation* and I would have escaped yet another selection.

If this isn't how it happened, then I must return again for an explanation to blind luck or even, dare I still believe it after all this time, some sort of divine intervention.

I suppose I was in hospital for three or four days, getting a little stronger each day because of the relatively good food. Then they moved me out. I expected to go back to the *Rampe Kommando*. It was appalling, tragic work – 'Tell them you're eighteen. Tell them you can work.' It had got so I was as experienced as Mengele at making selections, at least in my head. He of course continued to do it for real; so did Kurpanik. But the Rampe job had gone to somebody else and I was marched back to the familiar huts and fences of the Quarantine Block. And Unterscharführer Karel Kurpanik would be my charming host once again.

But now I was streetwise and knew the score. I'd been at Auschwitz-Birkenau for six months and knew to keep my head down and avoid trouble. The ground around the huts had been levelled, killing God knows how many in process, and in that bitter, snow-crusted winter, there was surprisingly little for us to do. One day, perhaps in January 1944, I was standing gazing out beyond the perimeter wire when something odd caught my eye. A group of women prisoners were hacking away at a ditch with picks and shovels, watched, as always, by their *Kapo*. We didn't see women often at Auschwitz, except those on the Rampe. The women's quarters stood away to the west, beyond the railway tracks and near the gas chambers and Crematoria II and III. They had gone, I assumed, through the same processes that we had. They wore badly-fitting clothes, rough clogs and scarves over their shaved heads to make them look a little more human. They never worked with the *Rampe-* or *Sonderkommando*, but in every other respect, their lives must have been as miserable as ours. As I stood there that morning, watching them and making sure none of the SS or *Kapos* were watching me, I wasn't looking for my mother or for Hendla. I knew there was no point.

What really held me transfixed was the women's *Kapo* and I couldn't take my eyes off her because I knew her. She was from Bedzin, a distant cousin of mine and her name was Gutscha.

She saw me virtually the same moment I saw her and she crossed to the fence, 'Szlamek Pivnik, is that you?'

The sound of her voice, the smile on her face, whirled me back to a lost time I knew I'd never see again. I just nodded, unable to say anything.

She thanked God I was still alive. She knew better than to ask after my family. She came as close to the wire as she dared. A *Kapo* she may have been, but talking to a male prisoner, other than to scream an order at him, was

putting her life on the line and she told me that I needed
to get out. They were going to kill us all here. Any chance
I got, I was to get out. Did I understand? I still hadn't
spoken, hadn't moved. She went on that if they wanted
volunteers for work, I had to go. She made me promise
that I'd do that.

From somewhere I found my voice, 'Yes,' I nodded, 'I
promise.'

'Good,' she smiled at me. 'Now go. Don't let them see
you talking to me.'

And she turned away, bellowing at the women scrabbling
at the frozen ground.

'*They're going to kill us all here.*' I knew that already –
how could I not? But there was something in the way Gutscha
said it and something in what she asked me to do. Volunteer
for work. The alternatives – that some people had tried,
lashing out with a shovel, making a run for the perimeter
wire and the guard towers – that wasn't an escape attempt,
it was suicide, guaranteed a bullet, electrocution on the
fences or the walk past the garden to the gas. But volun-
teering for work outside the camp . . .

In the insane world of Auschwitz-Birkenau that made a
kind of sense.

8

The Prince's Mine

It must have been January when my chance came. At Auschwitz you didn't volunteer. It wasn't like school when you put your hand up to answer a question – 'Please, sir! Me, sir!' If there was to be a 'me' at all at Auschwitz, if I was to go on living, I had to keep my head down, keep quiet, not make eye contact. That was what the SS expected from their lofty Aryan pedestals and that was exactly what we inmates gave them. The only 'progress' at Auschwitz was by means of selection; somebody else's choice. It was like the worst kind of nightmare interview – you had no idea what the selectors wanted. You could only hope for the best.

I remember we were shivering in the snow on a bitter January morning roll-call, the wind biting through our thin striped jackets, our breath snaking out on the air. Grey faces under a grey sky. I could see Kurpanik across the square, deep in conversation with another SS man, wrapped in a greatcoat with his collar turned up. I always looked out for Kurpanik, the man who still haunts my dreams. It was a little comfort to me to know that he was some yards away that morning because that in itself meant he wasn't within hitting distance.

I found myself looking, guardedly under my eyelashes, at the SS man with him. I'd seen him before, on the Rampe and around the camp. He was in his mid forties, I suppose, his hair blond under his peaked cap with the death's head, his shoulders square and broad. I'd never seen him at close quarters and didn't realise then that he only had one eye. The missing one had been replaced by a glass one that didn't move, a reminder of the war against the British on the Western Front in 1940. But I knew his name and I knew his reputation. He was SS-Hauptscharführer Otto Moll and at Auschwitz-Birkenau he was responsible for the gas chambers and the crematoria.

My stomach lurched as Kurpanik broke off the conversation and marched over to us, his jackboots crunching on the ice. He muttered something I couldn't catch to our *Kapo*. It was the start of another selection. All of us, I know, were thinking the same thing: what do they want? What's the purpose of this one? There was a rising panic in all of us, but nobody moved. To do that, to break out of line, meant a bullet. In the twisted world of Auschwitz at least that made some sense. You broke the rules, you died. It was as simple as that. Everything else was just unnatural selection.

'You. You. You.' The *Kapo* wandered the lines, pointing at five, six, seven men. By the time he'd picked the eighth it was obvious that these were not fodder for the gas and the crematoria. He was choosing the strongest, the fittest of us. That was a relative term of course in Auschwitz, but we'd all long ago lost any ability to compare ourselves with the outside world or the world we had lost.

The *Kapo* got to me. I was seventeen and stood perhaps five foot three. God knows what I weighed. He looked me up and down and passed on. No 'You'. No selection. My brain was whirling. 'Get out,' Gutscha had said to me. 'As soon as you can. Get out, Szlamek. They're going to kill us all. Get out.' There were fifty or sixty men standing in the chosen group, all of them older and bigger than me. 'Get out, Szlamek. Get out.' So I did. I just walked out of line and tagged on to the chosen group. I didn't look to left or right, just straight ahead, so I didn't see it coming. If it had been a bullet I wouldn't have seen it wherever I looked. As it was, it was a stick with a burly *Kapo* on the other end of it and it thudded across my shoulder. I reeled at the sudden shock and pain; the *Kapo* snarled, 'Where do you think you're going, you little bastard?'

'Leave him,' I heard the chief *Oberkapo* say from behind me. 'If he wants to go, let him,' and he carried on along the ragged lines. 'You. You.' It was my lucky day. Another time I'd have been beaten to death. More blood on the snow. Another example to encourage the others.

With the Nazis it was all about control. Heel-clicking and saluting and attention to duty. We 'healthy' ones stood in line again, shivering in the morning while the *Blockschreiber* took our numbers and wrote them down in his ledger, part of the tonnage of paperwork of which the Third Reich was still, at this time, so proud because it was the timetable of genocide. Then they ran us – presumably just to prove that the fitness selection was justified – over the snow to the guardroom at the north end of the Quarantine compound. My shoulder hurt, my feet were numb and my lungs felt like bursting. But none of that mattered. We were going out of the camp. We were leaving Auschwitz-Birkenau. Alive.

Three grey-painted Opel trucks idled beyond the

compound gates, their engines rattling, their exhaust fumes thick in the cold morning air. There was a Jeep there too; all of the vehicles had SS registration plates. We were loaded onto the lorries, herded together, packed tightly like the cattle-trucks. There were barked orders in German that we all knew so well – '*Schnell. Schnell.*' There were SS everywhere, bristling with machine-pistols. Then one of them slammed shut the tailboard of my truck and slid the bolts. The gears jarred and we skidded our way out onto the road.

We could see the camp through the canvas sides of the trucks as they flapped in the wind. The barbed wire, the lamp posts, the rows of huts and the crematoria endlessly belching smoke. What new madness was this? Were they taking us to the ovens by a more direct route now? Or were we actually riding in one of those death-trucks we'd all heard about, where carbon monoxide was pumped into the inside? A moment's thought would have dispelled that fear. You'd never gas anybody in a truck with canvas sides.

Then the time had passed and Auschwitz-Birkenau was a ghost that faded in the mist. We were bounced around on the ice-rutted roads of a Polish winter and the wind was cutting but we didn't care. We were alive. We were out of Auschwitz. And I, for one, had forgotten how beautiful were the forests of silver birch.

I don't remember how long that journey lasted. I suppose it was an hour and a half on the frozen roads. In a way I wanted it to go on forever. Somebody once said it is better to travel hopefully than to arrive and that was certainly true of that truck journey that day.

The arrival was at another camp, but it was altogether

different from Auschwitz-Birkenau. It had an atmosphere of work, of purpose. The place was rectangular with a high brick wall around a central compound. The barracks here were single storey and looked new, built of brick and timber. There were guard towers at each corner of the place. Whatever this was, it was still lorded over by the SS and who knew what twist was waiting for us? I'd noticed mining gear as we'd driven in, the sort of derricks I remembered from Bedzin. There were railway sidings too with locomotives snorting and belching smoke. This was a coal mine.

The inmates were the same as us. Ghosts in striped uniforms coming and going, watched carefully by the SS in combat greens with machine-pistols and rifles slung across their arms. And then, of course, it all started again. They'd counted us all out of Auschwitz-Birkenau; they were counting us all in here. We stood in frozen ranks in the central compound; they took our numbers. Then we had hot showers and were deloused. You can't believe the joy of warm water when you've had so little of it. Delousing didn't work very well but it was a sign they wanted you to live. Little signs of optimism. Little flashes of life.

I was inspected by the camp doctor. I knew better than to make eye contact, but I knew this wasn't Mengele. We hadn't come round in some terrible circle of Hell to be enrolled in Auschwitz-Birkenau again. A medical orderly forced open my mouth and lifted my arms. I stood as straight and tall as I could. This was a more thorough check than the lightning, casual 'You. You. You,' of Auschwitz. This was a work camp; that much was clear. If we didn't make this selection, they'd have sent us straight back to the ovens. Would I, I wonder, have noticed the silver birches then?

During that first day as we were allotted to our barracks. I noticed, we all did, that the inside walls were spattered with dark brown streaks. It was blood that had run in rivulets to the floor. People had died here, recently and in large numbers.

That night, I learned where we were. You won't find the place on any map today although a society of Holocaust memorial people have marked it with a huge cross in the forest. The place was called Fürstengrube, which roughly means the Prince's Mine and it was one of the many sub-camps of Auschwitz-Birkenau that had an industrial purpose. Long before the war it had been called Harceska, a typical, small-scale coal mine that had been shut for years because the tunnels had become dangerous. It stood next to the village of Wesola and the nearest town was Myslowice. I didn't realise the exact position and if I had, incarceration here would have been all the harder to take. I was no more than sixteen kilometres from Bedzin. In the good old days, I could have caught a train and been there in less than an hour, back at Modzejowska Street with mother and father and Hendla and Nathan in my dreams . . . Just as well I didn't know.

Mines like Fürstengrube had acquired a new lease of life when the Germans invaded Poland. Uneconomic mines and qualms over dangerous shafts and tunnels belonged to the niceties of a free world at peace. They had no place at all in 1944. The industrial giant I.G. Farben had bought the mine three years before and had re-opened it. The coal extracted was used to make synthetic rubber for the war effort.

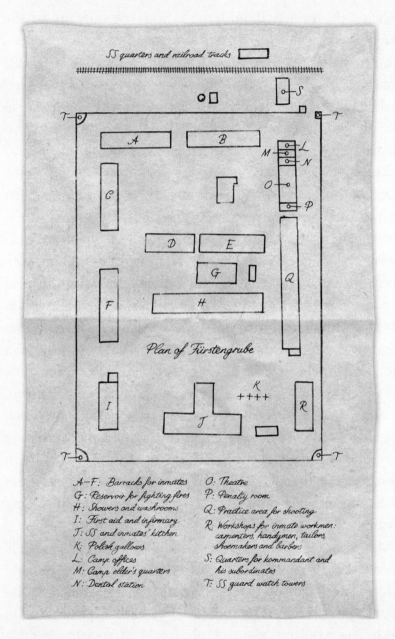

SS quarters and railroad tracks

S

T   T

A   B   L
M   N
G   O
         P

D   E
G   Q

F   H

Plan of Fürstengrube

K
++++

I   J   R

T   T

A–F: Barracks for inmates
G: Reservoir for fighting fires
H: Showers and washrooms
I: First aid and infirmary
J: SS and inmates' kitchen
K: Polish gallows
L: Camp offices
M: Camp elder's quarters
N: Dental station

O: Theatre
P: Penalty room
Q: Practice area for shooting
R: Workshops for inmate workmen:
   carpenters, handymen, tailors,
   shoemakers and barbers
S: Quarters for kommandant and
   his subordinates
T: SS guard watch towers

Plan of Fürstengrube. Based on a drawing by Hermann Josef, 1965.

None of us realised our new situation or fully grasped its significance. We were now part of a labour force, albeit slave labour, and were doing our bit for the German economy. While back in Berlin, Hermann Göring spoke of guns, not butter, the desperate tunnels of Fürstengrube were churning out coal to be trained to Monowitz where the production plant carried out the necessary chemical processes. The SS charged four Deutschmarks a day for an unskilled labourer like me; six marks for a skilled man. None of this of course appeared as wages and very little was used to maintain the mine. I suppose the SS attitude was that they had a virtually inexhaustible supply of slave labour and any one of us could easily be replaced.

They had started serious work at Fürstengrube in the summer of 1943 and Jewish labourers had built the camp under the guns of the SS. Within weeks, they were shipped out and new people like us were brought in from Auschwitz I and from Birkenau. And there were Russians there too, prisoners of war from Stalin's Red Army. There was an irony here that was not lost on us Polish Jews. In 1939 the *Wehrmacht* had overrun Poland so quickly because they knew their forward units would not tangle with the Russians who had already agreed to carve my country up with the Germans. The shoe was on the other foot now and these men had been imprisoned by their former allies.

Actual living conditions in Fürstengrube were not very different from Auschwitz-Birkenau. For all the barracks were newer, they were still spartan and extremely basic. Ours was a rectangular building in the centre of the compound, specifically housing skilled workers. Here was the building school with shoemakers' and tailors' workshops next door. We were packed like sardines in three-tier bunks and the 'beds' consisted of a straw-filled sack-cloth palliasse which formed a mattress. The single blanket was made of burlap, but it felt like it had been knitted from barbed wire. The food was the same too – breakfast was the usual ersatz coffee, made of barley or acorn. That was used to wash down a single slice of bread and piece of sausage. More coffee in the evening when we had the watery soup made from potatoes or turnips.

My first job was not unlike the one I'd left behind – welcoming new arrivals. Yet it was in another way totally different. There were no cattle-trucks here, no Rampe and no one was passing in on their way to the gas chambers. Under the orders of the ever-watchful SS guard commander, I opened and closed the main gate at the north-east corner as trucks and SS vehicles went in and out. After a few days, there was another selection. As usual, the standing in line, the pointed finger, the sheer randomness of it all. But as things turned out, this one wasn't actually random at all.

This time I landed on my feet. If Fürstengrube was the way out of Hell, the *Maurerschule* was halfway to Paradise. A group of us were sent to this Builders' School in the centre of the compound and taught a trade. It might have been what I would have ended up doing at home if there had been no war – working for one of the big industries in Bedzin. There were carpentry workshops with the tap-tapping of hammers and the smell of planed wood; bricklaying with its mysteries of the German-bond pattern brought in wherever the Swastika flew; there were cement works with shovels scooping and mixing the great piles of grey sludge.

In the rather more normal atmosphere of the *Maurerschule*,

some of us became friends. We were all wary about this, because selections were still so arbitrary, violence still so random, that forging lasting friendships wasn't wise. We'd all lost family in these madhouses; we didn't want to lose friends too. Even so, Henry Bawnik and I became friends. We called him Herzko and he had flat feet. We became amicable rivals in the building trade in the days and weeks ahead.

And so, Szlamek Pivnik, Number 135913, became a first-class bricklayer. I learned to take accurate measurements, make rough and ready sketches and plans, learned how to dig foundation ditches and build walls which, like the Reich for which I now worked, would last for a thousand years. My instructor was one of the team of civilian builders who worked on the site. It took a lot of imagination after Auschwitz-Birkenau to realise that these men went home after a day's work. Their home life probably wasn't as normal as all that, because although we didn't know it, all Hell was beginning to close in on the Third Reich. The Red Army had not only held against the assaults of the *Wehrmacht*; it was now actually pushing them back and winning victories. It's ironic that I can't, after all this time, remember the name of my bricklayer instructor. He was an SS man of course, a *Volksdeutscher* lance-corporal who had been a builder in Silesia before the war. He wasn't kind exactly, but he treated us as human beings at least. He never raised his hand to any of us nor even shouted and if that description has elements of Mengele, it is difficult to imagine two men more different.

For two weeks we learned our trade in the *Maurerschule* and then we were unleashed to carry out the work itself. This was a new experience for me, not only working along-side contract-worker civilians from all over Europe – there were a surprising number of Belgians – and local Poles, but having skilled status. My SS value would have gone up to six marks a day had I but known it, but that was translated in a way into more food. We were given a *Premiumschein*, a ticket for the camp canteen which gave us *thick* soup, bread or a couple of cigarettes. This of course, as in civilian prisons all over the world, was currency. I didn't smoke then – that was a bad habit I picked up later – so I found myself operating in a black market. Cigarettes bought more food, some of it smuggled in by the contractors coming through the gates each day. They were rarely searched, perhaps because the SS couldn't imagine any Christian Pole wanting to trade with a Jew.

I suppose somewhere along the line during training I must have impressed someone, perhaps the Silesian bricklayer, because as we began work for real I was made *Vorarbeiter*, foreman. There was a strict hierarchy at Fürstengrube, as at all camps – it was a Nazi and a German preoccupation. At the top of the tree was Moll, the *Lagerführer* or commandant and below him a team of underlings with various responsibilities – the training workshops, the hospital, the kitchens, security and so on. Below them came the *Kapos*, that mixed bag of saints and sinners – mostly sinners – who were the banes of our lives. As at Auschwitz-Birkenau, have a good one and life was bearable. Have a bad one – Rudi, for instance – and you might as well throw yourself on the wire. Most of these men were working class and had already proved themselves as efficient workers with a ruthless streak. The Gentile *Kapos* barked, 'You fucking Jews,' at us morning, noon and night. The Jewish ones, hardened criminals with a grudge against society, said things like, 'You ate roast duck and mouth-watering cakes at home while I went hungry.' Yes. I lost count of the roast ducks we'd eaten in the Kamionka!

Vorarbeiter was a long way down the chain of command, but I was no longer right at the bottom. I got better food, a half-decent pair of shoes and something akin to respect from the newcomers. On the other hand I was seventeen and had no idea how to handle even this tiny bit of power they had given me. It was a two-edged sword. In Fürstengrube you were either the solution or you were the problem and I discovered how difficult it is to run with the hare and hounds at the same time. I now had responsibility. Until that February all I had to look out for was Sam Pivnik. Now, if anybody in my squad was slacking or something went wrong, a *Kapo* would come to me. 'Pivnik, sort it out. That man. See to him.' That man could be my friend. Perhaps we'd bunked together at Auschwitz-Birkenau, frozen alongside each other in the lines in the compound, sweated side by side carrying bricks until our hands were bleeding and raw. I couldn't save him. I wasn't in a position to administer a light reprimand. There were no slaps on the wrist at Fürstengrube, just sticks, fists and boots.

One of the bigwigs at the camp who had been brought over by Moll from Auschwitz-Birkenau was Otto Breiten. He was *Lagerälteste* when I first arrived and I never really got to know him because he left that February for the Eastern Front. Breiten was a political prisoner, one of those whose status had always been higher than us Jews and as camp senior he commanded considerable respect. That month, a circular was sent round all concentration camps – any political prisoner who applied for frontline service would be given amnesty. This was Breiten's way out of his own particular hellhole and he took it. He couldn't have known what that transfer actually meant. Like most other volunteers, he ended up in the SS *Sturmbrigade Dirlewanger*, one of the most despicable and desperate units of the Waffen-SS. They were a bunch of criminals who were unleashed against Jews in Byelorussia and Eastern Poland under the excuse of anti-partisan warfare. Oskar Dirlewanger himself, it became widely known after the war, was responsible for thousands of deaths of men, women and children in the Wola suburb of Warsaw during the uprising there. Breiten probably took part in this because it happened six months after he left Fürstengrube.

Breiten's place as camp senior was filled by an *Oberkapo* who had a fascinating background. He wore the red triangle of the political prisoners but he was in fact a half Jew. He was Hermann Josef referred to by the Nazis as a *Mischling*, the product of a mixed marriage, and he always looked over his shoulder as a result. He came from Augsburg in Bavaria and was an architect before the war, born of a Jewish father but a Christian mother. This, in the racially, blood-obsessed world of the SS, made Josef a second-class citizen. And doubly so, because in the Thirties he had been an active member of the Social Democrat Party in Germany, firm (if liberal) opponents of the Nazis. He was in his late thirties, I think and cultured. He was tall and strikingly handsome, with an aristocratic manner reflected in the expensive leather boots he always wore. We called him Schwarz (Black) and I have no idea why. He was important to us because he represented something of a go-between for us and Hauptscharführer Moll.

I had little to do with Otto Moll and that was fine by me.

Close up, his unmoving glass eye was terrifying. He drank vodka like it was going out of fashion and when he was drunk he was dangerous and unpredictable. I remember one occasion when Moll was strolling near the water storage tank in the camp compound with a couple of SS men. Until this day I had rather a soft spot for that water tank. To begin with, I'd helped build it on the suggestion of Oberkapo Hermann and Herzko and I got to grips with the corners and the fancier brickwork, each of us watching the other to make sure he didn't do *too* good a job. When the work was finished and the water pumped in, Hermann would sometimes, on a Sunday afternoon, let us swim there. It was here that Herzko's flat feet became very evident and we didn't let him forget it. Neither of us knew that in the future our swimming skills would be necessary to stay alive.

On this particular day, Otto Moll was celebrating his departure for another camp and intended to have some fun on his last day. He was drunk and a prisoner walked past him too close for the *Hauptscharführer's* liking. He pushed the man into the water. I don't know whether he could swim or whether the icy water would have killed him anyway. I didn't find out because Moll pulled his pistol out of his holster and shot the man dead, like a fish in a barrel. I stood transfixed for a moment, then realised that I might be the next bit of target practice for the *Kommandant* and I got myself out of there. Looking back, a lot of the SS drank heavily, especially in the afternoons and evenings, and it's not difficult to see why. I have no sympathy for them after everything I have seen but they were, I now realise, locked into the same nightmare as I was.

Moll had been a landscape gardener before the war and I

think he actually supervised a little of that at Auschwitz-Birkenau before the killing took over and his special responsibility became the gas chambers. He liked to watch football and on Sunday afternoons when we were given the only real rest period in the week, we'd organise teams and kick a ball around. I suspect this had more to do with the civilians on site, who had better food and more energy than the rest of us, but I used to play because kicking a ball somehow symbolised reality. This was what I used to do as a kid; it was how 'normal' people passed their weekend.

If I'd played well, Hauptscharführer Moll would clap me on the shoulder or ruffle what hair I had. And this, I learned later, was how I was selected for the *Maurerschule* in the first place. It wasn't simply a pointed finger, a meaningless choice. Oberkapo Hermann had set up the school in my first days at Fürstengrube and both he and Moll had been quietly impressed by my footballing skills – hence the selection in my favour. There were those in the SS who would have been appalled by Moll's behaviour – to have favourites among Jews would have been frowned upon and to touch a Jew was just not done. On the other hand, remembering how that monster touched me makes my skin crawl even today.

And crawling was what I was doing now on a regular basis. You get used to the darkness underground, the rats and the heady fumes of the coal itself. What you never get used to is the fact that you can't always stand upright, but have to move at a crouch or push yourself into the blackness on your elbows. I have enormous respect for men who work underground; it's not something I ever want to do again. We worked eight-hour shifts, from six in the morning till two in the afternoon; or two until ten; or the night shift, ten to six. I was on the night shift where the *Kapo* was Hans, a Christian political prisoner with a red star. He had been a miner before the war and had bad legs and a clicking hip to prove it. Needless to say, he kept this little fact from the SS with his happy-go-lucky personality. These shifts were another little reminder of the outside world, because civilian miners from all over Europe worked them too, and because Hans had been a trade unionist before the Nazis made trade unions illegal. There was always the risk – the dripping water that could become a torrent, the cracking timber that could bring the roof down. Added to that, we were slave labour and we were expendable. I was as black as the miners themselves, our eyes oddly bright against the masks of soot and even though it was my job to check the timbers and the joists, I breathed in the same dust as they did. Coal gets everywhere – in your nose, your lungs. It clogs your ears and becomes ingrained in your skin. And on the way back from our shifts, the SS would insist that we sang. Anyone who wasn't opening their mouths, making a noise or was missing the beat got a rifle butt for their pains.

In that atmosphere, cramped and confined as we were, accidents were bound to happen. I was on the night shift – this might have been in March or April, I don't remember – and I was fixing joists. There was a creaking sound, almost a groan deep in the tunnel. When you hear that, you run. It's instinctive. You're not going to be able to fix it, to take the weight of the world on your shoulders, so you get out. Except that I wasn't ready for the terrifying speed of what happened next. I'd got maybe a couple of yards and the roof came down, grey rock thudding and crashing in the clouds of black dust. I was thrown onto my back by the impact and my legs were pinned by rubble. I shut my eyes, expecting the rest of the tunnel to follow, burying me alive. But there was nothing. Just the rattle of small stones and the gradual settling of dust. I'd lost my lamp and was in total blackness. I daren't move for fear of dislodging more of the tunnel.

Then I heard the shouts, the clatter of shovels and the tapping of picks. 'Over here!' I heard somebody shout and shafts of light from torches were darting everywhere as they hauled me out. My back was wrenched – and it still plays me up today – and I'd cracked a rib so that earned me two nights in the infirmary. About the only drug they had was aspirin and because I was a *Vorarbeiter* I was given some. It didn't help much to fight the pain but at least I knew I'd get over this. There'd be no Angel of Death hovering by my bedside with another selection.

But the next brush with death was entirely my own fault and it led to a change in my status I wasn't altogether sorry for. We were working above ground and I was supervising my squad putting up scaffolding for some new building near the main entrance. With us were the *Baumeisters* or *Steigers*, the civilian engineers engaged on the construction of the new mine. I heard a commotion and went to see what was going on. One of the *Steigers* had hit his head on a piece of scaffolding that was sticking out. He was in charge of the Russian prisoners of war, his head was bleeding and he was less than pleased.

He bawled at me and called me a stupid bloody Yid. 'Can't you see that's dangerous?' he shouted. 'I could have really hurt myself.'

I should have grovelled, of course. I should have bowed my head, pulled off my cap and mumbled my apologies.

I should have dragged the man who'd put the scaffold bar there in front of the *Steiger* and reported him to the *Kapo*. But I'd been *Vorarbeiter* for a couple of months by now and it had gone to my head. Without thinking, I told the *Steiger* to piss off. 'You should have been looking where you were going!' I said, proving that a Yid could shout too.

You could have cut the silence with a knife. Nobody, least of all a Jewish prisoner, spoke to a *Steiger* like that and he went straight to the SS, to report to Rottenführer Berger. A lot of the punishments meted out in the ghettoes and the camps was instant – a slap round the face, a cane across the back, a bullet in the head. Mine wasn't. All day I was expecting it and that night, after roll-call, it came. I was marched out on the *Appellplatz* in full view of everybody. My wrists were tied to a wooden post and my trousers were dropped. Maximum humiliation, maximum effect. They were treating me like a naughty schoolboy, not *Vorarbeiter* of a construction squad. Kapo Wilhelm came up behind me. I could see the walking stick in his hand and after the first stroke I couldn't bear to look. I have never experienced pain like it, before or since. I'd taken the odd switch with a ruler from a teacher, felt the sting of my father's belt, but nothing like this. I gritted my teeth as the tears of pain and shock ran down my cheeks. I was given twenty strokes of that stick, but I lost count after the first five or six. I am not ashamed to admit that I lost control of my bowels at some point and shit ran down my legs. There was nothing I could do about it and all the time I was thinking of the man with dysentery in the Quarantine Block in my first day at Auschwitz-Birkenau. He had been beaten to death. It felt as though I was detached from my body, looking down at that stupid Yid Szlamek who didn't know when to keep his mouth shut. It was a lesson learned.

I don't really remember a group of the lads from my squad dragging me away. I could barely walk and spent the night lying on my front on my bunk while my arse must have looked like a patchwork quilt and my back was in agony. Getting up in the morning was almost impossible and I needed serious help. I got to the wash block which wasn't far away but it felt like kilometres and actual washing was hell. Even half turning to wipe off the dried blood was agony and I should have stayed in bed. That of course would have been suicide. It would have meant selection. Men who couldn't work routinely found themselves on trucks going back to Auschwitz-Birkenau.

I stood as straight as I could for the roll-call to be told that I'd lost my position as *Vorarbeiter*. My replacement was Hersh Goldberg, a man in his mid-twenties I'd got to know quite well. He was solidly built, with a ruddy complexion you didn't come across often in the camps. He had a brother, Yonnie, and a cousin, Shlomo. It was nearly two kilometres to our building site at the mine's entrance and I was going to need all my strength just to get there.

'Szlamek,' Goldberg whispered to me as we moved off, 'March on the inside of the squad.'

'Why?' I asked, green as grass for all my months in the camps.

'Because Rottenführer Berger is looking for an excuse to shoot you, that's why.'

I didn't risk looking across at the man, in case that look was interpreted as excuse enough. Berger was an SS NCO from Silesia and he hated my guts. I suspect that the scaffolding incident was the last straw. Fürstengrube was different from Auschwitz-Birkenau. Harsh and often bewildering as they were, there were rules here that smacked of the outside world. In Auschwitz, Berger would just have put a gun to my head and pulled the trigger and some other poor bastard among the special units would have had the job of scraping me up. Here, Berger needed a reason – dragging behind the squad or sloppy marching might have been enough – but if I was half-hidden by the others, he'd find it more difficult to winkle me out. After all, we all kept telling ourselves, we were skilled workers for the Reich. Killing one or more of us would affect productivity and Hauptscharführer Moll and Herr I.G. Farben wouldn't have approved of that. The strategy worked and I always listened to Hersh Goldberg after that.

Losing my job had its compensations. As a skilled worker I still got the *Premiumschein* so food and cigarettes still came my way with their huge black-market potential. Now, without having to worry about the squad – that was Goldberg's headache now – I could get on with my work. I specialised in doorways, corners and windows and kept my head down. And I had an assistant. He was years older than me, an intellectual who had been a professor at the University of Kraków. He was a political prisoner or perhaps some kind of hostage – you didn't talk about such things or pry too deeply at Fürstengrube. His unusual status meant that he got mail from outside, including the odd food parcel that he'd sometimes share with me. I think this was the SS idea of a joke: an uneducated working-class teenager giving orders to an academic. He mixed mortar and fetched and carried without complaining once and I never knew his name. It's funny how the little civilities survive even the worst barbarism. In the outside world, in the Poland we all knew before 1939, he would have been addressed as 'Panier'. And that's what I always called him in Fürstengrube, even when he was staggering under the weight of bricks, covered in dust and cement. He was a nice man. And he was always 'Panier' to me.

However much I might be able to make capital out of my skilled-worker status, it was never possible to forget where we were and what was happening. This was still part of the Auschwitz complex and the unskilled workers around us were dropping like flies that spring. I watched them day after day, turning into *Muselmänner* in front of us, their bones sticking through their jackets and trousers, their faces pinched and drawn. They didn't get enough food, enough rest or enough medical treatment and yet they were expected to carry the heavy bags of cement and loads of bricks. They still dug ditches and laid pipes, the backbreaking work that would take its toll on fit, well-nourished men before the war. One by one, the worst of them fell to the selections.

After all this time, I can barely remember most of the men in the *Maurerschule* and in my Block, with the obvious exception of Herzko Bawnik. Yankl was the camp barber and Sol was in the next bunk. During the working shift I met Josek Zoller, whose *Vorarbeiter* was the fair-haired Peter Abramovitch. And there was a man called Velvell and an electrician Srulek Lipshitz, whose brother was there too. Srulek was in his mid twenties, a powerfully built man with darker hair than his kid brother, who wasn't much older than me. Kapo Shlomo Barran was a jack of all trades. Most *Kapos* had a specific role, but Shlomo seemed to be all over the place. He was huge. Mendeler Davidovitch was a shoemaker, with a square face and constant grin. Somehow, he had been able to hang on to his glasses. Most of these men had come direct to Fürstengrube from the Lodz ghetto; they had no experience of Auschwitz-Birkenau, the Rampe or the crematoria. As far as they knew, or at least hoped, their families were still coping, somehow, in their home town. I knew that mine weren't, so I kept off the subject. What did we talk about, buried deep in our tunnels or crammed in our bunks? God knows. What I understand as a joke now, was not a joke then.

And no one talked about religion either. The Jewish faith was of course taboo to the SS and the idea of holding even limited services was laughable. Some survivors whose accounts I have read since talk about feeling God with them in spite of everything. I couldn't feel that. Auschwitz-Birkenau and Fürstengrube didn't make me an atheist. They just made me realise that God wasn't allowed inside the perimeter wire.

If you got ill – as I had done on the Rampe – you had two weeks (if you were lucky) to get better. In the end, I had to go to the Infirmary at the far eastern corner of the camp. This was presided over by Dr König, who was a genuinely nice man, like doctors are supposed to be. I had painful, inflamed swellings in my neck and I knew the risk I was taking. Somehow, though, I knew I'd survive this and I was back at my bricks the next day. If you didn't get better, you were on the truck for Auschwitz-Birkenau. Most of these were swept up from the infirmary, but some were shunted out of line at roll-call or on the deadly march to or from the mine. Their response was always the same. They became quiet, sunk in on themselves. A few would cry. Some, the ancient traditions of my people bred in them, prayed to a God I knew wasn't listening. I never saw anyone try to escape or fight back. They were too far gone for that, physically exhausted and mentally dead already. The fight had gone out of them with the debilitating drill of each murderous shift. The guards marched them back to their barracks for the rest of the day. No one spoke to them. No one had the words, not even Panier with all his sophistication. Late in the afternoon or early in the evening a truck would arrive, engine growling at the main gate. It had a red ambulance cross painted on the side; that was supposed to allay fears and maintain the lie that these men were being taken away for convalescence. The sad little column would shuffle out, nobody speaking, nobody making eye contact. Then it was out on the free road, out past the silver birches making for the distant gates that led to the crematoria.

Work was never going to set these men free. For the *Muselmänner*, freedom was the gas chamber if a new consignment had arrived from somewhere else. If not, to save on Zyklon B, it was a bullet to the back of the head. Either way, it was the end.

In the March of 1944, Hauptscharführer Moll handed over command to his Number Two and went back, we heard on the camp grapevine, to Auschwitz-Birkenau to supervise huge consignments of Hungarian Jews who were on their way. The Rampe, I knew, would be busier than ever.

Moll's Number Two was Max Schmidt, not that much older than me in his early twenties. He had the smooth face of a country boy and wore his blond hair combed back. He had been with Moll the day his boss shot the man in the water tank and liked to stride around Fürstengrube with his Alsatian and his riding crop, ready to use either on us if the occasion arose. He came from a farming family in northern Germany, not far from the Baltic coast, and Nazism was in his blood. His father had been a party member for years and had served in the brownshirted *Sturmabteilung* long before they became subservient to the SS. Schmidt himself had been a combat soldier in the Waffen-SS, along with his two brothers, one of whom was missing. In common with several of the SS men in both the camps I knew, he had been wounded, invalided out and posted to the Auschwitz Guard Regiment. Shortly after I arrived at Fürstengrube, Schmidt had married Gerda Bergman, the pretty blonde daughter of one of the civilian engineers working on the mine. The Schmidts lived in nearby Wesola.

Even though I was no longer *Vorarbeiter*, I was savvy enough to know by now how the camp politics worked. Moll was violent, drunk and dangerous when he was in his cups. Schmidt was steadier and came increasingly under the thumb of Oberkapo Hermann Josef, who, now camp senior, exercised an almost paternal influence over the *Oberscharführer*. Josef, like all *Kapos,* walked a deadly tightrope and he could usually play Schmidt like an old fiddle. If things weren't worse than they were in the spring of 1944, I thank Oberkapo Hermann for that. Hermann Josef would tell investigators long after the war that Schmidt was not a natural sadist like Moll, but, completely imbued with the culture of Nazism and very ambitious, he did all he could to impress his superiors.

But sometimes things went wrong. It may have been April when there was a sudden burst of activity. Prisoners were hurried from the mine, cleared out of the workshops.

Tools were downed and abandoned. The civilian workers, who had already been ordered to remove their headgear so that we shaven-headed ones couldn't sneak out of the gates with them, were sent home. We were all marched back to our huts at double speed, the *Muselmänner* keeping the pace as best they could. This was a lock-down, searchlights probing the far woods, dogs barking in the darkness. We crowded to our slatted windows trying to see what was going on, but the windows faced the *Appellplatz* and we couldn't see the wall or the wire at all.

Rumours of course ran like wildfire. Somebody had heard something and they'd passed it on to somebody else. Was it true? Who knew? But lock-downs didn't happen for no reason. The story went that there had been an attempted breakout. One of the Block Seniors had led a group in digging a tunnel, pointing north under the camp perimeter between Blocks A and B. One of them had been caught inside it. Was this just luck on the part of the SS guards, to catch them red-handed? Or had someone blown the whistle? The bottom line was, don't teach men to be miners and not expect them to put their skills to good use.

The prisoners were taken away and no one expected to see them again. But of course we had reckoned without the theatricals of the SS and their need to make a point. None of us had any notion of the romantic escapes of British and French prisoners of war from the *Stalags* further west. In theory those men were covered by the Geneva convention, even if it was sometimes ignored. There was no convention for Fürstengrube and no convention for Jews. And it must have been Friday when we saw the truck full of fresh timber arriving and a gang hammering and sawing on the *Appellplatz*. They were building a gallows.

Sunday. The Christian Sabbath. A blessed day of rest at the mine. But there was no football match today, no chance to ease exhausted, aching limbs. We were ordered out onto the *Appellplatz* early in the afternoon as though for a roll-call. The gallows stood stark against the grey of the sky, the timber pale and almost gleaming in its awful newness. I could see a row of chairs set out in line facing the posts. This was a circus for the entertainment of the SS and we were to consider ourselves privileged to watch the show too.

After a while the snarl of car engines reached us from the main gate and a convoy of SS vehicles arrived, swastika flags snapping on car bonnets. The men who got out wore the silver braid of senior SS officers from Auschwitz and there was much saluting and heel-clicking, the Prussian military obsession long overlaid with Nazi formality and the inevitable '*Heil Hitler!*' Schmidt was there, the perfect host, smiling and nodding as though he were presiding over a garden party. And in a way, of course, he was.

I knew all the men who had tried to escape and been caught. Three of them had come from Auschwitz-Birkenau with me. And I saw them now, brought out from a guard hut with their wrists shackled and their eyes vacant. There was the Frenchman, Leon. Maurice, the happy-go-lucky *Blockältester* who came from Belgium. My fellow Pole Nathan, who had been a gangster before the war in Lodz to the north of Bedzin. And the fourth man whose name, I'm afraid, I have now forgotten. He looked after Max Schmidt's chickens. I can see him now, throwing some of the grain to the half wild pigeons that flew into the camp, reminding me of home. All four looked like *Muselmänner* now, scrawny and ill, with sunken faces and shambling walks. And they'd all taken one hell of a beating over the last few days.

Four nooses swung from the cross beam, rough hemp creaking. Below each one was a plain wooden chair and leaning against one of the uprights a small wooden stepladder; the furniture of death. Schmidt and his visitors took their positions on their own chairs that gave them ringside seats. Then, as if we hadn't had enough of them, another selection. Unterscharführer Anton Lukoschek was running the show and no doubt he wanted to impress his superiors with his efficiency. He stood in front of us, one arm behind his back, the other outstretched with the pointing finger. He told us he needed five of us and he raked our ranks with his lethal gaze. 'You,' he barked, 'You. You. You. And . . . you.'

The finger had pointed at me. We all looked at each other. We were all teenagers. We all knew each other. Felt each other's pain in all the terrors of Fürstengrube. And now we were an execution squad – an *Einsatzgruppe* with no zeal, no motivation, and no alternative.

'You,' Lukoschek said to one of the others, 'are going to put the nooses around their necks. The rest of you,' he looked at each of us in turn, 'will kick the chairs away when I give the word.'

We forced ourselves to look up. The SS guards had lifted the dead-men-walking onto their chairs. Lukoschek handed the stepladder to the lad he had chosen. 'Get up there and put the rope around their necks. The rest of you, stand in front of the chairs.'

I did as I was told and I was standing in front of Maurice, the Belgian. I couldn't look at him. Instead, I focused on

Leon to his left and watched the rope pulled tight around his neck. In the terrible silence of those seconds, I heard his erratic gasps, fighting for breath already even before his chair had gone. When it was Maurice's turn I heard a slight sob but now I was looking at the ground, at the chair, *anywhere* but into the face of the man I was about to murder. One of the condemned men roared a Polish battle cry, defiant to the last.

I was aware of Lukoschek looking over towards Max Schmidt for the signal. There were no speeches, no reaction from the watching crowd. 'Right,' Lukoschek barked to the boy in front of Leon, 'you first.' I saw the boy's foot lash out and hit the chair, but it barely moved.

'You'll have to do it harder than that,' the *Unterscharführer* tutted. The lad kicked again, but still not hard enough and Leon's feet were still on the seat. I heard him snort in terror and the lad doubled over, yanking the chair legs with all his strength. The rope creaked and stretched as the chair clattered away. Leon's feet flailed in mid-air, desperately trying to find the ground, to take the appalling pain away from his throat and windpipe. His jaw was rigid and his bulging eyes stared wildly ahead. All this took seconds, but it felt like years.

'Now you,' Lukoschek was snarling in my ear. 'Pull it.' I heard a sigh and I looked up. God knows I never meant to, but I did and found myself staring into Maurice's face. Tears were trickling down his cheeks and he had this profound look of sadness. I heard him say, 'Long life.' The others there heard it as a rallying cry, one last, proud, fierce gesture from a brave man. But I heard it as a whisper, to me only, to the stupid, naïve kid who was ordered to make sure that *his* life wouldn't be long at all. I turned away, grabbed the chair legs and pulled. Maurice's feet danced in the air as he writhed in his death agony, kicking my arm in his convulsions as he died.

Nathan and the chicken man were next, but these went badly. When you hang a man on a chair, his neck doesn't break. There isn't enough drop and there isn't enough weight. The old executioners will tell you it's an exact science, that the neck snaps at the third vertebrae and death is almost instantaneous. It wasn't like that, that Sunday in Fürstengrube. Those men strangled to death and Nathan and the chicken man took minutes to die.

We were ordered back into line as the visitors' party got up, hardly noticing the hanged men at all. They walked over to the administration building, nattering casually about this and that, no doubt looking forward to their schnapps. After all, it was a long drive from the Auschwitz main camp. They'd earned it.

We were turned away, away from the men we'd killed, back to our barracks, back to the humdrum routine of Fürstengrube where men died every day because they were largely of no consequence.

Only I had looked into Maurice's face. It is a face I see in my dreams to this day.

'Long Life.'

9
Death March

The hangings of Maurice and the others didn't mark the end of the escape attempts. Someone I remembered from Bedzin, but whose name I never knew, had the idea to hide out in a disused tunnel. This was never likely to work; he knew as well as any of us that the evening roll-call would find him out; it would only be a matter of simple deduction by the SS to realise he must be somewhere in the mine. I often wonder what he intended to do, how he would have got through the gates or past the wire. In the event, he didn't get the chance. Either the SS had worked out his plan or someone, for extra soup or half a sausage, had informed on him. When the SS found him, crouching in the blackness of his tunnel, Oberkapo Michael Eschmann was given the 'honour' of shooting him on the spot and they left his body for the rats.

The Russians didn't have much more time for us Jews than the Nazis, so it was odd to find a Jewish officer arriving at the end of June from the Red Army. He was a quiet, determined man, probably in his mid-twenties, and wore a red triangle on his prison jacket to show his status as a political prisoner. Officially, such men were called *Schutzhäftlinge*, protective prisoners, and whereas most of these were harmless victims of the Nazi state, some were actually dangerous partisans. This man was and the guards watched him like hawks.

The chance he took was huge but it could have worked. He realised that of the four guard towers at the camp's corners, only two were manned during the day. If he could get close enough, he could get into one of the empty ones – he chose the tower to the east – and out of a window on the outside of the wire. He would then have to run for it before the alarm was raised, but once at the trees, he had a reasonable chance to keep going. What he couldn't have expected was that Oberscharführer Schmidt would be waiting for him on the outside with a squad of men. We heard the shots at our various work stations and carried on working. You didn't look up, express concern, show any sign that anything out of the ordinary had happened. They brought the Russian back into the camp on a plank carried by two prisoners, his arms and legs dangling grotesquely.

This was the last escape attempt I remember, perhaps because of the way it ended. Schmidt and his thugs weren't just waiting beyond the perimeter fence by accident. They knew exactly when and where the Russian was going to make a break for it. And that could only mean one thing: someone had informed on him. There was no shortage of suspects and the rumours, as always, spread like wildfire. There was no solidarity in a place like Fürstengrube. The *Maurerschule* and our work on the mine gave me a sense of purpose and even pride in our work; the hangings of Maurice and the others ought to have drawn us together. But it doesn't work like that. For every good deed in the camps, there were dozens of bad ones. Heroes are the men on the outside, who can still come and go as they please; men who have free will. We couldn't come and go unless a *Kapo* or the SS said we could. And many of us had no will left.

Who had blown the whistle on the Russian officer? It might have been the Russian lad in the kitchen who had smuggled food for the man's escape? It could have been Hermann Josef or any of the senior *Kapos* keen to cosy up to Max Schmidt. But there was another school of thought and that one gained ground as time went on and that was Bronek Jakubowicz. He was already at Fürstengrube when I arrived and had been brought there with his father and brother. He came from Dobra, near Lodz, and had been a dentist before the war. To everyone's surprise, Otto Moll had set up a dental laboratory in the camp and equipped it with the latest equipment – this at a time when there was nothing as impressive at Auschwitz-Birkenau – and installed Jakubowicz as the camp dentist. He never treated fellow Jews of course – dental treatment was reserved for the SS and the occasional political prisoner. There was never any conclusive proof that Jakubowicz had been the informant but he spent too much time kissing arse with Max Schmidt and Hermann Josef for the liking of most of us.

Shots ringing out in Fürstengrube were rare. It was not an extermination camp like Auschwitz-Birkenau and shootings only happened when Otto Moll had been drinking or there was some infringement which the SS thought merited execution. But we heard them one day at the end of my shift in the mine. Covered in coal dust and clinging, sticky mud, we had the untold luxury of a shower, part of the SS obsession with cleanliness. On this particular day however, there was no hot water. The boiler had broken down and the orderly, a prisoner called Chaskele, had not had time to fix it before the end of the shift.

We trudged back to our barracks, cold and filthy, under the gaze of Oberscharführer Schmidt. The man suddenly went berserk and to this day I don't know why. Did he see it as a reflection on him, that his camp was running at less than 100% efficiency? Was he in a bad mood about something else already and was this the last straw? He stormed off in search of Chaskele, bawling him out in a way that echoed around the whole compound, telling the man his future except that he had no future. Schmidt whipped out his pistol and shot the man twice at point-blank range. Again, no one 'noticed'. We continued in a line to our hut, looking neither left nor right. The murder of Chaskele happened a little out of my eye-line. All I saw was Schmidt, face still taut with fury, striding back to his office and holstering his gun. He slammed the door. I suppose it had the desired effect. If a boiler breaks down at Fürstengrube, they kill you. Another lesson courtesy of the SS.

It must have been the August of 1944 that another hanging took place. By now, time was running out for the Third Reich. The British, Americans and Free French were pushing across France from their D-Day beachheads of two months earlier and in Warsaw a Home Army was beginning to carry out operations in preparation for the arrival of the Russians. Snippets of this reached us from somebody who had spoken to somebody who had heard the news over the radio from the BBC. We had no way of knowing what was true and what wasn't in this mad game of Chinese whispers; and of course the BBC were playing a propaganda game too.

What we did know was that five Poles, Gentiles, were taken away under heavy armed escort for the Auschwitz main camp. The story went – and this one came in an unguarded moment from Hermann Josef himself – that they had been in contact with partisans of the Home Army that was causing chaos in Warsaw. Exactly how they could have done this and to what effect was never seriously considered. We were again on the *Appellplatz* towards the end of that month when the five were brought back, battered and bloody, to be hanged for the entertainment of the SS and as a warning to us. This time, thank God, I was not chosen as an executioner, was not the one to rip a stool away from a man, leaving him to strangle to death in the stifling August air. But the rumours ran like wildfire that Hermann Josef was the man responsible for bringing them to the attention of the SS. Each of the five roared at him across the *Appellplatz*, screaming that he was as guilty as they were and demanding to know why he wasn't up there on the gallows with them. The cry was taken up by many of us in our lines and it took nearly an hour for the SS to maintain order and carry the executions out.

That was the summer that the Hungarians came to Fürstengrube. They brought with them grim news from Auschwitz-Birkenau. The speed of extermination was increasing – not until after the war would the world find out that nearly half a million people were gassed during this period. If you read the statistics today you will learn that on two days and nights in July, 7,000 people from the family camp of Theresienstadt Jews were gassed. On 2 August the gypsy camp at Auschwitz-Birkenau was similarly liquidated – nearly 3,000 died.

By November the world had turned again. We didn't notice any change at first. The roll-calls, the work at the mine, the accidents and the brutality continued. But the selections stopped. Nobody was being sent back to Auschwitz-Birkenau, not even the *Muselmänner* or accident and disease cases. Gentiles were being shipped out, it was true, but they were relatively strong and healthy so we had to assume they were being shipped to another sub-camp. Our numbers were falling and that should have been good news for us but the food supply was becoming increasingly hit and miss as the war began to pinch the Reich and even us 'privileged' workers felt it.

I had turned nineteen that September and spent yet another Hanukkah behind the wire. It was early in January 1945 that I heard a noise I hadn't heard before – at least not on that scale. It was a vibration really, something that always worried men who eked out a living underground. We glanced at each other when we heard it under the watch of the *Kapos* and the SS. We whispered about it in the tunnels and our bunks. I don't remember who said it first, but someone realised what that vibration was; it was artillery fire, the roar and crash of the Russians miles away. But it was getting nearer.

Did we feel elation? Delight? Near hysteria at the prospect of liberation? Perhaps; but if any of us entertained those thoughts, we soon dismissed them in the face of our reality. The wire was still there, the watchtowers, the perimeter guards. They could still hang us on the *Appellplatz* or shoot us in our bunks; set up explosives and bring the roof down on our heads in the tunnels. What would the SS do? Smile and shake our hands and say it had all been some sort of bad dream? A joke?

19 January 1945. That day the Russian General Ivan Konev took Kraków and Tarnov and Marshal Georgi Zhukov liberated Lodz. It was probably Konev's guns we had heard. I had no idea how close freedom was, but at Fürstengrube what was happening had an immediate effect. As we stood in the ice and snow of the *Appellplatz* that morning, we suddenly heard a crash and roar. The camp's administration block was going up in flames, black smoke belching into the sky. The SS stood by, petrol cans in their hands, admiring their handiwork. They were burning records, the names, the numbers and the details of men long dead or still barely alive, trying desperately to conceal the evidence of the greatest mass murder in recorded history. At camps all over Europe, similar bonfires raged, similar lines were being drawn in the sand.

Oberkapo Hermann Josef broke the news to us. Sounding as matter of fact as if he were sharing holiday plans with us, he told us we would be moving to a camp in Austria, starting with a march to the railway station. We should bring any food and warm clothes we had.

I remember being struck by the rich irony of Oberkapo Hermann's words. The SS had warm overcoats and plenty of food still; the *Kapos* would get by. The rest of us had our thin uniforms. In a way, I was lucky. I'd traded some cigarettes the day before for a solid pair of workman's boots. They were old and the leather was cracked but they were paradise in comparison with the clogs I'd brought from Auschwitz-Birkenau. All I had in the way of food was the bread ration I'd saved, as usual, from breakfast. But they gave us extra bread and a tiny portion of butter and marmalade.

We were formed up into a column. And they made us wait all afternoon. This was different from the usual trek to the mine entrance. There must have been 700 of us, wrapped in whatever rags we had, shuffling along as best we could, sliding and scraping on the ice. Nearly 300 men stayed behind, too ill and too weak to walk. In the Quarantine Block in Auschwitz-Birkenau these 'idlers' would have been beaten and shot, but not now. Now, as we marched away through that bitter January evening, we saw them still standing on the *Appellplatz*, shoulders hunched, eyes sunken in their heads. The SS marched with us, to the head and rear of the column and along our flanks. They looked as grim and miserable as we did, collars turned up, rifles and rucksacks on their backs. No one looked behind. No one was going back.

What began on that icy January evening has come to be known as a death march. Dozens of them were happening all over Europe in the winter and spring of 1945 and they have been extensively researched and analysed by historians. I am not an historian. I am not a psychologist or a sociologist. I can't begin to tell you what impelled Oberscharführer Schmidt to take us west except for a natural impulse to get the hell away from the Russians. I can't explain why he felt it necessary to take us all with him or where he thought he was going. All I can tell you is what happened to me.

The weather was terrible. Polish winters are always grim, but for men weakened by slave labour and starvation, it was lethal. And I couldn't help thinking that this was what it was all about. The SS, the *Wehrmacht*, the entire Reich, were on the run and the end of the war was in sight. But it would not be a rout, not yet at least. The SS still, literally, called the shots. They still had the power of life and death over us and they would decide how, where, why and when at last we died. Anyone who stepped out of line, anyone who staggered and fell by the roadside, went down to an SS bullet. If you wanted to pee, you did it walking along, the warm liquid soaking into your trousers rapidly cooling and then freezing. If you wanted to shit . . . you didn't want to shit. There was no talking, just the clatter of clogs and boots on the crunching snow. This monotonous rhythm was punctuated now and then by the crack of a rifle and another heavy bullet, fired at close range, slammed into a fragile body. No bullet ever missed. No target ever survived.

Evening of 20 January, the end of the second day of our march. Oberkapo Hermann Josef had told us we were marching to the railway station; where the hell was it? Another Nazi lie? Another ruse by the SS so gifted in the variety of their torture methods? We were crammed into a barracks once home to the Polish army and more recently to the *Wehrmacht*. There were thousands of us there, in every makeshift uniform you can think of, the stripes of the concentration camps most evident. Many men couldn't fit into the buildings and had to sleep in the sub-zero temperatures outside. Men from Auschwitz I, men from Birkenau, men from Monowitz. Many – perhaps the majority – were Jews. It was like a nation on the march again, like the refugees we'd seen fleeing through Bedzin all that time ago, like the Pivniks were when we were herded out of the Kamionka. We got no food that night and precious little sleep for all we were exhausted. And the place, someone told me, was Gleiwitz, where all this madness was supposed to have started the day before my thirteenth birthday, when Poland attacked, without warning or provocation, a German radio station.

Except that now, Gleiwitz was another concentration camp linked to the collapsing industry of the Reich. The women made lampblack; the men made weapons of war.

The next day dawned raw and cold. I had eaten almost nothing for two days and breakfast of a bread crust and ersatz coffee barely made any difference. We were formed up into a column again and marched along icy roads to the promised railway siding. Hermann Josef hadn't told us the station would be two days' excruciating walk away. The freight cars were open-topped trucks, of the type they used to haul coal and coke. It would be worse than freezing in those but it was better than walking and in that sense not as appalling, perhaps, as some of the other death marches. They loaded us onto the train and I was grateful for the overcrowding because it gave us greater body warmth. But we weren't going anywhere. The train just waited in the siding, steam crystallising on the morning air. The mid-morning brought the sound of artillery fire again and occasionally even the crack and rattle of rifles. This was the Soviet 17th Army pushing ever westward out of Kraków and Katowice and it terrified the SS, who ran for it.

I didn't know what was happening and instinctively we

all crouched below the frozen sides of the trucks, keeping our heads down, so I didn't actually see the SS go. Others did; they just vanished into the woods. A stationary train in a railway siding makes a tempting target for aircraft or long-range artillery and from what we'd heard of the Red Army, they weren't going to ask any questions or worry about what today you'd call friendly fire. The train carried Reich markings so it was a legitimate target.

Some of the prisoners, too exhausted or desperate to take the tension any more, climbed over the truck rails and dropped to the tracks or the platform. They ran for the woods where I knew the SS would be waiting and I didn't have the nerve to try it myself. How long the panic lasted I don't know, but bullets started whizzing overhead and bouncing off the metalwork on the trucks, tearing through the planking. One or two of the men were hit, dropping like stones to the truck floor or falling on the living, their blood warm and dark against the icy grime of the rest of us. The SS were back and this was their announcement of the fact. We cowered under the brief barrage and then the engine snorted into life and we were rolling.

I often think it ironic that I arrived at Auschwitz in a passenger car which still had, for all its grim connotations, a modicum of pre-war civilian civility about it. It was taking men, women and children to their deaths but it had a veneer of sophistication. These coal trucks had nothing, except an increasing number of corpses, and we rode the rails for seven days. Men died in that appalling week, of cold and exposure, of exhaustion and malnutrition, of wounds old and new inflicted by the SS and the *Kapos*. We hauled some of them over the side and watched them flop onto the frozen embankments before rolling away into the bushes and the dead grass. Others became useful seats. You forgot they were once people. Now they were relatively soft padding where you could perch while you tried to rub some feeling back into your frostbitten feet.

For those seven days we rattled through the Czech countryside, the trucks bouncing and swaying with no predictability at all, so we were thrown against the walls and each other. There was no food, no water except for the icicles we could crack from the rims of the trucks and the snow that fell, which we collected in a tin can, and there was no shelter. We hurtled through stations, never stopping, never slowing. Police, *Wehrmacht* officials in uniform, stared at us from platforms. Just another trainload of Jews. We'd started the war in the first place, hadn't we? The Führer had said so. Nobody had cared what happened to us from the first day and now everybody was too concerned with what would happen to them.

And on that train, men ate each other. The criminologist Brian Marriner has written '. . . in life threatening situations human beings lose all their inhibitions . . . We become what we were designed to be: animals. And there is no shame in that.' They say cannibalism was a feature of life for the Russian peasants when I was a boy at home in Bedzin and that it happened in KL Bergen-Belsen a few weeks after our particular train journey. The army doctors who examined the corpses there found that one in ten had bite marks on their legs. One of them saw an ex-prisoner, even after liberation in the relative comfort and safety of an American field hospital, use a knife to cut off a portion of flesh from the leg of a corpse in the mortuary and slip it surreptitiously into his mouth. 'No shame in that'? I am not so sure. Desperate, freezing men from Eastern Europe – and I'm not sure where – used whatever sharp-edged objects they could find to rip open the frozen corpses and cut out the liver, eating it raw as it warmed their frostbitten fingers.

Food – it was all that mattered. Czechoslovakian civilians clustered at various bridges under which our train whistled, throwing bread to us. The SS guards, in wagons between the open trucks, swivelled their machine-guns upwards and scattered these Good Samaritans with their bullets; killing people who were just trying to feed us. They also turned their guns on us, peppering anybody who caught the bread. That was overkill. We were already killing each other in those trucks. The law of the jungle that ruled in Auschwitz-Birkenau and Fürstengrube had now spread to this train. We fought and jostled, punching, gouging, kicking with the desperate energy of the starving. It was literally survival of the fittest. The biggest, the strongest, the most vicious, got the bread. The weakest, the smallest, sank to the truck floor in their hopelessness.

It was on the seventh or eighth day that we rolled into Mauthausen. Nearby, although we didn't know it, was the city of Linz where Hitler in his madness was still trapped in his bunker below the streets of Berlin, planning to rebuild as Germania, the most colossal city in the world. Mauthausen stood on the north bank of the Danube, a beautiful part of Europe whose beauty was lost on us, the starving; we had come deep into Austria. It was not actually an extermination camp, which you might find odd if you look at the camp's *Totenbuch*, the ledger of the dead.

It records the fact that 36,318 executions took place there in the six and a half years of its existence – a drop in the ocean, of course, compared with Auschwitz-Birkenau.

We'd heard there were gas chambers and crematoria at Mauthausen and we could see from the trucks the huge gates and the giant eagle and swastika above them. We'd heard too about the stairs of death, one hundred and eighty-six stone steps of different depths up which *Muselmänner* were forced to carry stone as I'd been forced to carry it in the Quarantine Block in Auschwitz-Birkenau. Men died in their dozens each day, the collapse of the front row on the highest steps crashing backwards in a deadly domino effect on those behind. Most of the prisoners here were originally Polish intelligentsia who had been worked to death through slave labour.

The previous year large numbers of Dutch and Hungarian Jews had been bought into Mauthausen, many of them thrown to their deaths at the so-called Parachutists' Wall, their bodies bouncing off the rocks on the quarry floor. One of the survivors of Mauthausen, Dr Antoni Goscinski, recorded years later in his memoirs that he counted sixty ways in which the SS murdered their prisoners. At Nazi headquarters in Berlin, Mauthausen was known as *Knochenmühle*, the bone grinder.

Still no food. Still no shelter or warmth. Whatever negotiations took place between our SS and Mauthausen's commandant, the place was full and there was no room for us. We were shunted on to Buchenwald. This was one of the earliest and largest of the concentration camps, set up to house political prisoners before the war. It was built on a wooded hill a few miles from the town of Weimar,

associated in German culture with the names of the poets
Goethe and Schiller. I doubt if either of them would have
understood Buchenwald. The factory here operated twenty-
four hours a day making machine-guns and shells for the
Wehrmacht, now retreating – we heard in snippets of
railside gossip – on all fronts. Buchenwald was also a place
where, like Auschwitz-Birkenau, they killed people in their
thousands, to realise a madman's dream.

There was a sign over the main gate, although I never saw
it, which read, in wrought iron, *Jedem das Seine* – to each
his own. The inmates apparently had their own reading of
that – everyone gets what he deserves. Many of them got
far worse than they deserved in the 'singing forest', the
macabre name given to the woods beyond the camp where
men were hanged upside down from the trees. Testimony
of the survivors would record that Walter Sonner, the
'hangman of Buchenwald', once followed the biblical end
of Jesus' disciple Peter and crucified two priests upside down.

I can't describe the pain in my stomach and the cramps
in my legs as Buchenwald turned us away too. The train
was split now, half the trucks taken in one direction, half
in the other. I suppose you could say it was symbolic. The
more we thought about it, the more obvious it became that
the Reich had fallen apart. There were no decisions coming
from the top now; there was no cohesion, no plan.
Everybody was operating on tittle-tattle, rumours of troop
movements and the word 'liberation' was on everybody's
lips. Why were the SS keeping us? As hostages, pawns in
some desperate deal to save their skins? Or could this, even
now, be an ongoing part of the Jewish policy that the Nazi
state had been carrying out for the last six years?

We rattled into Dora-Mittelbau near Nordhausen in the Harz mountains. The haunting beauty of this range was lost to me, crouching, frozen and starving, in a coal truck with corpses for company. At last we left the train. It had been nine days and I could barely walk. Dora-Mittelbau was a large complex built in natural caves in the mountains and tunnels linked with workshops that made Germany's top-secret V-2 rockets which were still raining down on Britain, bringing death and destruction of a kind I never saw in Bedzin. Everywhere was high-security, electrified fences, painted skulls and crossbones and signs to 'Keep Out!' We slept in a disused hall and we got food for the first time in a week. It was the usual thin soup with two cabbage leaves chasing each other around the bowl, but it *was* food. The place had no heating and there were no beds, but it was indoors, under a roof and after so long in the trucks, a little touch of paradise.

We spent two days there and Oberscharführer Schmidt turned up. We hadn't seen him for the whole of the march and the train journey, but then we hadn't actually *seen* much at all apart from what was happening in our own truck. It had been a surreal experience being penned in that rectangular box of wood and metal, like a little world of its own where men died of hunger and cold and there was nothing but the snow beyond it and the rhythm of the rails.

Schmidt collected several hundred of us, the living debris of the camp, and we were marched off to a sub-camp called Tormalin. It was only much later I discovered that the camp's actual name was Regenstein, that it was near the little town of Blankenburg and was named after a ruined medieval castle nearby. For whatever reason – and it was probably to cause the maximum confusion to the Allies trying to find them – a number of camps were given the names of minerals. Regenstein became Tormalin. This was another Fürstengrube, as though the whole journey between these places had been pointless – just a new means for the SS to kill us. There was an *Appellplatz*, rows of huts, blocks, electrified wire and four guard towers. The sleeping quarters were new and looked temporary, as if the SS were just making us squat here before the Russian artillery moved us on. There was no permanent kitchen and only a makeshift water supply. The food was the same monotonous round – hard black bread, watery soup, 'coffee' – and on it we were expected to work on a new tunnel that led to the underground rocket factory. Technically, although no one told us this at the time, our employers were the Hitzbleck company from Duisberg, Brandt from Magdeburg and the Scheffer Organisation from Blankenburg. Behind them were the industrial giants in the whole Dora-Mittelbau complex like Junkers, Heinkel, Siemens and BMW. We made the joists that held up the roof – the same sort of work we'd been trained for at the *Maurerschule* in Auschwitz-Birkenau – and the pace was murderous. The chemical stench in the tunnels was awful, the kind of sulphur you associate with Hell. There'd been trouble at Tormalin before we arrived and camp gossip told us that Russian prisoners of war had attempted various acts of sabotage. Everybody involved had been shot.

Here was one of the most ghastly sights I had seen in the camps. Would-be escapees were hanging from the walls in the tunnels of Tormalin, meat hooks wedged into their flesh. There they stayed, putrefying to blackness, as a warning to the rest of us.

And here I began to turn into a *Müsselmann*. On the Rampe and at Fürstengrube I'd been able to *organise*, to scavenge some extra food here and there to stay alive. At Tormalin there was no chance of that. Here, we were all equals, all, whatever our individual skills, doing the same job. They were working us to death and on that dreadful diet, a lot of us made it easy for them.

There were civilians here too, of course, because of the technical nature of the work. And there was the same kind of sporadic, unpredictable brutality that there had been at Fürstengrube. Most of the time we got along tolerably well but there was the occasional outburst when the SS complained about sloppy workmanship and the whips snaked out, whistling through the air to thump on backs where shoulder blades were already painfully obvious.

It was here that Kapo Hans and Shlomo Barran were executed, along with four or five others on the orders of Oberscharführer Schmidt. I no longer remember what crime they were supposed to have committed, but since Hans was a Christian, it couldn't have been simply a case of anti-Semitism.

It all changed again early in April. On 6 April, although we didn't have any accurate news at the time, the Red Army was at the gates of Vienna. Far to the East, Poland was once again in Russian hands and what ought to have been liberation was anything but. Before dawn we were up as usual, shouted orders, short patience. We downed our breakfast, such as it was, and I tucked the usual grey crust into my jacket for later. But the *Appell* that morning was different. The *Kapos* and *Vorarbeiters* from Tormalin weren't there, just the SS. And under the death's heads caps and *stahlhelmes* were faces I recognised; these were the old guard from Fürstengrube, with Oberscharführer Max Schmidt at their head. Did I imagine it or was the roll-call, that interminable torture that could last hours, quicker this morning? Schmidt had something to say and once the headcount was over, he told us we would be leaving and must be ready by 0700 hours. That wasn't difficult. I had the clothes I stood up in, a metal bowl and a tin cup I'd scrounged from somewhere. There was a real buzz as we mustered. For days now we'd been aware of Allied aircraft high overhead, sometimes swooping lower to investigate, looking for the *Wehrmacht* who must be hiding out or offering token resistance here and there. We never, in the snatched moments we looked up at the sky, saw any sign of the Luftwaffe. The Reich was bleeding to death.

But dying animals still have it in them to kill, and snatches of whispered conversations all around me, on the *Appellplatz*, in the barracks that morning, said it all. Schmidt had warned us that any stragglers would be shot. Were they taking us to yet another camp? Could there still be any left? If we were to go on the road again, would we meet a Russian platoon or a British tank unit? Above all, the fear that gripped us most was what the SS would do to us. Once they'd been so proud of their meticulous paperwork, their quick, efficient removal of an entire race. Now, not only were we an encumbrance as they retreated, we were walking evidence of their inhumanity. Could they possibly keep us alive?

Once we'd got our flimsy gear together there was another roll-call on the *Appellplatz* and they counted us again. We were about 200 strong and they marched us out in fives, escorted by the Waffen-SS, armed to the teeth. There was no mention of a train now. The man who had spoken of one back at Fürstengrube had been Oberkapo Hermann and he vanished into the distance ahead of us on the back of Max Schmidt's Zundapp motorbike.

Another death march. Another trek along rutted roads where the sudden arrival of spring meant nothing. The ruts weren't frozen solid any more and the snow wasn't falling; but the mud was clinging and made walking difficult. How long my Fürstengrube boots would hold out I didn't know. They weren't much better in this situation than the clogs of the Quarantine Block and they chafed my feet, raising blisters that burst and rubbed with every step. Men staggered and dropped by the roadside and no one turned back to look as we heard the dull crack of the pistol shot as the SS killed them.

The only time we stopped all day, trudging through the foothills of the Harz mountains, was to let the SS have a drink or a cigarette. We got no water, no food, no idea of where we were going. In fact, we were going to Magdeburg and we got there as dark fell. This medieval city was only about ten kilometres from Berlin, the capital of Hitler's Reich that now had the fury of the Red Army unleashed against it. I had never actually seen a bombed city before. The planes that had hit Bedzin on my thirteenth birthday had targeted industrial areas only and I realised now what little damage they had done. This place was a shambles. The Elbe slid a sludge-brown in the gathering gloom. There were no lights anywhere and the huge towers of the cathedral loomed black and broken against the night sky.

The streets we trudged along were littered with rubble and broken glass. This city had been destroyed before, burned to the ground in the Thirty Years War in the seventeenth century, and now it had taken another pummelling. There was a fortress here, but it was also a key communications centre with a tangle of railway junctions, and the real reason for Allied bombing was the huge Krupp armaments factory just out of town. The people we saw here were shabby and dirty and looked just as hungry as we were. In Czechoslovakia, people had thrown bread to us on our open trucks. In Magdeburg they had no bread to give and they ignored us completely.

By nightfall, the SS had assembled us at one of the quays along the waterfront. We were corralled into an open-sided shelter and told to rest. My feet and back were in agony and I just huddled the night away in the darkness, listening to the gurgle of the river and praying for food. There wasn't even any water, even though the mighty Elbe was just feet away. We noticed the SS ranks had thinned during the night, but whether they'd be back at dawn we didn't know. Those who remained watched us carefully, rifles at the ready, eyes alert. Just in case we doubted that they were still in charge.

At first light we were ordered to our feet again and I wasn't sure how I could walk on through the pain. Max Schmidt roared up on his motorbike; he'd found a drum of water for us. There was still no food but we queued patiently, as most of us had queued for five years now, to dip our tin mugs into the water and gulp it down. Then, another roll-call. And we marched to the water's edge.

Riding at anchor in front of us were two river barges. They were filthy and rotten-looking, flat boats with an open cargo hold and a small wheel house at the stern. The SS divided us into two groups and we were loaded into the holds, gritty and dusty with coal. I was used to this, both from Fürstengrube and from the open coal trucks into Mauthausen. It's funny how you can take comfort from such little things, familiarity breeding a kind of hope. There was no shelter of course and nothing by way of a toilet but at least we weren't walking and I was grateful for that. I noticed Schmidt lolling against his motorbike chatting to the harbour commander, but I couldn't hear the conversation. The Elbe ran north to the sea, I assumed, but at the time I didn't even know which river this was, still less exactly where it went.

North. We were definitely going north, chugging down-stream, belching black smoke into the April sky. There wasn't much conversation in those holds. We were crouched or sitting as best we could, a hundred men watching the world go by. We saw villages along the riverbanks, smoke rising lazily from chimneys. We saw children playing in back gardens. Now and then, we even caught the smells of cooking. This was a different world. A world where there was no war, no camps; a world of peace we could see, smell and almost touch. Of course, had I thought about it, this was also a world without Jews. I wonder what those laughing, happy children made of us, with our shaven heads and our filthy, lice-infested uniforms, staring back at them: a floating concentration camp.

For three whole days we steamed on, speculating on where we were going. If Kapo Wilhelm, on the barge with us, or Hersh Goldberg had any idea of our destination, they weren't telling us. At one point, watching the bank sliding by, I saw refugees streaming along the road, carrying the kitchen sink on their shoulders, in their carts and prams. A people on the move. But not the Exodus this time. These people were Gentiles, Aryans beaten out of their homes and fleeing – though whether from the Russians or the Americans and British, we didn't know. From time to time we saw Max Schmidt, with Hermann Josef behind him, weaving his motorbike through this trickle of the dispossessed.

Each evening we moored somewhere along the river and on the second morning, a van drove up. Out of it got four civilians who bought us bread and ersatz coffee, the first food we'd tasted since leaving Tormalin, and it was relative heaven. The final morning of the journey came on the third day and we tied up in a canal on the outskirts of a port. This was Lübeck, we heard hours after we arrived. Its name, apparently, means lovely one, but it wasn't very lovely when we arrived. The medieval church was a ruined shell and the place was in chaos, with trucks, ambulances and people everywhere. The port installations and U-boat building yards had been the target of the British RAF for the past three years and it showed.

But as things turned out, we were only passing through. From the barges we were marched north through flat, prosperous-looking farmland. Away from the shelled town you could again believe there was no war on. We were halted outside a large barn beside a road in a hamlet called Neuglasau. We stood in our rows of five, exhausted, confused. Some of the older men knew roughly where we were. This was Schleswig-Holstein, specifically Ostholstein, on Germany's northern coast and we had marched with the Bay of Lübeck on our right. This was the scene of the last of the murders of the death marchers. As we shambled past a line of ancient oaks along the road that led into Neuglasau, a prisoner went down to a pistol bullet.

We spent three or four days in this barn or in the yard outside, all 200 of us, exhausted and scared. Schmidt was absent most of the time and we didn't know why. He may have been scouting ahead as he'd done throughout the death march or he may have been visiting SS headquarters which, it was rumoured, had moved into the area away from the firestorm that was Berlin. In his absence, four men were brought to this barn by the local police. They were probably partisans or escapees from another death march. I saw Schmidt's number two, a red-headed sergeant whose name I never knew, take these men one by one at hourly intervals behind the barn and I saw him draw his pistol. The crack of the gun, drifting smoke and bodies flopping to the grass.

The next day, the *Oberscharführer* returned and played God again and carried out another selection. About twenty of us were chosen and we were on the road again. We came to yet another barn, smaller than the last. It was Oberkapo Hermann Josef who made things clear to us now. This was Max Schmidt's home, the farm owned by his parents. And we were going to work on it.

To this day I have no idea what was in Schmidt's mind. Was he ordered by somebody higher in the SS to bring us here? We couldn't know at the time that the SS, which had decided whether we lived or died for the past six years, was on the point of collapse, everybody frantically shifting for himself. Did Schmidt have some fantastical idea about keeping us Jews prisoner to the bitter end, to continue to do his bit, as his Führer had once said, to bring about the end of Jewry in Europe? Did he hope to trade us as hostages to save his own skin?

One thing we were all sure of: this was not a humanitarian gesture. There was nothing remotely humanitarian about Oberscharführer Max Schmidt.

10

Cold Comfort Farm

We had been rousted out of the barn by shouting SS men, but you couldn't equate it with Fürstengrube or Auschwitz. And we got fresh bread and real coffee rather than the ersatz rubbish we'd had since, in my case, 7 August 1943, my first full day in the Quarantine Block. I can't describe the taste of that bread. People living around this farm had had this every day and I could barely remember what it tasted like. But if my mind wandered back to Wodzislaw and the Garden of Eden and all the comforts of my childhood, it was soon shaken back to reality. All around me in that damp-smelling barn sat exhausted, half-starved prisoners of the Nazi state, our heads still badly shaved, our striped uniforms hanging in tatters and our clogs caked with blood. And around us the SS were still in charge, if only because they still had guns.

It was now that Schmidt made another selection. Were they going to divide us into small, manageable units to shoot us on the edge of burial pits they would make us dig first? In the end, this was the most benign selection I'd ever faced. We were broken up into small groups and one by one they marched off across the flat fields of Ostholstein. My group stayed put, the boys of the *Maurerschule*, and if I didn't exactly feel a burst of pride about that, at least I was among friends.

The Schmidt farm became a sort of home to us over the next few days. We lived in a hay loft over a pigsty which said it all in terms of how the Schmidts regarded us. And they made us work. For two weeks we broke our backs building walls and mending roads, lashed at first by the stinging rain or chilled to the marrow by the winds howling in over the flatlands. But by comparison with what we'd all known, this was a sort of paradise. There were no more selections on the Schmidt farm. We worked hard because we could. I didn't get much more food than at Fürstengrube or on the Rampe, but it was *quality* that counted; it was real and it was fresh. Our morning bread was made with flour and had butter on it. Our soup had actual vegetables and sometimes pieces of meat. If this sounds childish, it's not meant to; it's just that none of us had had such luxuries for so long.

Occasionally in that fortnight we'd be marched out to other farms and here the fare was even better. One of the men we worked for was Herr Miller. He was ill and couldn't do the jobs himself. His wife was so grateful to us that she cooked potatoes in schmaltz for us and we all had extra helpings. On the Schmidt farm were two Ukrainian girls, forced labourers who did odd jobs cleaning the farmhouse and cooking. Their fried potatoes were to die for; I hadn't seen food like this since before we moved to the Kamionka.

The situation in the Schmidt household was surreal. After my years in the camps with rough male company and the daily terrors of selection and the *Appellplatz*, the atmosphere here was very different. I remembered I had seen Schmidt's wife, Gerda, at Fürstengrube. She wasn't much older than me, very pretty, with golden hair she usually wore in the braids so beloved of German woman-hood – every inch a Valkyrie. Her father was there too, the civilian engineer Herr Bergman from Fürstengrube. When we were at the camp the Bergmans lived in Myslowice nearby but I guessed that part of Poland had now been overrun by the Red Army and the Bergmans had fled to one of the tiny 'islands' where the Thousand Year Reich still prevailed. Schmidt's parents were in their early fifties, I supposed. My time in the camps made it difficult to guess ages and the whole experience was tinged with that deadly, hopeless mantra from the Rampe – 'tell them you're eighteen'. The senior Schmidts were prosperous-looking 'good Germans', both well-built. He had the short cropped hair popular among middle-aged men with a Prussian back-ground. She was very much the North German *Hausfrau*. I wondered if they knew exactly what their son did for a living and whether they were proud of him. There were local men too, labouring with us in the fields but they didn't talk to us and we in turn left them alone.

It was nearly the end of April now and the weather had turned to spring with greenery on the trees and blue between the clouds. From time to time we heard the drone of aircraft and saw the black outlines of bombers high above. We couldn't be sure but they were either British aircraft – Wellingtons, Halifaxes and Lancasters – or American B-52s and the sky belonged to them. There was no sign of the Luftwaffe. Every night we saw the sky glowing red over Hamburg to the south. We heard artillery fire too on the ground and it was coming not from the east, where the Red Army was forging ahead across a shat-tered land. It was coming from the west and I remembered that day, the day I turned thirteen; how we all stood on the pavements in Bedzin waiting to welcome what we thought would be British or French tanks. And soon, very soon now perhaps, as we worked in those German fields, they'd be here. Six years too late, General Miles Dempsey and the Second British Army were on their way.

One evening we were sitting in our pigsty eating our soup when Schmidt and his father wandered past, deep in conversation. For days now his men had been getting increasingly nervous, fingers on triggers, tempers frayed, watching the skies and watching the roads. There was the steady thud of distant shells as dusk fell, a deadly barrage which we know now was costing the British £2 million a day to maintain and which was sounding the death knell for the Third Reich. I heard Schmidt say to his father, 'It's getting bad.' He crossed to the pigsty and rested on a metal barrier looking at us. Was this it, I wondered? Would he pull out his revolver as he had at Fürstengrube when the boilers wouldn't work? Had he decided to get rid of his troublesome burden once and for all? He said nothing. His face gave nothing away. He turned on his heel and walked into the house.

Why didn't we run? That night, after soup in the pigsty? The next day under the Ostholstein sun, in the fields of springtime – why didn't we run? Yes, Schmidt was there. So were his men and their guns. But we weren't supervised all the time, other than by unarmed, harmless-looking farmers. We *could* have run, *could* have made it, *could* have reached the welcoming arms of the British, who surely wouldn't fire on scarecrows wearing the stripes of a concentration camp? But we didn't. None of us. And it's something

I've read about since in the memoirs of other survivors. The years of terror, of barbed wire, of electric fences, they never leave you. You turn in on yourself, hiding in the only Hell you know. Why? Because out there, in those fields and woodlands, across the ploughed farmland of North Germany was a world I didn't know at all. I was just thirteen when the *Wehrmacht* invaded my homeland and in a way my life had been put on hold ever since. In a word, I was too scared to run away.

But all that changed one day. It was 1 May. To the southwest of us, Hamburg radio announced that Hitler was dead. The madman who wanted to build his own Garden of Eden in my country had gone. His successor was Admiral Dönitz, a man I'd never heard of, and he told his distraught listeners, 'It is my duty to save the German people from destruction by the Bolshevists.' As the Red Army got to the Reich Chancellery, they found the charred remains of Hitler and his wife in the little garden there. There was a kind of poetry in that, although it would be years before the world knew the full details.

We had our breakfast as usual that day but now we were ordered into column again. There would be no more work on the farm. We marched back through Ahrensbök, the little village with its Christian church and its weekly market where the locals tried to pretend everything was normal, even when shaven-headed men in stripes walked among them. The other prisoners from the outlying farms joined us and once again we were going north, heading for the sea.

I don't remember who heard it first, us prisoners or the trigger-happy SS walking alongside, behind and ahead.

There was the unmistakeable whine of an aircraft banking high to our left ahead of us and straightening as it roared towards us almost at tree-top level. It must have been a British fighter but nobody was taking time to look for markings. Even before we heard the SS order to scatter, the column had broken up and we all dived for cover. I must have run for thirty or forty metres before I threw myself into a ditch at the roadside and waited. Heads were popping up everywhere, but the danger hadn't passed. The plane banked again and was coming back for another look. Columns on the road could have been troops or they could have been civilian refugees. The last thing the RAF would have been expecting would have been the remnants of a death march. Again the plane roared above us and I saw the red, white and blue roundels this time. There was no gunfire though. The Luftwaffe would have recognised our stripes at once and riddled us just for the hell of it.

This time I stayed put, crouching in my part of the ditch, feeling wet and uncomfortable in the earthy hole. I suppose the fighter made three or four passes and then became a speck in the blue before disappearing altogether. When I put my head up again, there was no one there. I can't explain to this day how that happened. Why didn't I hear the SS orders to form up again and the clatter of clogs on the metalled road? The point is I didn't and I suddenly felt the most terrifying panic. I couldn't remember when I had last been entirely on my own, but it must have been before my thirteenth birthday. Even when I was living at 77 Modzejowska Street and going to school, there must have been times when I was just by myself. After the German invasion, that never happened.

The fields and trees of a beautiful early May stretched away in the Ostholstein countryside and everything seemed so normal. Why had the column marched without me? My experiences of the *Appellplatz* had taught me that the living – and the dead – were counted again and again. But this wasn't the old SS, the lethal institution that had so many ways to torture people. Our guards were as scared as we were, perhaps more so because they knew retribution was waiting for them. No one was coming back for me and I had no one to go to. My father, my mother and all my siblings were dead in the gas chambers of Auschwitz-Birkenau. Nathan had been taken from us as we moved into the Kamionka; my grandmother left behind at the Hakoah months before that. I had to assume they were dead too.

I didn't know exactly where I was. As I write it now, it's obvious. You can Google Ahrensbök on a computer and fly over a digital version of the road I crouched beside on that day in early May. All I knew was that I was inside the heartlands of the Third Reich and the people there hated Jews. How long would I last in the open, on my own? So I decided to go back, back to the Schmidt farm with its cold comforts, to the most recent place I could call a sort of home. I waited in the ditch until dusk was falling, then made my way back.

I was careful in the twilight to avoid the main road through Ahrensbök. There were SS installations nearby and every house, I supposed, was the home of a rabid Nazi. I kept to the fields, crouching low and running along hedges, from barn to barn and outbuilding to outbuilding. In one of them I found some raw sugar beet and ate it, the first food I'd had since breakfast. Then I recognised the pigsty and its loft and crawled in there, tapping the grunting inhabitants aside and stretching out on the straw.

It was probably dawn the next day when I heard a commotion below me. I must have stirred waking up because a floorboard creaked and I found myself looking straight into the tanned, weatherbeaten face of Max Schmidt's father. He swore in German, more surprised than angry, and demanded to know what I was doing there. I told him I got lost. It wasn't very convincing but when I added I felt I ought to come back, he seemed satisfied. I wasn't going to give him any trouble. He told me to stay put and that's exactly what I did, resting back on the straw again.

It was a while later – I can't be sure how long – that Max Schmidt appeared. I heard his motorbike growl into the yard and snatches of conversation between him and his father. The next thing I knew was that Oberscharführer Schmidt was standing outside the pigsty looking at me. He wanted to know why I wasn't with the others and I told him I had got lost when a plane flew overhead. He shook his head, more in sorrow than in anger, and for a moment I felt like a naughty schoolboy again, throwing snowballs at the lady with the funny hat in Bedzin. The difference now was that rather than my father's belt or a stern word from Mr Rapaport, my old headmaster, this man could put a bullet in my brain.

'Come with me,' was all he said and I followed him to his motorbike. He straddled it, revved the throttle and told me to get on the back. The last person I'd seen in this position had been Oberkapo Hermann Josef on the death march and I felt terrified. I'd never ridden on one of these things before and it took me a while to realise I had to lean with Schmidt and the bike. I didn't know where to put my hands. Hugging an SS man, the *Kommandant* of Fürstengrube, a Jew-hater and a murderer, was something I couldn't bring myself to do. So I held on to the bar behind the pillion seat and hoped for the best.

None of this made any sense. Even a few weeks ago, Schmidt would have beaten me half to death for 'getting lost'. He'd have shot me rather than let a Jew so close to him. But now . . . now, though I didn't yet know it, his Führer was dead and the Third Reich had only four days of life left in it. Oberscharführer Schmidt was hurriedly re-inventing himself, to present an altogether more human face to the world. And the first part of this was to make sure no concentration camp survivors were found at his parents' farm.

We roared out of Ahrensbök and after about a kilometre or so saw another marching column ahead. They wore the stripes and the clogs I knew so well but these weren't my boys of the *Maurerschule* or even from Fürstengrube. Schmidt spoke to the NCO in charge of the SS escort and signalled for me to join the rest. I watched Schmidt climb back on to his bike and ride south and I hoped I'd never have to see him again.

We marched north again as the sun climbed, but by mid-morning a thick, grey sea mist had enveloped us and you could barely see the men in the row ahead. Out of the gloom I could make out the buildings of the outskirts of a town. This was Neustadt and we were back at the Baltic again.

Survivor

There are twenty-two Neustadts in Germany. This one
was a naval base and we could just make out the ghosts
of what appeared to be warships riding at anchor in the
bay. The whole place was full of prisoners like us, sitting
around in their striped uniforms with the SS prowling the
perimeter. What was different was the presence of the
motor buses with well-dressed civilians standing near them.
On the sides of the buses were huge red crosses.

I was still staring at these when a voice I knew made me
turn. 'Szlamek, where the hell have you been? Get your
arse over here!' It was Oberkapo Hermann Josef and he
beckoned me over to the huddle on the ground. One by
one the faces flashed before me. This was the Fürstengrube
contingent I'd last seen scattering into ditches near
Ahrensbök. Herzko Bawnik, Peter Abramovitch, Hersh
Goldberg; I was back with the boys of the *Maurerschule*.

Everybody was whispering excitedly. The Red Cross had
a reputation that cut across national barriers. They had
even, although I never saw this, muscled their way into
Auschwitz. The war was over, everyone said. The Red Cross
were going to take us all to Sweden. After the hysteria of
these early moments on the dockside, cold reality began
to dawn. If the war was over, why were the SS still there,
with guns and vehicles? And why were we going to Sweden,
a neutral country, when we should have been allowed to
go home to Poland? And there was an even colder reality.
How could the thousand or so prisoners crowded on that
concrete all get on three buses?

The answer came soon enough. A knot of Red Cross
officials and SS officers had been deep in conversation near
the buses. An SS man broke away from them and started

marching around us. 'Prisoners from the West!' he shouted. 'Any prisoners from the West. Move to the buses now.'

Left. Left. Right. Left. It was another selection, just as surely as if Dr Mengele was standing in front of me, flicking his grey gloves to right and to left. But almost always to the left. Now it wasn't a matter of whether you were eighteen, fit and able, or old and crippled or with a family. Now it was a matter of where you were born. The accents all around me were unfamiliar. Away from the Yiddish and Polish of the *Maurerschule* I could hear snatches of French, Walloon and a completely alien tongue somebody told me was Danish. These men were on their feet, forming into the lines which were bred into them by now, shuffling forward. I heard my mother's voice – 'Szlamek, save yourself' – and felt her hand, loving but firm in the small of my back. I remembered the line of able-bodied men on the *Appellplatz* in Auschwitz-Birkenau, the men who were going to Fürstengrube, to life. And I knew that my time had come again. As a group trudged past me, I scrambled upright and joined the column. I daren't look back, at the faces turned to me. I knew no one would call out, give me away, and I suspected many of them had the same idea I did.

It felt like kilometres to those buses, standing there with their doors open and the safety of their leather seats. I could smell the gasoline; almost feel the lurch of a bus I hadn't ridden in for nearly six years. I was at the door now. And bureaucracy stood in my way. A brown-overcoated civilian stood there, with a clipboard and a pen. Next to him stood a *Hauptsturmführer* of the SS, still immaculate beneath the death's head, still in charge for all that the war was supposed to be over.

He asked me, in a German accent I'd never heard before, where I was from and I told him I was French. He narrowed his eyes and spoke again. This time the language was incomprehensible. It must have been French and he was trying to catch me out. If so, he succeeded. For a split second I thought of my old school in Bedzin and wished I'd been less keen on gardening and keener on languages. I pretended to be deaf, but that didn't work either. Reverting to German, the SS officer told the Red Cross official that I wasn't French. The official looked me up and down, still a kid in my stripes with my hair growing back and tears in my eyes. He leaned towards me.

'Where are you actually from, lad?' he asked.

I hadn't heard that soft a voice from an official of any kind for years and I confessed at once. 'Poland,' I told him.

He smiled. He said he was sorry but they could only take prisoners from the West at the moment. There was only so much room on the buses. Then he straightened and said, louder than he need have done, I thought, 'The war will be over in a few days. You'll be safe then.'

I turned back to the Fürstengrube people and noticed others being turned away too. I wasn't ready for my welcome, but I suppose I should have been. I felt a stinging slap around my head and Oberkapo Hermann Josef was looming over me, calling me a stupid bastard between clenched teeth and asking if I wanted to be shot.

'Any more nonsense from you, Szlamek and I'll beat the shit out of you. Sit down!'

I did and watched the lucky ones, those born by the accident of fate in a Western part of Europe, climb aboard the buses and rattle away through the sea mist, disappearing

Me (left) with my brother Nathan shortly after liberation. Taken at Konstanz am Bodensee where we were helping with illegal transports of Jewish refugees to Palestine.

Aunt Rachael and Uncle Solomon Abramovitch, my relatives in London with whom we stayed when we first came to the UK.

Nathan and me in Trafalgar Square in the 1950s. We had recently become naturalised citizens.

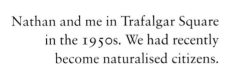

Going to the war –
Nathan took this
photo of me just
before I left London
for Israel.

Me (front right) with my
army colleagues training
in France for the War of
Independence, 1948.

Posing with my rifle as part of the
Machal, the Volunteers for Israel.

Driving a half-track in Palestine. We weren't prepared for the heat.

מדינת ישראל

משרד הבטחון

צבא ההגנה לישראל

Mr. Sam Pilnick

In recognition of your contribution	על חלקך ותרומתך
to the defence of the State of Israel	לבטחון מדינת ישראל
in the War of Independence	במלחמת העצמאות
1948	1948
With deepest gratitude	תודה

Yitzhak Rabin

Prime Minister & Minister of Defence   10.12.1992

יצחק רבין

ראש הממשלה ושר הבטחון

The certificate presented to me by Prime Minister Yitzak Rabin
for my service in the War of Independence.

Nathan and me at our home in London, 1965.

Outside my gallery in Notting Hill, 1985.

Oberscharführer Max Schmidt
with his parents in Ostholstein.
No doubt they were proud of
their boy.

The nearest I got to an
'apology' for the Holocaust –
Max Schmidt's letter to me.

The barn at Neuglasau where I
stayed towards the end of the Death
March. Taken during filming of a
German TV documentary, 1986.

The marble monument where the Great Synagogue stood in Bedzin.

Standing by the monument in 2009 to remind us of the Kamionka ghetto and the Jews deported to Auschwitz.

In 2004 when I went back to Bedzin. I am standing in the courtyard of my family home in Modzejowska Street. The pigeons are still there.

On the Rampe at Birkenau in 2004 with a group of Jewish students from the UK.

Me at Birkenau in 2009. I said a last goodbye to my family
and I don't think I will ever go back.

into freedom as if it was a distant, unattainable land I wasn't going to be allowed to see.

How long we waited there I don't know. Perhaps they intended to keep us there, sitting curled up on the quayside until the war ended. Perhaps they were going to throw us into the sea. I'd never seen the sea before. Bedzin, Wodzislaw, Auschwitz-Birkenau, Fürstengrube: all the places I'd called a kind of home all my life had been far from the coast. And it was made all the more mysterious to me because I couldn't really see it, just a lapping greyness that merged with the rolling mist.

And out of that mist came a fishing boat, engine chugging and with nets and weights hanging from its hull. It manoeuvred into position and the SS piled fifty or so prisoners on board. As it moved away into the grey distance, a second one came in; then a third. The fourth boat had my name on it and we Fürstengrubers, with an armed *Rottenführer* leading us, clambered aboard. I didn't like the wobble and sway as we rocked at the quayside. There was nowhere to sit and anyway there were too many of us on board to make sitting possible. The engines roared and we too were swallowed up by the mist.

I don't know how far out we'd gone into the Bay of Lübeck when I realised that the sea mist was thinning. Looking back there was no sign of the quay or the little town beyond. Looking ahead a large grey ship loomed out of the gloom. It had three funnels and was huge. I'd never seen a ship like it, not even in pictures. Its grey hull was streaked with rust rivulets and it had obviously seen better days. Halfway up the hull was an open door cut into the grey metal and a deadly-looking rope ladder trailed from it to just above the water level.

A ship's officer appeared in this doorway in the uniform of the *Kriegsmarine*, the German navy. He shouted down to the *Rottenführer* that the ship was already crammed with prisoners. They couldn't take any more.

'I've got my orders,' the *Rottenführer* shouted back. This phrase and others like it I had heard before and would hear again over the years from ex-Nazis anxious to excuse themselves from the madness they'd taken part in.

The naval officer told him to try another ship. We could all see the others, three of them moored nearby, but they were all smaller than this one. If *this* one was full, what chance would there be on the others? The boat's pilot had let us drift along the giant hull during this shouted conversation. Now he swung the wheel over and we circled back to the ladder and the doorway. As he did so, I saw, under the grey camouflage paint of the *Kriegsmarine*, the original name of the ship.

It read SS *Cap Arcona*.

11

The Cap Arcona

The reports of the Royal Air Force bear out my memory of 3 May 1945. It was a Thursday and low cloud obscured the south-western coast of the Baltic Sea, especially along the coastal strip at Neustadt and the Bay of Lübeck. One by one we grabbed the swaying rope ladder and scrabbled up. There was hardly time to be terrified before I was stumbling in through the hole in the hull and facing, for a moment, impenetrable blackness.

It was the smell that hit me first. As my eyes acclimatised to the dim electric light I could see heads and shoulders as prisoners like me sat in every available space, crammed together like sardines in a tin. The smell told me that these men had been here, in this sea-borne concentration camp, for days and we were among the last to arrive. This was a floating Hell and there was nowhere to go in the congested space. The dead, we discovered, had already been thrown overboard, to float like human debris in the black waters of the Bay of Lübeck. Even our SS guards were rattled and they spoke to the crewmen, asking where they should take us.

The atmosphere crackled with tension. It was clear we'd come aboard against the wishes and the better judgement of the ship's crew, who resented being ordered around by the SS. What we didn't know – and the world would not know until much later – is that the *Arcona*'s captain, Heinrich Bertram, had held out for a whole day against the SS claiming, quite rightly, that his ship's sanitary arrangements could only cope with about 700 prisoners. We had no way of counting heads but that morning in the Bay of Lübeck we were nearly 4,500. The SS had turned up with an order for the captain's execution and he had reluctantly given up. He knew perfectly well that if he didn't the SS would shoot him and load us all on the *Arcona* anyway.

We were ordered up top and followed our *Rottenführer* through the mass of stinking humanity. Most of these men, we learned later, were from KL Stutthoff and unlike us, they'd had no respite on the Schmidt Farm. I lost count of the stairs we climbed until we reached what had clearly once been a passenger lounge. There were people here too, of course, hundreds of them, sitting in their own filth and muttering among themselves. The scene was like something out of an old painting of Hell because the porthole windows had been painted over and only a grey dim light filtered through onto the huddled 'passengers'. At least there was just about room to sit down, and I was climbing over people to find my own space when all Hell broke loose. The ship lurched violently with an almighty bang and I went sprawling, along with anybody else who had been on their feet.

I was on all fours now, heart pounding with fear, but with an overriding sense of confusion. What the hell was going on? There was a second lurch and crash and this time the windows blew in, showering us all with flying glass. We were under attack.

If you read the calm collected account of the sinking of the *Cap Arcona* written by military historians today, it all sounds so orderly, so everyday. There were three prison ships in Lübeck Bay – I'd seen the other two briefly before I got on board the *Cap Arcona*. The others were the *Thielbek* and the *Athens* and there was a fourth vessel too, the *Deutschland*. All four of them were believed by the Royal Air Force's Intelligence Units to be carrying SS and probably *Wehrmacht* in an attempted breakout for Norway, perhaps to continue to fight the war from there. As such they were legitimate targets for Allied bombers and it was only the bad weather on the morning of 3 May that had held off an attack until midday.

The first attack came at 1200 hours when four Typhoon IBs, fighter bombers of the RAF's 184 Squadron, hit what their reports described as 'a two-funnel cargo liner of 10,000 tons with steam up in Lübeck Bay'. This was the *Deutschland*, which had only days before become a hospital ship. Only its funnels were painted white, rather than the whole ship because of a shortage of white paint, and the red cross was only painted on one funnel, facing *away* from the raiders. The Typhoons fired a total of thirty-two rockets, four of which hit the ship and set it alight.

I knew nothing of this attack at the time and have only read about it since so the *Deutschland* must have been too far away, in the hazy mist, for us to be aware of it. What I was aware of, though, was the second attack because it was the one that had knocked me off my feet. This was the one delivered by 198 Squadron under Group Captain 'Johnny' Johnson, one of Britain's most celebrated air aces, that tore into the *Arcona* a little after 1500 hours. Nine

Typhoons snarled out over the Bay and sent forty rockets into the stricken ship. I heard and felt the first two of these. The reports state that the shells hit the *Arcona* amidships, between the funnels. These shells contained 60 pounds of high explosives and the subsequent hits reverberated together with an appalling noise.

What followed was the worst sound I've ever heard. It rumbled and boomed away from somewhere below us and it took me a while, kneeling and dazed, to realise what it was. It was the sound of thousands of men screaming in terror, echoing and re-echoing up stairways and through corridors. The *Arcona* shuddered and now I could smell burning. As if someone had blown a whistle, we were suddenly all on our feet at once and all shouting together in a mad scramble to get out and find the light. Somewhere above me a hatch was thrown open and I could see the grey of the sky. With whatever strength I had left – and it's astonishing how much strength you still have when your life depends on it – I tried to reach that hatch. I couldn't, my fingers clawing the smoke-filled air, but my Fürstengrube friend Peter Abramovitch was there, shouting instructions and getting me up on his shoulders. I grabbed the cold metal and hauled myself upwards, taking my weight on my arms and dragging my feet out onto the deck.

The whole ship was vibrating and shuddering under me but all I could see were the planes, painted in camouflage, green and grey, snarling overhead. Time and time again they wheeled and banked, flame bursting from their wing rims as they screamed past me. It was Bedzin all over again, that day when I was playing football and the war came to our world. I was thirteen that day. Now I was eighteen and

I'd seen more horrors than most people do in a lifetime. Then the Luftwaffe had been aiming at factories. Now the RAF were aiming at me. And they were supposed to be on our side!

People were running in all directions over the deck and thick grey-black smoke was belching from the area below. Somebody shouted that we were sinking, and I spun round to scrabble in the open hatch and grab Peter's hands. But they weren't there.

'Peter!' I yelled into the blackness. 'The ship is on fire! We must get off!' There was no answer. Peter had gone, carried away in the headlong panic below decks as men desperately looked for a way out.

One of the many rumours today is that the SS had removed the lifeboats and deliberately turned the *Arcona* into a death ship. This doesn't take into account the fact that the SS men on board, not to mention the ship's crew, would all be committing suicide. It also ignores the fact that I saw the lifeboats myself and prisoners desperately trying to release them. The crew were there too, hauling at ropes already on fire and jumping in and out of billows of smoke. Us prisoners had no idea how to release the boats and some of the manila housings gave way, burnt through and more than one boat plummeted downwards to crash into the foaming sea, empty and useless. Others were still welded to the ship's gantries and impossible to use.

I didn't give a thought to the men still below decks even though Herzko was there and Peter, Joe and the other lads of the *Maurerschule*. Sailors on the *Arcona* who testified to the Allies later, said that the fire on the upper decks spread so fast that there was no time to get the fire-hoses into action and they couldn't reach the pumps.

Over the side as I clung to the rails in an agony of confusion and indecision I could see the fishing boats that had brought us out to this inferno coming back. It became obvious as I watched what their instructions were. They were picking up anyone in uniform, the *Kriegsmarine*, the SS, but not us. Anyone in stripes who tried to jump into a trawler was shot at by the SS, either those still on deck or in the boats themselves. Including the people they fished out of the churning sea, the records show that sixteen of the eighty crew were rescued and perhaps 400 of the 500 SS guards. They didn't collect a single prisoner.

Panic was everywhere. The *Cap Arcona* was blazing from stern to bows and all I knew was I had to get off. I'd never been a great swimmer and this was a sterner challenge altogether than paddling in the Lesnica river back in the Garden of Eden. I looked over the side. I must have been twenty metres up, the height of a nine-storey building, and the sea far below was littered with debris that the Typhoon's rockets had blown out of the ship and with the bobbing heads of those trying to swim for it.

I became one of those. I held my breath and jumped. The air rushed into my nose and mouth, billowing up my jacket and stinging my eyes. There wasn't time for my life to pass before me before I hit the water. It felt like a wall. I didn't hear the noise and the word 'splash' just doesn't do it justice. The water was like ice and the impact knocked the breath out of me. I went down into the blackness, the daylight on the surface above flashing like searchlights in my head. How many feet I went down I don't know but it seemed to last forever until I felt myself carried upwards again and broke the surface, taking a huge, agonising gulp of air and trying desperately to remember how to swim. I hadn't done this since the water storage tank in Fürstengrube but you never forget how it's done and I doggy-paddled towards a large piece of planking floating nearby.

As I reached it my frozen hands grabbed someone else's and another half-dead prisoner got there just as I did. We probably both had the same idea, to forget all thoughts of humanity and kick the other bastard away. Other men in the water around us were doing just that, fighting and screaming at each other in a desperate quest for survival. In fact, with both of us clinging to the timber, it became more stable and we were each grateful for the presence of the other. We both hauled ourselves up onto our elbows with our legs dragging in the water.

I can't describe the noise. The *Arcona* loomed above us, a blazing wreck, bangs reverberating from the ship's metal, twisting and buckling in the intense heat. The fishing boats were snarling all around us too, their engines revving and smoking as their crews worked desperately to haul SS men out of the water. Now and again there were bursts of pistol and machine-gun fire as those in the boats scattered prisoners trying to board them. At one point a German torpedo-boat, fast and deadly, roared out of the drifting smoke and its crew sprayed the sea around them with their machine-guns. I saw the spurts of water in neat rows where the bullets ripped the surface and terrified men writhing in the sea as they were hit, falling backwards and plunging below the surface.

I don't know how long I'd been in the water when I saw

the planes coming back. The pilots' logs will tell you that it was 1600 hours when nine Typhoons of 263 Squadron hit the *Deutschland*. Minutes later a fourth attack hit the same ship, already on fire. 197 Squadron dropped eight 500-pounders onto the deck. I had once made wooden packing cases for bombs of this size in Herr Killov's factory back home but of course I had no idea of the weapons carried by the planes snarling over the *Cap Arcona* again and one of them swooped low over us firing its cannon at us thrashing about in the sea.

Should any of this have happened? Today there is the suggestion that the RAF's intelligence was faulty, that they should have known the ships they were destroying carried concentration camp prisoners. In that situation, travelling at high speed over a burning sea through dense black smoke, I expect one struggling swimmer looks much like another. I believe the man who pushed the cannon button in his cockpit thought he was killing Germans. That was his job. It was his duty. He flew low over the Bay of Lübeck and then headed west. It was probably his last mission.

Eventually the shooting stopped and the planes had gone. A third prisoner had joined us and together we made a sort of plan. We had no idea what happened when a ship sank, how the downpull can drag anything with it for hundreds of metres around. Almost the last thing that happened on the *Cap Arcona* was an enormous explosion. There is a theory today that the whole ship had been rigged as a floating bomb by the SS, the fuel tanks filled with gas and incendiary devices. If this was true then it was a fittingly fiendish way for the SS to carry out yet another elaborate form of execution on us. More likely the *Arcona* went up because of vaporisation of the fuel in the tanks. Whatever the cause, the ship rolled like a dying whale onto her port side to lie half submerged and still burning fiercely. The hull was too hot for anyone to stand on – I could see the metal bulging and buckling. Anybody still left on board must have been dead.

The wind and tide by early evening were driving us towards the shore and the fishing boats, loaded with *Kriegsmarine*, police and SS, were still prowling the waters, looking for survivors. We all knew perfectly well that anyone in a striped jacket was likely to receive a bullet. It must have been about six o'clock and we'd been in the water for over two hours. I was exhausted and couldn't feel my legs for the cold. Even so, about a hundred metres from the shore we decided to swim for it.

Gunfire from the beach stopped us. I could see two policemen as we bobbed nearer, firing their pistols into the breakers. We couldn't see their targets but we knew they were half-dead men, like us. We decided to wait until dark and by now my feet were touching the bottom. But time and tide wait for no man and before night fell we were buffeted onto the sand and were too weak to do anything about it. If the SS had found us then, it would all have been over. I couldn't walk, so I crawled up the beach, flapping like a seal in the sand. There were corpses lying in the surf, battered and rolled around by each incoming wave. Too exhausted to move and unable to stand, I may have fallen asleep.

I heard voices from far away: perhaps people further along the beach or else the ghosts of the *Cap Arcona*. They grew louder and I realised that someone was shaking me by the shoulder.

'Wake up!' the voice said. 'If you lie here you'll freeze to death.'

I tried to make my eyes focus, my mind concentrate. It was the Rampe all over again as Jew fever swept over me, but now a kindly man in a striped concentration camp jacket was helping me sit up.

There were other men around, dark shapes in the evening who helped me hobble up what felt like a shingle slope. My clothes were saturated, clinging to my body, and I'd lost my boots. I remember the glow of a fire in some trees and two men half carrying me to lie next to it. As my circulation came back, I started shivering. Part of it was the cold of my body and my wet clothes. Part of it was shock. There was no food, no water and no blankets but I drifted in and out of sleep until dawn.

The first thing I remember the next day was birdsong. And I realised after a while that this was the first morning since I'd got to Auschwitz-Birkenau that there was no morning roll-call. No barked orders, no clubs, fists, boots. In fact, and this was so odd, there were no other sounds at all. There were five men sitting around the ashes of last night's fire. One of them had been floating with me on the debris from the *Arcona* that had saved both our lives. The others, who must have found us both on the beach, were strangers. No one spoke. We were all too shocked and too exhausted.

Perhaps my ears were sharper than the rest, because I was the youngest there; I heard the throaty rattle of an engine. I expected a truck or perhaps a motorcycle with SS plates but as I saw it coming along the road that ran beside the grove of trees I could see it was a battered flatbed, an old Ford, and it was driven by an old civilian. The brakes screeched as he pulled up and leaned out of his window. He asked in his heavy North-German accent if we were from the ship. Somebody told him we were.

'Get in the truck,' the old man said, jerking his thumb to the flatbed, 'I'll take you to Neustadt. They'll give you some food.'

So we drove into Neustadt, each one of us still silent, jolted around in the truck. There wasn't a swastika in sight, just grim-faced men in khaki uniforms who stared at us. That day, if you read the history books, you'll find that Admiral Dönitz, Hitler's successor, sent his officers to Luneburg Heath, to the headquarters of the British Field Marshal Bernard Montgomery, to talk surrender.

It should have been flowers and laughter and homecomings and relief. Instead six Jews sat on a flatbed truck in an alien town, soaked to the skin, thirsty and hungry and cold.

For some of us the war would never be over.

12
Liberation

There is a photograph of me taken a few weeks after the war ended. I am eighteen. It's the only photo I have that even vaguely reflects my childhood. All the others – and there probably weren't that many anyway – were thrown away and destroyed by the Nazis in their attempt to obliterate my life and a whole *way* of life. In the photo my hair is growing back and I had enough to comb a parting into my curls.

'He looks pretty good on it,' the Holocaust deniers will say, 'considering all he's supposed to have been through.' Yes, I do. By the time this photo was taken I'd been getting decent food for several weeks. My prison stripes have gone and I've scrounged a military shirt from somewhere. It doesn't fit me, any more than the stripes did, but it's warm and soft and comfortable and that means a lot. I don't think I look eighteen and in an odd sort of way, this photo is more than just a snapshot. It is a memento of my teenage years. I didn't look so very different from that day in Bedzin when I was thirteen and the planes came. Six years. Six years during which time stopped and a nightmare took its place.

The kindly old German had dropped us off outside the huge, brick-built naval barracks. The place was in darkness and we couldn't find the light switches. We knew the war must be over but there was no sign of the British Tommies. There was a sense that no one wanted to become a casualty with a ceasefire so close, so perhaps everyone was just keeping their heads down, avoiding any more confrontation. Over the coming weeks we heard horror stories of the fierce resistance some of the Waffen-SS units were putting up as the Reich surrendered.

Our first priority, as it had always been, was food. However well I look in that photo, back then I was seriously underweight and the fact that the British had taken Neustadt didn't guarantee us a meal ticket. We were allowed into the naval barracks and could help ourselves to any surplus clothing lying around. For the first time in nearly three years I stripped off my striped rags and put on 'real' clothes. The irony was that these were the Nazi uniforms of the *Kriegsmarine*, the German navy. We ripped off the Nazi insignia with delight, partly because we were tearing up the remnants of the most appalling regime in history and partly because the last thing we wanted was to be interned by the British as German prisoners of war.

The barracks was crawling with refugees, camp survivors like us and people from God-knows-where who had long ago lost their homes and lost their way. It was like the Tower of Babel, with everybody gabbling excitedly in a bewildering range of languages. What there wasn't was any food. Hours passed and locals turned up with bread and cheese, the first we'd had since we'd left the quayside for the *Cap Arcona*.

Most of the talk was about the sinking, the garbled stories of who saw what, of who died and who was still alive; people we didn't know who had so nearly survived the nightmare only to die just before the dawn came. In these hours I realised that most of the *Maurerschule* had gone – Peter Abramovitch's brother and cousin; the Engel brothers, Willi and Viky; Max Schmidt's camp barber; the list was endless. Some would have been machine-gunned in the water, others mangled by the torpedo boat's propeller blades. Many would have drowned or been shot as they reached the shore. Most, perhaps, were burnt to death in the inferno of the *Cap Arcona*'s hull. I remember particularly listening to survivors from the *Athens*. She was a small freighter and her captain, too, had tried to refuse the SS's demand to take prisoners on board. Like the *Cap Arcona*'s captain, they had threatened to kill him and the ship had been used to ferry prisoners out to the *Arcona* moored further out in the Bay.

When the Typhoons came over, the captain ordered the white flags to be hoisted and the planes passed overhead. The *Athens* came under her own steam into port and unloaded the passengers she carried. We wondered how many SS men had managed to slip away from the quay before the British ground troops arrived.

We got confirmation the next day that the war was finally over. People were running in all directions in the barracks square, shouting and laughing hysterically, hugging each other and slapping each other on the back. 'We're liberated, we're free!' rang out in a dozen languages. The words sounded good in all of them. I didn't have much to do with our liberators. We began to see the occasional armoured car and heard the Tommies' boots crunching in the streets as they took full occupation of the town. There was no fighting, no pockets of resistance. Now and again there'd be a commotion as somebody caught a German soldier trying to escape and gave him a good smacking or a kick up the arse.

In those days of course I couldn't speak a word of English and had only the vaguest notion of those times back in Bedzin when my father would entertain us with the snatches of the language he'd picked up when he lived in Stamford Hill. Food came from these liberators in their typically reserved way. We heard as time went on that further south the Americans who had liberated Buchenwald were giving out chunks of chocolate they called candy and allowing ex-prisoners like us to help themselves from shops and warehouses. That didn't happen in Neustadt. Instead, the British let various refugee agencies try to tackle the problem.

It must have been chaos everywhere in the days and weeks after the German surrender. There were people all over the place, desperate, confused, hungry and broke. I know – I was one of them. A British soldier gave me a khaki tunic to wear in place of *Kriegsmarine* blue. It was so different from the grey-green of the Waffen-SS I had seen every day for the last six years. It was what the British called a battle-dress, itchy and short, but after the stripes of Auschwitz-Birkenau I felt like a millionaire. Food came from one of the refugee agencies; papers were supplied by the Jewish Refugee Committee, an American organisation. The roof over my head was by courtesy of the German Navy, requisitioned by the British Second Army.

It's odd, but I don't remember any real restrictions in the days after the war. There ought to have been a curfew, no-go areas, everything you'd expect from martial law imposed by a conquering army in enemy territory. In fact we were allowed to go where we liked and I remember feeling very bored, especially in the evenings. This sounds ungrateful but it's not meant to. My days had been filled for so long with backbreaking physical work and constant terror, to find myself at a loose end now was a very strange sensation. The British laid on films for us in the naval barracks and through the cigarette smoke (currency wafting into the thick atmosphere) I watched again those black-and-white Westerns I had loved as a kid back in Bedzin. I didn't understand a word of the dialogue of course, but I knew who the good guy was from the colour of his hat, and how difficult can it be to follow a plot where a fist fight breaks out in a saloon? And there was another oddity about liberation. I slept in my own bed on my own for the first time in my life. And the bed had sheets and a pillow.

Of all the emotions that whirled in our heads in those first days of freedom, the strongest was of revenge. This was a time before Simon Wiesenthal's Nazi hunters, before what had happened was given the name the Holocaust, before all that developed into an industry of its own. All we knew was that the murderous face of Fürstengrube and the death march looked very like that of a farm boy from Neuglasau, hangman and killer of Jews – Oberscharführer Max Schmidt. Three or four days after the liberation, a group of half a dozen of us found a horse and cart from somewhere and piled on board. We'd hired the vehicle and its driver in exchange for cigarettes and our direction was the farm at Neuglasau.

It had been less than a week since we'd left there, marching on the road towards our rendezvous with death on the *Cap Arcona* and I remember passing the spot where I'd thrown myself into the ditch as the British plane flew overhead. The farm of course looked the same – the house, the barns and outbuildings, the paving stones we'd laid in the yard, the pigsty loft where we'd slept. But everything else was different. We'd left that place *Untermenschen*, life unworthy of life. And now we were back, if not exactly as conquerors, at least with the tables very definitely turned.

Herr and Frau Schmidt were painfully polite and almost apologised for the fact that their son was not there. It was as if we had come along with our football to see if Max could come out to play and his mummy had to tell us he couldn't. There were eight of us, all Jews, all survivors, but it turned out that not all of us had a common motive at this stage. Herzko had survived the bombing of the *Cap Arcona* and I had been so happy to find him still alive in Neustadt, his flat feet pounding the pavements of a town that had never known a ghetto. The dentist, Bronek Jakobowicz was there with his brother Josek and the electrician brothers, the Lipshitzes. So too was Kapo Janek, a huge man with dark hair, Peter Abramovitch, who had helped me onto the *Arcona*'s deck and the *Mischling* architect Oberkapo Hermann Josef who I had last seen on the quayside when he gave me a clip around the ear for trying to get taken away by the Red Cross. The one who wasn't there when we arrived was the shoemaker Mendeler Davidovitch. He had been hiding out on the Miller farm, almost certainly with the connivance of Max Schmidt, and so he'd escaped the horrors of the *Cap Arcona*.

The Schmidts insisted we stay for a meal and it turned out to be roast pork. They said we could select a pig and kill it ourselves. I knew this would be beyond me as I'd never killed an animal in my life and didn't know where to start. It turned out that none of the others had a clue either and we spent several fruitless minutes hurtling around the pigsty, trying to catch the squealing beast. In the end, Herr Schmidt put both it and us out of our misery, slinging a rope over a beam, deftly looping it round the pig's back legs, hauling it up and cutting its throat. With a final squeal and shudder, the animal was dead. After the horrors of our collective diets for the last three years, we weren't going to stand on any sort of Jewish dignity over the fact that this was forbidden meat, and we ate heartily. I wondered what my father would make of it all. In that bizarre dinner party we all spoke German, drank schnapps and made small talk. Did I imagine it or was Herzko making eyes at Gerda Schmidt? And most of all, did she seem to be enjoying his attention?

Perhaps it was because I was the youngest there that Gerda's sister seemed to take a liking to me. She was pretty and sixteen but after all this time I can't remember her name. Despite what I'd seen of the Theresienstadt women, I had no clue about sex. Like everything else which a boy would normally have been getting up to during his teens, I had no direct experience of anything like that. I was probably blushing when she spoke to me, laughing and smiling, and I tried to copy the much more worldly Herzko without making it obvious.

When it came to evening and darkness closed in, it was decided that we would stay. Most of us squeezed into the attic rooms at the top of the huge farmhouse, so different from the pigsty loft that had once been our home. Herzko,

I noticed, slipped off to a room rather closer to Gerda Schmidt's.

Over the next few days, as Mendeler came out of hiding and we all strolled in the spring sunshine of Neuglasau, I became ever friendlier with Gerda's sister. Now, in the contemplation of my old age, I may have all sorts of issues about sleeping with a Nazi, the sister-in-law of an SS *Oberscharführer*. Then, we all had an air about us of what Jews call *hefker*; we'd abandoned any sense of responsibility and we just enjoyed our freedom. I don't think anyone could have blamed us, and certainly the sixteen-year-old girl who wandered with me in the sprouting corn of Ostholstein seemed to feel the same crackle in the air. Perhaps, if things had turned out differently, I could have faced my future with the pretty blonde girl whose name I can't now recall.

I don't remember either how long we stayed on the farm or what the Schmidts made of our presence, but I do remember the evening their son turned up. It is one of the most bizarre transformations I've ever seen. So bizarre that each of us there has a different memory of it. Gone was the SS uniform and the tall, elegant stride. The *Oberscharführer* was no more and plain old Max Schmidt, the farmer's son, stood in his place. His head was shaved, rather more neatly than ours had been in Auschwitz-Birkenau and Fürstengrube and he joined us at the dining table and made small talk as if we were all old buddies having a post-war reunion. I didn't know it at the time, but he may well have had in his pocket the papers of Kapo Hans the Miner, whose body he had left at Tormalin. We had one plan; ex-Oberscharführer Schmidt had another. It made my blood run cold to see the way he behaved. Had there been a war? Was there such a place as Auschwitz? Had anybody died over the last few years? It was incredible.

After dinner, out of earshot of the Schmidts, a full-blown row broke out among us. Hermann Josef was arguing that Schmidt had done his best to help us in recent weeks; he'd brought us to his parents' home and saw that we got decent food. He'd let Mendeler hide in the Miller's farm – though none of us understood *that* – and had let him (Hermann) ride everywhere on his motorbike. Jakobowicz talked of forgiveness, of the need for us all to move on and reclaim what we could of our lives. Schmidt had helped him, he said, on no less than three occasions. On the death march when Jakobowicz was on the point of collapse, the *Oberscharführer* had turned up on his bike and ordered vodka to revive him. Schmidt had given permission for Jakobowicz to set up as a dentist in Ahrensbök, allowing him to visit various friends in the process. Just before we were marched to Neustadt, Schmidt had taken Jakobowicz aside and told him of the impending visit of the Red Cross, implying he should pretend to be from Western Europe, so he would be taken to Sweden. As for Schmidt, the best way to repay his kindness was to give him the best alibi possible. If any British soldier stopped Herr Schmidt, all he had to do was to roll up his sleeve and show a tattooed number, the mark of shame that was Auschwitz.

As we argued this way and that, I realised that I was, in the end, a lone voice for the arrest of Schmidt. Herzko wasn't there at the time. Neither was Mendeler Davidovitch. Hermann Josef wasn't an *Oberkapo* any more but he was a powerful persuader with a towering personality and it ended up with Kapo Janek slapping me across the face and telling me to shut up. My head was buzzing, but as I remember it, Bronek Jakobowicz had the job of rolling up Schmidt's sleeve and tattooing a false number on his forearm. This was all the more peculiar because, as I would learn afterwards, Schmidt took the identity of Hans the Miner who, as a Christian prisoner, was not tattooed. The rest of it would be up to Schmidt's imagination. If anyone challenged him in the days, weeks, months ahead, he had enough inside knowledge of Auschwitz-Birkenau, Fürstengrube and even the death march to give a convincing account of himself from a prisoner's point of view. The tattoo would be the final 'proof'.

Why didn't I do something about this appalling situation? Why didn't I go into Herr Schmidt's living room, take his shotgun from its rack and blast the *Oberscharführer* to death? Perhaps I'd seen too much killing. Perhaps I am not a murderer. It turned out I couldn't even kill a pig. I wanted Max Schmidt to face legal retribution, not a kangaroo court and certainly not a random execution. And I missed my chance. My face was still stinging from the slap I'd received as Max Schmidt, Hermann Josef, the Jakobowicz brothers, the Lipshitzes and Schmidt's father-in-law, Bergman, the I.G. Farben engineer from Fürstengrube, all left. To this day I can't understand why the Lipshitz boys went. Jakobowicz had been kissing SS arse for a long time and naturally his brother went with him. Hermann Josef had been hand-in-glove with Schmidt, virtually since the man had taken over Fürstengrube from Moll. But the actions of the Lipshitzes didn't make sense to me then and

still don't make sense today. Schmidt had just lost a war
– what possible future could there be with him?

It might have been the next day or the day after that the
British came. A khaki-painted lorry arrived and a handful
of Tommies tumbled out. There had been complaints,
apparently, from the local Lutheran pastor that there were
ex-prisoners on the Schmidt farm who were disrupting the
tranquillity of village life. The irony of this amazed me
then as it does still. Men like that Lutheran pastor had
knuckled under when Hitler came to power in Germany
and his church had become by and large a Nazi organisation. Here he was still banging on about the unacceptability
of the Jews. He didn't want us in his backyard and extraor-
dinarily, the British were on his side. As we climbed into
the truck I realised that Herzko was missing. He hadn't
been there during the row over Schmidt's future; he wasn't
there when the British took us away. That man could vanish
for Poland! I heard later that he was hiding in a toilet and
I suspect this was with the connivance of Gerda Schmidt
who had taken more than a liking to Henry Herzko Bawnik!
He was probably disrupting the tranquillity of village life
all by himself.

I stayed in the *Kriegsmarine* barracks for perhaps two
months. There was a formality about the British that we
found awkward, especially as rumours were reaching us
from further south how the Americans treated refugees
like us. Near Buchenwald, as the GIs liberated the camps
around there, General Eisenhower had given specific orders.
'Open the stores,' he had said. 'Let the prisoners take
whatever they like. Give them whatever they need, from
town, from the bakeries, from the butchers, give it to them.'

That didn't happen in Neustadt. It was an occupied town at the end of the bloodiest war in history and everybody had their own agenda. For Joe Zoller and me it was still about survival, as it had been for years.

I hadn't known Joe very well before Neustadt. He had been on a different shift from me at Fürstengrube, sleeping in a different block. But we both had a basic ability to *organise* and we went into business together. Neither of us smoked back then, but we scrounged cigarettes and traded them on the black market. In the back streets of Neustadt we traded anything – watches, cameras, anything the SS and the *Wehrmacht* had left behind in their hurry to get out. Looking back, Joe and I weren't very good black-marketeers and we ended up with a lot of stuff we couldn't shift.

I got hold of a German motorbike in the course of this wheeling and dealing and Joe and I roared off to Bergen-Belsen to sell herring we'd acquired from local fishermen in the Bay of Lübeck. The *Cap Arcona* still lay there, a black carcass washed by the grey sea; corpses floated out of her charred hull for weeks. We took pictures with the cameras we got and what an historic record they would have made today if I'd ever got the film developed or bothered to keep it.

What we were really on the lookout for were girls. My fling with Gerda's sister had whetted my appetite I suppose, and what else were two nineteen-year-olds with cigarettes and a motorbike going to do with themselves? There were professional black-marketeers in Neustadt who could run rings around us – let them get on with it. We just wanted a good time – *hefker*, a lack of responsibility which we both found exhilarating.

That was not how the British saw it. We were not confined to the naval barracks but it was clear that they saw their job as building bridges, literally and metaphorically, with the locals. Black-marketeering was a crime in Britain and the Tommies had a habit of searching young men on the streets, confiscating their contraband and locking them up for the night. When I tried to get petrol for my motorbike, a British soldier wearing sergeant's stripes refused to sell me any.

There was one day, though, when I had enough petrol to go back to the Schmidt farm. A lone visitor on a motorbike, wearing a British Army jacket, didn't cause much of a stir. Ostensibly I went to the dairy to get fresh butter and cheese but in fact I'd really gone to see Gerda's sister. We didn't tumble in the hay that day. Did we exchange promises? Vow to stay in touch? If we did, I don't remember and there were more pressing needs, and I left with the produce of the dairy stuffed into my saddlebags. Back in the barracks that night, we all ate well.

At the back of my mind, in that early summer of 1945, was what I would do with the rest of my life. I'd used up far more than my nine lives and I wasn't yet twenty. Neustadt was a surreal adventure after the hell of the camps, but it was hardly a way of life and I had to move on. For many camp survivors at the end of the war, moving on meant moving back. Home. Family. The life we'd known. Some went back. Joe Zoller did. He had a sister he believed was still living, somehow, in Poland and he went off to find her. As for me, I knew my family had all gone. Grandmother Ruchla-Lea couldn't possibly have survived. My mother, my father, Hendla, Chana, Majer, Wolf and

Josek had been in Heaven for two years, by way of the chimney at Auschwitz-Birkenau. The last I'd seen of Bedzin was Christian Poles, on a sweltering August day, carrying away our furniture from the Kamionka. For months before that, somebody else was already living in my house along Modzejowska Street. The only possibility – and it was a slight one – was that Nathan was still alive. I had last heard of him nearly three years earlier when he was in the labour camp at Blechhammer. But Nathan had a hernia and had to wear a special belt. How long could he have survived in that condition in a world where the Nazis were bent on creating a perfect Aryan state and imperfections weren't tolerated?

In those weeks in Neustadt there were rumours everywhere. People were moving in all directions, on the road, hitching rides on trains and trucks, looking for people who were probably long dead. The Jews in particular were looking for more than that – we were looking for our past, our history, our way of life. And it didn't seem to be anywhere. It was on this rumour mill that I heard of a cousin of my father's who had ended up in Bergen-Belsen and at some time in June I hitched a ride there and started searching.

KL Bergen-Belsen had been liberated by the same British Army division that were billeted in Neustadt. It was one of the first to be liberated by the Allies and the appalling conditions there shocked the world. Captured SS men at the camp had no accurate idea how many inmates there were; they guessed perhaps 40,000. The dead lay in heaps in the barracks or on the *Appellplatz*. Men too weak to move lay in their own filth on their bunks and their shit trickled down to the tier below. There had been no water for a week when the British got there because bomb damage had destroyed the pumping system. Red Cross boxes in the camp's stores contained tinned soup, milk and meat sent by various Jewish societies. Much of this had been stolen by the SS and nothing had been distributed. On one day after liberation, the official Second Army History will tell you 548 prisoners died. They died free men.

There was nothing for me at Bergen-Belsen, just another camp to be bulldozed, another German town made to confront its recent past. Still homeless, still wandering, I made my way back to Neustadt. And as I reached the *Kriegsmarine* barracks, there, on the tarmac outside, stood Nathan.

He didn't look any different, my big brother. And yet in so many ways he was. We both were. We fell into each other's arms and cried. We were both hugging our mother and father, old Ruchla-Lea, Hendla, Chana and the boys, Majer, Wolf and Josek. We were hugging ourselves for all we'd seen and been through. We were hugging a way of life that was gone forever.

Nathan never asked me what happened to our family. He didn't have to. He knew already. Heaven via the chimney – it was as simple and as stark as that. Eight people we both loved more than anything in the world wiped out to realise the dreams of a madman. That madman had not gone up the chimney, although as the years went by we learned that Hitler's body had indeed burned, on his own final orders, in the garden of the Reich Chancellery in Berlin. Was there any comfort in that for Nathan and me? None at all.

My brother's story would take another book to recount in full and over the next few days in Neustadt we swapped our experiences. In a way it was easier then than it is now. We were still both boys and although the memories were still new and raw, there hadn't yet been time for the nightmares and sadness to sink in and become a way of life for us. Nathan had been transferred to camp after camp until he was sent to Blechhammer, and by the time he got there, it was under the auspices of the huge Auschwitz complex. I remember thinking, as he talked, that had he gone to Auschwitz-Birkenau with us on that terrible day in August 1943, he would have gone with the rest of the family to the gas chamber, because of his hernia. That kind of physical problem would not have been tolerated by Mengele's welcoming committee and the doctor's elegant gloved hand would have flicked to the left. And if Nathan had gone to the flames, I would have gone with him as I saw too many people do on the Rampe; people who chose to stay with their families, no matter what. I remembered two brothers in particular. One had had his arm broken in a beating by a *Kapo* and his brother had walked with him towards the terrible gates, supporting the lad and cradling his arm.

In the camps where Nathan worked, there was no brutal stripping, no selection and no gas chambers. Once under the Auschwitz umbrella, of course, that changed. Nathan had to give up his civilian clothes and wear the blue and white stripes that marked us all in Auschwitz-Birkenau. He was also tattooed; his number was something like 176000. As we chatted in the safety of the *Kriegsmarine* barracks, with our hair growing back and our mixed bag of clothes

on, Nathan mentioned the name of our old friend Vladek
Lipanski. He had been working at Blechhammer at the
time that Nathan was there and he often visited us before
the Kamionka move made that impossible. We'd both
played football with him; he bought Nathan's bike from
us in exchange for potatoes. And he had never once
mentioned Nathan. To Nathan he had said, 'I knew you'd
end up here. And here, you're going to die like a dog.' That
was our friend. That was a Gentile Pole.

In one of those bizarre coincidences which can happen
in wartime, Nathan and I *almost* met. The Blechhammer
camp had been every bit as brutal as Auschwitz-Birkenau.
Hours on the *Appellplatz* in freezing conditions, standing
in rows of five. Beatings and killings by the *Kapos* and the
SS. *Muselmänner* being worked to death. What was
different about Blechhammer was that, unlike Auschwitz-
Birkenau, Nathan's camp was bombed by the Allies. Ten
times between July and November 1944 bombs hit
Blechhammer. I had probably seen those bombers droning
overhead from Fürstengrube, not realising they were
targeting my brother.

Nathan had left his camp on foot in the bitter January
of 1945, one of the last groups to leave, three days after
we left Fürstengrube. His experiences on the road were
every bit as ghastly as mine with the desperately starving
breaking formation to grab cabbage stalks in the snow-
covered fields, only to be shot dead by the SS, red staining
the green and white. He too rode the open coal trucks and
at Buchenwald, we actually rode the same train. There, as
the SS desperately looked for some kind of plan as their
world was collapsing, Nathan's trucks rattled into

Buchenwald itself and ours went on to Nordhausen and Dora-Mittelbau. The coincidences of war.

When we met again in the naval barracks, Nathan was living in Konstanz am Bodensee, on the pretty lake there, in the French zone. If it wasn't apparent already, it quickly became clear that the Allies of 1941–5 were Allies no more. Before 1941, the Russians had carved up my country with the Germans. Before 1941 and the Japanese attack on Pearl Harbor, the Americans had shown little inclination to get involved in another European war. During the war most of France had collapsed against the *Blitzkrieg* of the *Wehrmacht* and the area that hadn't, Vichy, were straightforward Nazi collaborators. There was no love lost between East and West, Stalin's Communism against Churchill's democracy, and the British and French had fought each other for a thousand years, recent experience notwithstanding. Each of the Allies controlled their captured bit of Germany jealously and with a careful eye on each other.

This was how Nathan had found me. He caught a train from Konstanz with a friend who was looking for his family. At a camp called Feldafing near Munich, he met somebody from Bedzin who had seen me in Neustadt. By the time Nathan got there, I was already in Bergen-Belsen, looking for him.

There was nothing to keep me in Neustadt and I went with Nathan on those brilliant, scruffy, unplanned, free trains to Konstanz in the late summer of 1945. I had never been this far west before and we were suddenly in Baden with a tranquil lake crowded with brightly painted steamers and the mountains of Switzerland reminding us that some countries at least had been spared the horrors of war. We both knew that no Swiss Jews had been sent via the cattle-trucks to the chimneys. The French First Army, with its borrowed American armour, had taken the town without opposition at the end of April and Konstanz was now the centre of the French zone.

Nathan lived in a palace! I had never seen anything like it. Gailingen had been a Jewish settlement for centuries but the Nazis had destroyed it, burning the great synagogue there shortly before the war. The house I now moved into belonged to the Rothschild family, those wealthy Jews from the international banking community that Hitler had been gunning for most of his life. In fact, the Nazis had only just vacated the house because it had been a hospital during the war and a Jewish Committee had recently taken it over. I slept in a bed more comfortable than the *Kriegsmarine* barracks and ate decent food provided by the Joint Refugee Committee.

We played football; we learned Hebrew. We looked to our future and we looked to our past. The future was Palestine – the biblical Canaan, a land flowing with milk and honey and almost every day lorries came through Konstanz carrying Jewish refugees who had decided to get there. We put them up for a day or two and sent them on their way. Like us, they were the flotsam and jetsam of the camps, men and women young and strong enough to take everything the Nazis had thrown at them. They had lost their prison stripes and put flesh on their bones before taking off into the unknown.

From us, rested and refreshed, they went on over the border into France or Italy, with forged papers and cash to bribe frontier guards. From there, the Holy Land of Palestine beckoned them.

It didn't beckon us – not yet. Our past lay in Poland, in Bedzin or with our mother's relatives in the Garden of Eden. Yet we each of us had memories that were too bitter to contemplate a return. We knew that the synagogue in Bedzin was a burnt out shell. The Kamionka, I assumed, had collapsed into decay and in any case, it was too primitive to make a home there. The place was *Judenrein*, Jew free, and the Poles who had taken our home and our furniture and watched us board a train for Auschwitz weren't likely to want us back.

The only other home we could contemplate was England. My father had lived with relatives in Stamford Hill shortly before the First World War and there was at least one of his sisters living in London's East End. We wrote to our distant cousin in Bergen-Belsen who remembered the London address and, via the Joint Refugee Committee, we were sponsored to emigrate to London.

We rode the trains again, this time in an overcrowded passenger carriage. The last time I had done this I had been on my way to Hell with my family. Now it was just the two of us, the last of the Pivniks, and we crossed the Channel on a grey, rain-lashed day in the autumn of 1947.

I was twenty-one, officially a man in the eyes of most of the world's countries, and after the summer on Lake Constance, London was an impossibly miserable sight. Everything was grey and drab and the city that had withstood two Blitzes was still scarred and hurt. There were bomb craters everywhere, holes in the ground where houses, hotels and shops had stood. Rationing was still the norm and Britain was going through its Age of Austerity. Foreign holidays had been banned the previous month and the weekly meat ration had been cut by 2d. As Nathan and I gradually learned English and tried to cope with the contents of newspapers, we read that the government of Clement Atlee had just passed the Supplies and Services Act which was to force workers into certain industries. It caught my eye because the Tory Opposition called it the SS Act. If only they knew!

Thick fog enveloped the city that November – what Cockneys called a 'pea-souper'. I'd never seen anything like it. We were living in our aunt and uncle's house in the East End and it could only be temporary as there wasn't really the space. One of the songs I heard on the radio was 'Maybe it's Because I'm a Londoner' and I was struck by the fact that I wasn't. Nathan and I worked in our relatives' tailor's shop, both of us, as chance would have it, following in our father's footsteps. But no one wanted to know about the Jews, about what we'd been through. Everybody had their own problems – rationing, the loss of loved ones, the bombs, those 'doodlebugs' that I'd seen being made in the sulphurous tunnels of Dora-Mittelbau. The camps, Auschwitz, the Holocaust – all that was far away and somebody else's problem.

Since August 1943 I had been on the move – Auschwitz-Birkenau, Fürstengrube, the death march, Ahrensbök, Neustadt and Konstanz. And it was time to move on again.

13
The Land of Milk and Honey

'Next year in Jerusalem' was a slogan of the Zionist movement. If I hadn't grown up with this idea buzzing around somewhere in the back of my head, Nathan and Hendla had. Because they were both older than me they had joined *Gordonia* in Bedzin, an organisation which seriously looked at the idea of Jews returning to their first homeland.

I have read a lot about Zionism since I've had the leisure to do so and since I became a small part of it. 'We are one people,' Theodor Herzl wrote in my grandfather's time, 'our enemies have made us one whether we will or not . . . Affliction binds us together and thus united, we suddenly discover our strength. Yes, we are strong enough to form a State and indeed, a model State. We possess all the requisite human and material resources.'

Herzl was writing long before the Holocaust ripped away many of the human and material resources of the Jews but the heart of the idea of a Jewish homeland had not gone away. If anything, our collective experience in the years of the war had made the idea even more attractive, if not imperative. Survivors who went back to Poland to try to find their old lives found their houses occupied by someone else, their synagogues burnt down and their customs vanished. Some of them were beaten to death in the streets.

The British papers were full of Palestinian news during

1947 and the opening months of 1948. Since the area had been taken by the British from the Turks during the First World War, the Biblical land that flowed with milk and honey had effectively been British. Brought up as I had been with stories of the Flood and Abraham and Isaac, and staring at their pictures on the walls of the Great Synagogue in Bedzin, I probably had a vague notion that the people still dressed like that and tended their flocks and that the whole place was just a beautiful, empty wilderness where no one else lived. The Nazis had probably viewed their proposed Jewish resettlement area in Madagascar in the same way. I knew perfectly well it couldn't be like that and the newspaper headlines dispelled any notion of another Garden of Eden. Even so, the idea of an idyllic rural existence based on the kibbutz was one shared by millions of Jews all over the world.

There were terrorist attacks carried out in March, mostly in the Jewish city of Tel Aviv as various hotheaded groups tried to force the British to pull out and to force the Arabs – whose home Palestine had been, of course, for centuries – to make room for the Jews. The Stern Gang and the Irgun organisation, some dressed as I had been in Neustadt in British Army uniforms, blew open prisons in Acre and bombed the King David Hotel in Jerusalem. In the summer, the bodies of two British soldiers were found hanging in a eucalyptus grove near Haifa and, in a move that caught the imagination of the world, the Haganah ship *Exodus 47*, bringing 5,000 Jewish immigrants to Palestine, was boarded by the British. It was no *Cap Arcona* but there was fighting on board, tear gas was used against iron bars and food tins and three Jews died. The helmsman was beaten to death. The ship was turned back and its passengers taken to

Cyprus, which was fast becoming one vast prison camp. From there, it moved on to France, but the passengers refused to get off and it ended up in, of all places, Hamburg.

By September the British had decided enough was enough and agreed to pull out of Palestine. Two months later the blue and white Star of David flags flew over Jerusalem when the United Nations General Assembly agreed to the setting up of a Jewish state.

What this meant of course was open war between the Jews and the Arabs, the first in a long series of conflicts that continues to scar the Middle East. The newspaper headlines of 17 January summed up the tit-for-tat killing that is still going on today. Just after midnight on the previous day, a food shop near the Wailing Wall in Jerusalem was blown up by Arab terrorists. In reprisal, Haganah, the Jewish Defence Force, blew up a house and killed seven Arab children. Caught in the middle were the British who were trying to keep the lid on things by working with moderates on both sides. The trouble was that, as the death toll mounted, the number of moderates was falling daily.

Since the British government had clamped down on immigration to Palestine in what had become such a troubled hot-spot, I had to be smuggled out of the country illegally, crossing the Channel first, then across France by train until I could get a ship from Marseilles.

I couldn't believe the heat in Palestine, even in April when I arrived. Poland *never* had sun like this and I've never sweated so much in my life, not even at the end of the Kamionka ghetto before they took us to Auschwitz. It wasn't so much milk and honey as a parched, barren wilderness, with rocks, sand and more sand. Many of us volunteers from Northern Europe couldn't take the heat and there were serious attacks of sunstroke and badly burned skin. For virtually all my time in Palestine I wore shorts and a hat of some kind was essential.

By now my English was pretty good and I was billeted in the Telavinski camp, attached to a newly formed brigade, the 7th Armoured, which had a large English-speaking contingent and English-speaking leaders. Technically I was part of the organisation known as the *Machal*, one of 3,500 volunteers from forty-six countries. Many of us were camp survivors, drawn from all over Europe by our common experience and wanting to *achieve* something. Just staying alive had been an achievement in itself but I was twenty-one now and there seemed so much more to life than working as a tailor in the East End. If you look at photographs of the leaders in this war of liberation, as it came to be called, they are all young men, ready to take on the world. The photo of me on the dust jacket of this book was taken about this time and it represents a new Sam Pivnik. Gone is the scared, introverted boy of three years earlier. This version is a man, hard, steel-eyed, looking out into the middle distance of my future.

There were only 250 of us English-speakers in my section of the *Machal* and two of them I palled up with in basic training were Herschel Margules and Max Wolinski. I didn't know one end of a rifle from another, although I had seen plenty of them in use in the hands of the SS, and marching was a novelty too, about as far removed from the shambling of the death march or the shuffle to and from the Fürstengrube mine as it was possible to be.

One of the commanders in the 72nd Battalion of the 7th Armoured Brigade was Captain David Appel and he

impressed me as a great man, if only because he had far
more to lose than most of us on account of his background.
His real name was Thomas Bowden and he used David
Appel as a sort of *nom de guerre*. He must have been one
of the very few Englishmen who had seen the inside of a
concentration camp because when he was captured during
the war in Europe, letters from Jewish friends were found
in his battledress pockets and on the assumption that he too
was a Jew he was sent to Bergen-Belsen. He was married to
an Israeli woman and that had kept him in the Middle East
rather than going back to his family's farmlands in Norfolk.

Appel was looking for drivers. Today military historians
will tell you that the Jews actually put more troops into
the field than the Arabs in 1948 but it didn't seem like that
to us. It was David and Goliath and all we had was a
metaphorical slingshot against the huge power of the
enemy. We certainly didn't have military experience and
the advent of the Second World War had meant that very
few of us could drive. Back in Bedzin only the seriously
rich drove cars but I had learned how in Konstanz with
Nathan and so I volunteered.

I remember thinking how different all this was from the
Appellplatz at Auschwitz-Birkenau or Fürstengrube where
you never volunteered for anything. I told Captain Appel
I could drive and he ordered me to the 79th Battalion where
they needed drivers urgently. Here I stayed for the rest of
my time in Palestine.

At four o'clock on the afternoon of 14 May, hours before
the British Mandate in the country came to an end, the
leader of the Jewish Agency, David Ben-Gurion, announced
that he was the first Prime Minister of a provisional

government of the state of Israel. To millions of Jews worldwide, and especially the thousands who had survived the Holocaust, it was music to our ears. That music became louder and more joyous as President Truman of the United States became the world's first international leader to recognise the new state. Now all we had to do was fight for it.

There was a world of difference between driving a civilian car and driving a half-track tank for the Mounted Infantry. My instructor was a man who later became a good friend: Sidney Friedman, a Sheffield lad from the British Armoured Corps. Sidney taught me how to rattle through the gears, squelch through mud, up sandy hills and down the other side, taking ravines as a matter of course. Four-wheel drive, two-wheel drive, heavy vehicles, light vehicles. I had to be able to roar along primitive roads, turn on a sixpence and tackle sand in all its manifestations – red hot to the touch and stinging the eyes and face when a desert storm blew up. I also had to be able to maintain the damned things, often spending hours under a bonnet in the striking cold of a Negev night, clanging away with spanners and hammers. If you worked on the engines during the day, the metal was too hot to touch and you were eaten alive by mosquitoes.

I expect the regular armies of Europe would have been horrified if they could have seen our ramshackle outfit. Most of us didn't have army boots so we wore our civilian shoes instead. We wore British tin hats and most of us had Arab headscarves to keep the eternal sand out of our mouths. This was a surreal situation. We were fighting a war for Israel, a war of liberation for the Jewish state, but relatively few of us were Jews and most people were like me, with only a smattering of Hebrew at our command.

Our first commander in the 7th Armoured was Chaim Laskov, a Russian whose family had moved to Haifa in 1925. He had joined the British Army in 1940 as we were learning to cope with the German occupation in Bedzin and rose to become a major in the Jewish Brigade. For the last three years he had been heavily involved in the *Aliyah Bet*, which illegally brought Jewish immigrants to Palestine. There were rumours that he'd personally carried out the kind of vengeance I'd wanted to carry out on Max Schmidt, only he hadn't bothered with the courts. In the weeks before I'd got to the Telavinski camp, Laskov had been training desperately needed officers before being given command of the 7th.

While I was there, Laskov went back to recruiting with the rank of Major General and his place was taken by a relaxed Canadian called Ben Dunkelman, known in the desert as Benjamin Ben David. Like me, he was a tailor's son, but he came from Toronto and had come, as Hendla had wanted to, to work on a kibbutz in Palestine when he was eighteen. He'd tried to join the Canadian Navy when war broke out but, of all the ironies, anti-Semitism meant that that wasn't going to happen. So he'd joined the army instead and rose to the rank of major, dashing ashore in the crashing surf of Juno Beach in Normandy in the D-Day landings. Like Laskov, he hadn't long been back in Palestine when he found himself in the middle of another war.

Most of my mates in the 79th Battalion were ex-servicemen and once again I was the newbie, with less experience than the men around me. There were Americans, Canadians and South Africans and there was endless ribbing between the various nationalities. The Americans in particular would tease the South African Jews – 'I see your house-boy hasn't done a very good job on your shoes!' Nobody took offence, if only because that sort of harmless racism had already replaced the kind that had killed millions in the camps.

In that summer of 1948 I drove the third vehicle in our convoys along the roads into Jish, Safed and Galilee, liberating each town as we came to it. There were six of us in that wheeled tin can. I was crammed in the front next to the tank commander, with the litter of abandoned Syrian vehicles bobbing in front of my vision. Behind me were the gun crew with their anti-tank and anti-aircraft guns and their rapid-firing 20mm cannons. General Kaukji and his Syrians were holding a position near Galilee. The 7th was ordered to take it away from them and we did.

Another of my umpteen lives was used up on the outskirts of Jish during this campaign. You get used to the noise in a half-track, but on this one day we ran into heavy artillery fire. I don't know what happened because I was knocked out by the impact. All I remember was a devastating bang and then . . . blackness. When I came to, there was chaos, thick black smoke belching from the tank. I shook my head clear of the loud buzzing, trying to focus and make the two of everything I saw become one. Behind me one of my South African crew was lying dead by his gun and another was screaming as blood pumped from the ripped material where his left leg had been moments before. No war in the desert is pretty and the prospect of friends dying around me was precisely why I had kept to myself in the camps. When the surviving crew inspected the ripped vehicle, we realised that if the shells had struck two inches lower, the petrol tanks would have gone up, taking us all with them.

By the end of May we were in battle at Latrun. This was

the site of a medieval monastery just off the roads that run from Jerusalem to Jaffa and Gaza to Ramallah. It was a reminder that this was crusader territory and that East had faced West here for centuries. You can read all about the military manoeuvres in the weeks that followed for yourselves. I am no military historian and at the time of course all we were told was on a need-to-know basis. We were told to take the fortress of Latrun from the Arab Legion and that's what we tried to do. The first step was Operation Bin Nun Alef, named after Joshua, son of Nun in the Bible who had conquered Canaan. With the 7th were the Alexandroni Brigade and we were under the command of Shlomo Shamir who had served with the British in the war in Europe.

There were umpteen delays before Zero Hour finally happened and it wasn't until the small hours of the morning on 25 May that the guns opened up. Our artillery didn't have the range of the Arab guns and we had to fall back, without water and under murderous fire from the fort.

The whole thing lasted two months – two months of sporadic fighting, manoeuvring, marching and counter-marching. The history books will tell you that the Jordanians won and we lost, but it wasn't that simple. We couldn't take Latrun, but we did keep the road to Jerusalem open and that meant we could go on supplying the Jews there with weapons and equipment. Latrun to the Jews became what Dunkirk had been to the British. Dunkirk was a military disaster back in 1940 but if you listened to Winston Churchill (and millions did) it was a heroic victory for the British Army. In fact the whole of the war rested on this basis and the phrase 'the Dunkirk spirit' has become indelibly associated with all things traditionally British. So it was with Latrun. For Winston Churchill, read David Ben-Gurion. One hundred and sixty-eight Israeli soldiers died in these running fights, a fraction of the fatalities inflicted every day by even one of the gas chambers at Auschwitz-Birkenau, but the battle has become part of the myth of the formation of Israel and I was proud to have been part of it.

In the standstill after Latrun while the United Nations organised a truce, we waited. The Arabs had promised to drive us into the sea and that hadn't happened. If David hadn't actually killed Goliath, at least the boy was still on his feet.

When the war ended with a truce between Israel and Egypt in February 1949 we all breathed a sigh of relief. Ben-Gurion let those Arabs who had fled return to their homes and the roads to the kibbutzim in the Galilee region stayed open and free. I went to one of them, Kibbutz Dafna. The place had been founded in May 1939 by Jews from Poland and Lithuania. When I saw it, there was a great deal of bomb damage from the recent fighting, but the waters of the River Dan ensured a greenness that made the place a cool oasis of peace. It was here that I visited my cousin Zvi Wandasman, who I had last seen in Bedzin an eternity before.

I sometimes think I should have stayed in the Palestine that I, in a very small and unimportant way, had helped turn into Israel. It was a young country, with all the hopes and aspirations of a bright future, yet wedded to its past. Thousands of its first Jewish inhabitants were camp survivors like me. Now they faced a different enemy and one that was more persistent than the Nazis. They are fighting them still.

14
A Kind of Justice? A Kind of Peace?

London, 1951. The Festival of Britain lit up the city's skyline in what was supposed to be a 'pat on the back' for the people. Huge, prosperous-looking buildings sprang up along the South Bank, replacing the warehouses and little Victorian homes that Göring's Luftwaffe had reduced to rubble. The cost was a then unbelievable £8 million. All I remember is that a cup of coffee cost ninepence!

How I got back into England is one of those things I'd like to keep to myself. I'd been smuggled out illegally at a time when Britain was still fairly chaotic in the aftermath of war and getting back in was more difficult because everything had calmed down and normal service had been resumed. I travelled from Belgium to France and had to wait until the time was right to cross the Channel.

For Nathan and me, our new lives began officially on 15 September 1953 when the *London Gazette* announced that we were aliens who had been given our naturalisation certificates. Slomo Pivnik and Nathan Pivnik were living in a house we were buying together in N16 and my occupation was given as tailor and cutter. All very humdrum, all very safe. You could say that the *London Gazette*'s announcement didn't just mark the beginning of my new life, it marked the end of the old. But life isn't that simple. I had undergone a sort of 'resettlement in the West' but I could never forget the 'resettlement in the East' and all that that meant. In the camps nobody dreamed, but I dreamed now and those dreams were often nightmares. Like I said, for some of us the war would never be over.

Over the months and years that followed I began to piece together what happened to us during the time of the camps. Much of it remains unknown – and will always remain unknown; especially the unanswerable question of how a supremely civilised people like the Germans could become so seduced by a madman that they allowed the seemingly unthinkable to happen. In the 1950s no one wanted to know about the Jews. Back in 1939 there were a lot of people in Britain who thought that going to war over Poland was a wrong decision. I expect many more in France felt the same. British men and women had died to honour a treaty obligation with a distant country – that was how many of them saw it. And the last thing those who were left wanted was a bunch of Jews stirring things up.

Across Germany there was a rapid de-Nazification programme after the war. This was already happening when I was in Konstanz. People lost their uniforms, slipped off their swastika armbands and walked quietly away. Some of the most notorious were smuggled out of Europe to the anonymous mountains and jungles of South and Central America. The more ordinary just shrugged, denying any knowledge of the camps or of Nazi atrocities. Those who couldn't deny it, who were caught bang to rights, came out with the old nonsense that they were only obeying orders and had no choice. A brilliant study by the American historian Daniel Goldhagen – *Hitler's Willing Executioners* – which appeared in 1996 has conclusively proved that this is a lie.

But if most people in 1950s Britain didn't want to know, we, the survivors, *had* to know. Whether we'd gone to America or Israel or whether we'd tried to resurrect, however impossibly, our old lives, we *had* to find out. For years one of the problems in researching wartime Poland was the existence of the Iron Curtain. While I was still at Konstanz, learning to drive and surviving by my wits, Winston Churchill had made a speech at Fulton, Missouri in which he warned, 'From Stettin in the Baltic to Trieste in the Adriatic an Iron Curtain has descended across the Continent.' He went on to prophesy, in that over-the-top way of his, 'The Dark Ages may return on the gleaming wings of science. Beware, I say. Time may be short.' He was talking about the Cold War, the Communist threat which was then advancing west, and the ever-increasing risk of atomic warfare. The practical side of it from my point of view was that the Russians, enigmatic and humourless as ever, weren't giving out any information about what lay behind that Curtain, and the situation got worse rather than better as time went on.

I have tried to make it clear in this book that the men responsible for the Holocaust as I saw it were the ordinary, everyday members of the SS and the *Kapos* who all too often enjoyed carrying out their bidding. But for the record, the men at the top who engineered the whole thing met their ends in ways that could never atone for the millions of deaths they had caused – but they met them nonetheless. Adolf Hitler, consistently voted today as the most evil man in history, shot himself and/or took poison in the private apartments of his bunker under Berlin as the Red Army were battering the capital at street level. That was on 30 April 1945 while I was in Neuglasau waiting to be marched to the *Cap Arcona*. Thousands of books have been written by cleverer men than me in an attempt to unravel his twisted mind. Heinrich Himmler, *Reichsführer* of the SS that still haunt my nights, put on an eye patch and posed as a Gestapo agent, apparently blissfully unaware that anyone with Gestapo papers was to be arrested on sight. He was stopped by the British at Bremervörde and, during a routine examination by an army doctor, swallowed a cyanide capsule he had hidden in the lining of his coat and died almost instantly. Hans Frank, who had governed Poland from 1939 and promised to make us all slaves, was rounded up and faced judgement at the international court at Nuremberg. He pretended to be shaken by the testimony he had heard in court, confessed his guilt and told everybody he had found God via the Catholic Church. He was found guilty of war crimes and crimes against humanity and was hanged on 16 October 1946.

What happened to the people I knew – to those at the bottom, who were the victims of those monsters and to those who so willingly helped them achieve their insane goals? Liquidation came to Wodzislaw, my beloved Garden of Eden, at about the same time it came to us in the Kamionka. My aunt Lima Novarsky's landlady, whose name, sadly, I don't remember, was one of those rare Christian Poles who risked everything for us Jews. Lima's son – my cousin, Shlomo – was in his twenties by then and the landlady hid him in her house. Unfortunately, she got a little drunk in a pub one night and let slip the fact. It wasn't only in wartime Britain that 'careless talk cost lives' and someone informed the SS. The next day both of them, the old Christian Pole and the young Jewish man, were dragged into the town square and shot.

The last time I had seen my grandmother, Ruchla-Lea, the half-blind old lady had been standing, terrified, with the other old people of Bedzin that August day, the day of the *Aktion* at the Hakoah stadium, when day turned to night. She was herded onto a train and taken those fatal kilometres to Auschwitz. We heard that she lost her sight completely in her last hours; whether this was hysterical blindness caused by her fear, I don't know. I don't know either whether it was better or worse not to see what was happening on the Rampe, where months later I'd be working. Someone, I hope, helped her off the train and onto the platform. Someone, I hope, helped her onto a truck. Someone, I hope, helped her undress. And above all, I hope someone held her hand as she died.

'Already in Heaven', 'up the chimney' – this, I had known for a long time, was the fate of my immediate family: Lejbus Pivnik, the tailor who took his God and his traditions so seriously; Fajgla Pivnik, the mother who bore me, who gave me life and saved it; Hendla Pivnik, with her dreams of *Eretz Yisrael* and the Holy Land; the children, Majer, fourteen; Chana, thirteen; Wolf, eight; and little Josek, six. They were people – my people – but they became statistics and their names weren't even written down. We learned that Hendla had not in fact been selected for the gas chambers immediately as I had assumed. Long afterwards I met Gutscha Diamond, the *Kapo* at the women's camp at Auschwitz-Birkenau who told me to get out any way I could because they were going to kill us all. She told us that Hendla had lasted about ten days. She would have gone through a quarantine-style initiation which I can only hope was less brutal than mine. Her head would have been shaved, so would her armpits and between her legs. She would have been given a shapeless 'shift' dress and a pair of badly fitting clogs. She would have realised, as I came to realise, that her family had gone. And perhaps she gave up. Or perhaps she didn't. After all, she was a fighter was Hendla, a member of *Gordonia* and a big sister to me. Nathan never forgave Gutscha. To the end he believed that she could have done more for her, as a relative, however distant. But Gutscha's own children died in the camp. How could she have saved someone else's child and not have saved her own? After Hendla's ten days, somebody's hand flicked to the left and she walked to the gas chamber.

What about the people back home in Bedzin, those who we had known during the Occupation? Kornfeld, who had kept the pub where my father drank, was one of the first to go when the deportations started. Machtinger, the shoe-maker who was his brother-in-law, went too. A little later, Piekowski the horse dealer, his wife and the daughters I had seen being abused by Machtinger and the policeman Mitschker disappeared as well. Where did they go? Not Blechhammer certainly, because Blechhammer was a rela-tively small camp and it's likely that Nathan would have seen them there. But there were many labour camps in Poland and elsewhere – Auschwitz alone had forty-seven sub-camps – so God knows where they ended up or what their ultimate fate might have been.

I don't know either what happened to the Haübers, the kindly factory manager at Killov's factory and his wife, whose little girl I used to walk to school sometimes. She is still alive, I know, but her parents must be long gone, having walked that difficult tightrope of the war years when for a German to help a Jew meant death. One man who found that out was Alfred Rossner, who ran the factory where my father and Hendla worked. Although I don't remember it from the time, when the first deportations began in Bedzin in May 1942, he went around the streets of the town in his pony and trap, calling out in Yiddish – how many Christian Germans spoke that? – to ignore the orders of the *Judenrat* and refuse to be rounded up. My memory of 6 August 1943 as we waited, terrified, on the platform for a train that would take us to Auschwitz, doesn't include the removal of some people from the crowd. These were Rossner's key workers, all Jews, who were quietly taken back to his workshops, no doubt in exchange for huge backhanders to the officiating SS. Four months later, with a handful of Jews still working and by this time living in his factory, Rossner was arrested by the Gestapo. On charges that were never made clear, they hanged him in January 1944. Fifty-one years later, *Yad Vashem* in Jerusalem recognised Alfred Rossner as one of the Righteous Among Nations.

Old Dombek, the delivery man whose horses Nathan and I loved, ended his days in Auschwitz-Birkenau. I remember seeing him turning before my eyes into a *Müsselmann*; after they'd worked him half to death, the SS took him to the gas chamber. Like all of them, he deserved better.

He didn't live in Bedzin, but, indirectly, my uncle Moyshe had played such a vital part in my life and he never knew it. If, as I believe, Kapo Manfred put in a good word for me as I lay delirious with typhus in Auschwitz-Birkenau, it was because he knew Uncle Moyshe. Others who didn't know him however, sent him to Buchenwald, where he slept in a crowded bunk above Nathan. At some point and for some reason, a faceless SS bureaucrat moved Moyshe on. There were no gassings in Buchenwald; I can only presume that he died in another camp.

You have followed me from Bedzin in that grim train that sweltering August, with frightened men singing the psalms of David. You have followed me to Auschwitz. I left there in what must have been January 1944.

By the summer of that year, as I took my chances in the mine at Fürstengrube, the murder of prisoners was speeded up at Auschwitz-Birkenau. There were no selections any more; everybody who arrived on the Rampe was sent straight to the gas. You can read the statistics for yourself, but they only tell a small part of the story. As the Red Army got ever nearer from the East, a rising sense of panic set in amongst the German high command and the SS. Mass extermination officially stopped in November on direct orders from Himmler, although many survivors know from their own experiences how seriously those orders were taken.

In the last months of 1944 the old barracks we'd called home were dismantled and shipped elsewhere in the Reich. So were the contents of Kanada, the clothes, glasses and false limbs of the dead that still might have a use in the Nazi economy even now. From September the burial pits that contained bodies and the ashes of my family were cleared and filled in with soil, despite the best efforts of the slave labourers doing the work, to keep at least some evidence of mass murder for the liberation they prayed was on its way. The *Sonderkommando*, those poor bastards who dragged corpses from the gas chambers to the ovens, staged a revolt on 7 October. They were told they were being sent to the 'rubber factories' among Auschwitz's sub-camps but they knew perfectly well this was a death sentence. Using pickaxe handles and rocks they attacked the SS guards and set fire to the crematoria. One of the SS men was thrown alive into an oven at Crematorium II. The attempt had been brave but it underlined the hopelessness of open revolt, even as the camp was dying and the SS had their backs to the wall. An estimated 450 prisoners died as a result of the uprising as opposed to only three of the SS.

The last roll-call at Auschwitz was held on 17 January 1945, two days before we marched out of Fürstengrube into the freezing night. A total of 31,894 men and women stood on the *Appellplatz* that day, Birkenau itself having been contracted in size so that effectively the two camps became one. In the death marches that followed an estimated half of these people died, in exactly the same conditions we faced after Fürstengrube.

Auschwitz-Birkenau was liberated by the 60th Army of the First Ukrainian Front on 27 January. It was Saturday – *Shabbat*. There was some fierce resistance at Birkenau from the retreating SS but by three o'clock a makeshift Red Cross flag could be seen waving from the women's camp. One of the women shouted, in Russian, 'Welcome, victors and liberators.' And a soldier shouted back words that very few of them could ever have expected to hear – 'You are free.'

On that day there were 7,000 surviving prisoners at Auschwitz. By the most conservative of estimates, one and a half million died there.

What happened to the men who had run the camp, who had conspired in those years to make our lives Hell? The *Kommandant* there in my time, who I never remember seeing, was Rudolf Höss. I have read somewhere that his father wanted him to be a priest, but the boy had a calling of an altogether different kind. Caught by the Allies, he was put on trial at Nuremberg and his testimony there, along with private papers, has since been published in book form. It remains one of the most important pieces of evidence for the existence of the Holocaust ever produced. Holocaust deniers today can rubbish the memories of people like me as so much distortion and exaggeration, especially after so many years. But Höss actually ran the extermination process and his evidence was collected only months after it had finished. Holocaust deniers cannot dismiss him so easily. What is most chilling is Höss' calm description of genocide as if it's the most normal thing in the world, and the fact that he was more concerned to make a good impression on his superiors than worry about the inhumanity of it all. When his wife asked him if people were really being gassed at Auschwitz-Birkenau, he wrote, 'In the Spring of 1942 many blossoming people walked under the blossoming trees of the farmstead and most of them went with no premonition of their deaths.' How pleasant to note that one of the most efficient mass murderers in history was also – almost – a poet. They hanged Rudolf Höss outside Block 11 in Auschwitz I – the death block where so many had died under his orders. He had a last cup of coffee – the good stuff, not the ersatz rubbish we had – and died on a gallows that still stands today. His body hung for only thirteen minutes before a doctor pronounced him dead. It was the last public execution in Poland.

Hauptscharführer Otto Moll was captured by the Americans and tried by them. The transcript of his interrogation is available for anybody to read today. He insisted that Höss be present throughout so that he could check any errors Höss had already made in his lengthy statement. Even at this stage, when his guilt was evident, Moll tried to wriggle out of things. Yes, he admitted he was in charge of the crematoria, but it was the doctors who had shaken the Zyklon B capsules into the gas chambers and the doctors who selected those who died. As for the numbers involved, he was sure that was overplayed – the kind of nonsense the Holocaust deniers seize on today. Moll complained also about being shackled to a guard when Höss was not. His interrogator, Lt Colonel Smith W Brookhart, was unmoved – 'We are not interested whatsoever in your feelings in this matter.' Found guilty of war crimes at Auschwitz-Birkenau, Fürstengrube and against death marchers, Moll was hanged on 28 May 1946. He was thirty-one.

Today, among several others buried in the grounds of the old Landsberg prison where Hitler once did time, Moll's grave is tended by the State of Bavaria, as though this man should be shown any respect at all.

Unterscharführer Karel Kurpanik, the man whose face still haunts me in the darkness, led a death march in January 1945 and was wounded in an air raid in those chaotic months as the Reich collapsed. He was arrested in his home town of Neu Beuthen, now a suburb of Bytom, on 19 July and tried by a special court in Katowice, close to where so many of his crimes had been committed. They hanged him in February 1946.

I would like to think that all the monsters of Auschwitz received justice but that didn't happen. Dr Josef Mengele, the Angel of Death who had consigned my family to the gas chambers and who had done his best to do the same thing to me, was transferred to KL Gross-Rosen after the liquidation of Auschwitz at the end of January 1945. He served as a doctor with the *Wehrmacht* briefly before disappearing into civilian life. Despite plenty of evidence by survivors, there was little definitive proof which put Mengele at Auschwitz at all until 2007, when a photograph album was presented to the Holocaust Memorial Museum in Washington. The extraordinary photos show the SS at play, officers partying and having picnics in their leisure time when they weren't killing people. Mengele is there, smiling his gappy grin, enjoying the company of Cain.

He was smuggled out of Germany where he'd been working as a farmhand with stolen papers in Rosenheim, Bavaria and got to Argentina. In Buenos Aires he practised as a doctor, carrying out illegal abortions until the authorities rumbled him. Here he met Adolf Eichmann, more than any other Nazi, perhaps, the architect of genocide. But Eichmann's days were numbered by 1960 because he was being watched by Mossad, the Israeli Intelligence Service. When they smuggled Eichmann back to trial in Israel, Mengele ran again, this time to Paraguay, using his real name on his passport. By the late 1960s, the world's mood had changed. On the one hand, the Holocaust was an accepted field of study for historians and the stories of survivors like me were already being collected. On the other – even as early as 1950 – the Americans and even the Russians, who had suffered an appalling loss of 20 million of their people to the Germans, seemed less inclined to hunt Nazis. Even so, it was pretty unbelievable that the Israeli ambassador to Paraguay should say, 'I must confess I was not so eager to find Mengele . . . he was, after all, a German citizen who had committed his crimes in the name of the Third Reich. None of his victims were Israeli – Israel came into existence only several years later.' If even an Israeli is prepared to accept the 'I was only obeying orders' defence, what hope is there for justice?

Mengele almost certainly died in a drowning accident in Brazil and six years later his body, buried with the papers of 'Wolfgang Gerhard' was exhumed and autopsied. The telltale gap in his teeth alone proved who he was, but DNA confirmed it. His son is on record as saying that the Angel of Death remained an unrepentant Nazi to the end and claimed that he had never hurt anyone. Tell that to the hundreds of thousands who fell victim to the casual flicks of his doeskin gloves. Nobody wanted the body of Josef Mengele. To this day it lies in a vault in the Sao Paulo Institute of Forensic Medicine in Brazil.

Below the SS who ran Auschwitz-Birkenau were the *Kapos*, Jew and Gentile, who actively participated in the brutality and the murder. Men like Rudi in the Quarantine Block were too often able to vanish into the chaos of post-war Germany, knowing that most of their victims were dead, changing their names, keeping their heads down.

They became fathers, grandfathers, sweet old men growing older gracefully, and no one wanted to dig up graves or revisit the past. And of course, the *Kapos* had been vulnerable themselves, even in the camps. As long as they danced to the SS tune, they were useful, perhaps even indispensable. But if they transgressed in any way, helped themselves too much, showed kindness, then they would be on their way to the ovens too.

The one who stands out for me is of course Gutscha. I could never really see her as a *Kapo*. She was a nice lady, warm and kind, and lived out her years in Israel. I don't know what she did at Auschwitz-Birkenau. Research and the memoirs of others have confirmed that the women working in Kanada did not have their heads shaved like the others; that Höss set up a brothel, strictly for the SS and certain selected *Kapos*. It is very likely that several members of the SS put aside their ideological revulsion of Jews and had sex with the inmates of the women's camp. I never talked to Gutscha about any of this. All three of her children died in the camp; she'd been through enough. Starting a new life in Tel Aviv, she met and married Moniek Diamond and they had two children, Miriam and Emmanuel. Gutscha died in 2001. She was a lovely woman.

The other *Kapo* – the one who may well have saved my life – was Manfred. Because he was not in my block, I didn't see much of him at Auschwitz-Birkenau and I was never able to thank him for his intervention in the hospital. What happened to him remains a mystery.

What about the boxer, 'Kajtek'? The SS had used him as a punch-bag in Auschwitz-Birkenau, pitting him against bigger, fitter men as their idea of sport. And I am delighted to say he survived, returning to Poland after the war and coaching other boxers. He died in a respected old age in 2003.

Fürstengrube was the scene of a massacre after we left. The last I'd seen of the place was in the darkness of a January night after we'd stood for most of the day on the *Appellplatz* and the SS were burning papers. Those who made the stark choice to stay because they couldn't walk, probably somewhere around 120 of them, the *Muselmänner* and the diseased who had lost the will to live, were left there for a day or two with just a skeleton guard, without water and without food. Some of them, I'm sure, hobbled out of the camp now that the watchtowers held so few. How many of them made it and how many of them were given help by the locals, I have no idea. But the majority didn't even have the strength to do that and they lay on their bunks or wandered the *Appellplatz*, lost, starving and confused, until, even with the sound of Russian artillery getting ever closer, a Waffen-SS patrol turned up, machine-gunned men in their beds and torched the barracks. Anyone who had dodged the bullets burned to death. I don't think there is a record of how many the Red Army found alive a couple of days later, but it couldn't have been many.

Most of the people from the Prince's Mine joined me on the death march so their fates belong to the last phase of my story. My friends Herzko Bawnik, Hersh Goldberg and Peter Abramovitch emigrated to the United States after the war, where Goldberg and Abramovitch became builders. Herzko married and his children and grandchildren adore him still. Hermann Josef, that most slippery of survivors, served a prison sentence – where and for how long, I don't know – and he lived out the rest of his life working as an architect in Nuremberg.

Someone who did not join us on the march was Rapportführer Anton Lukoschek. I have no idea what happened to him until 1948, but on 20 February that year he was sentenced in a Kraków court to ten years' imprisonment. This was the man who had orchestrated the hangings of Maurice, Leon, Nathan and the man who kept the chickens.

Mauthausen was liberated on 5 May by twenty-three soldiers of the 11th Armoured Division of General Patton's Third Army. There were large numbers of Spanish political prisoners there, Communists interned during the Spanish Civil War. The SS had specific orders to herd the prisoners into the camp's tunnels and blow them up, but this didn't happen. A photograph taken the next day shows prisoners hauling down the eagle emblem over the camp's main gate and standing gratefully alongside a homemade banner reading, in Spanish, 'The Spanish Anti-Fascists Salute the Liberating Forces.' The previous night a kangaroo court made up of prisoners had tried and executed eight *Kapos* and six SS men. The 186 steps and the Parachute Wall would be used no more.

Buchenwald had been freed earlier, on 11 April, and by only four soldiers. It must have been surreal for those men of Patton's 6th Armoured Division as they walked in, unopposed, under the clock tower of the main gate. The day before, the prisoners had launched an attack on the SS guards, killed several and drove the rest to hide in the woods nearby. Captain Frederic Keffer, who commanded the unit, was thrown up in a blanket by the hysterical prisoners so many times that he had to put a stop to it. He recalled in an interview years later, 'My, but it was a great day!' If you go to Buchenwald today, you will find the clock tower more or less as Keffer found it and the clock is permanently set at a quarter past three, the time the inmates began to run the asylum and the SS were driven out of Buchenwald.

The Dora-Mittelbau complex, including Tormalin in the Harz Mountains, was liberated on the same day as Buchenwald, this time by the American 104th Infantry Division. They found 3,000 corpses and 750 *Muselmänner* and they took photographs of everything they saw. These are available on-line today – evidence, if it were needed, of the inhumanity of the Reich and the reality of the Holocaust. The Americans burned the disease-ridden barracks and forced local men, who of course professed their ignorance of the camp's existence, to bury the dead. It was the Russians who later filled in the tunnels where the V-1 and V-2 rockets were made.

But the Americans left an indelible stain on Dora-Mittelbau because on 20 June 1945 they whisked away a team from the camp's engineering section and eventually afforded them honour and distinction. I didn't know it at the time but the leading designer of the V-2 rockets, which caused such terror in Britain, was Wernher von Braun who had been a card-carrying Nazi since 1937 and a member of the SS since 1940. He constantly told people after the war that he was forced into both these situations so that he could work on his rocket engineering, about which he was fanatical. He denied ever having visited Dora-Mittelbau where an estimated 20,000 men died and claimed that when he heard about the brutality he upbraided an SS man who threatened to put *him* in a striped uniform if he didn't mind his own business. Since Von Braun was by then a *Sturmbannführer* (major) in the SS, this simply doesn't ring true. French prisoners at the camp claimed that he personally ordered them flogged for sloppy workmanship. I know who I believe.

Two years after I became a naturalised citizen in Britain, von Braun followed suit in America. His role in that country's space programme via NASA is well-documented. Less well known is the rewriting of his recent past by American authorities in 1945 in which he was 'de-Nazified'. I remember seeing a photograph in the early 1960s of von Braun in earnest conversation with President Kennedy – the leader of the free world chatting warmly to a *Sturmbannführer* of the SS. It made my blood run cold.

The desire for vengeance that many Jews of my generation have has nothing to do with cashing in and everything to do with justice. The world is an unjust place and today we have an insane contradiction to deal with. We have a blame culture – everything must be somebody's fault and the fault almost always comes with a price tag. On the other hand, we have a culture in which no one owns up, no one puts up his hand and says, 'Yes, I did it,' or 'Yes, I am to blame.' And since the end of World War II, the only way to gain justice after the appalling experience of the Holocaust is via the courts. The problem with that is that the courts are hidebound by abstract legal issues that rarely make sense to ordinary individuals and they are all too often run by people who are, conversely, too easily seduced by peer pressure. The issue of German guilt was of course hopelessly muddled until the last months of 1989 by the fact that there were two Germanies – East and West – each of them operating under different moral and political imperatives. One instance in which the courts *did* make sense took place in the late 1950s and it involved Nathan. He effectively sued the German government for wrongful imprisonment.

I still have the documentation and find the legalistic language almost laughable. 'The claimant [Nathan] was subjected to the National Socialist persecutory measures due to his Jewish descent . . . The International Missing Persons Service in Arolsen has confirmed the following details i.e. the claimant's arrest in Bendsberg [Bedzin] on 28.03.1943, the subsequent transportation . . . to Buchenwald concentration camp on 10.02.1945 . . . It was at the end of the war that he found himself in a German concentration camp and he had been imprisoned up to this point on the grounds of race.'

Nathan suffered ill-health all his life after the camps and this is why he was demanding compensation. He got it – 3,600 Deutschmarks for a two-year period, the judgment delivered in February 1957. And I got a German pension! Because I had worked in the Killov factory and had paid my 'stamp' at the time, I was entitled to one. It came through as a lump sum in the 1980s, a bizarre and quite extraordinary legacy of the German occupation of Poland, of one man's quest for 'living space' for his people.

Often, though, justice was not done, and that was the case of SS Oberscharführer Max Schmidt. I am no Simon Wiesenthal, no dedicated Nazi hunter determined to track down every last one of the bastards who killed innocent people for a barbarous cause. But Schmidt was different. We'd slept in his pigsty. In his house. As it happened, I'd also slept with his sister-in-law and Herzko Bawnik had slept with his wife. We'd eaten at his table. And we'd let him get away.

It didn't look good from the start. Between December 1963 and August 1965, twenty-one former SS officers from the Auschwitz camp complex faced trial at Frankfurt am Main. They ran through the whole gamut of excuses, from 'just obeying orders' to claiming to have had nothing to do with any brutality at all. I didn't recognise any of the names I read in the papers but I knew the charges against them were the truth. Of the twenty-one, six were sentenced to life imprisonment; these were cases of mass execution of a minimum of 475 people. Eleven received prison sentences of anything from three and a half years to fourteen years' hard labour. Three were acquitted. When I read these results, I couldn't believe it, but it was a measure of the times. Twenty years had gone by since the Holocaust came to an end and there were many in Germany and elsewhere who wanted to forget the past, draw a line and move on. So Pery Broad of the camp Gestapo was found guilty of twenty-two joint murders and complicity in the deaths of a thousand people – he got four years' hard labour. Dr Franz Lucas, a medical officer with Mengele, was found guilty of complicity in the murder of one thousand people. In the dock he said, 'I naturally sought to save as many Jewish lives as possible.' Naturally. He got three and a half years.

I began to assemble a case against Schmidt. I knew he

was responsible for the executions of Leon, Maurice, Nathan and the man who fed his chickens. He also ordered the hanging of the five Polish intellectuals at Fürstengrube. There he shot Chaskele, who had failed to maintain the boiler, and the Russian officer who had tried to escape through the watchtower. In his capacity as *Lagerführer* he ordered the execution of those left behind at Fürstengrube while we took to the roads on the death march and there was a similar massacre at Tormalin. He was responsible for the murder of Kapo Hans the miner. By this reckoning, Max Schmidt had killed, either by his own hand or by his order, several hundred people. And yet he was a free man. My only problem was how to find him.

I contacted the German embassy in London. They didn't want to know. They had lost a war and must have found it very difficult to be operating in a country that had brought them defeat and humiliation by the spring of 1945. One of the minions there actually said to me, 'What do you people want?'

'Justice,' I told him. 'No more and no less.'

In the end they had no choice but to file my complaint on Schmidt. After all, I knew where he lived, and my accusations were so explicit they could not be ignored. The problem of many people trying to bring Nazis to justice is that, years later, they were relying on their fading memories and pointing fingers at old men. Who could believe that that sweet elderly gentleman Klaus Altmann was actually Hauptscharführer Klaus Barbie, the Butcher of Lyon who sent the children of Izieu to Auschwitz, where I heard their screams and saw their bodies? But he was.

In the end the solution to the problem fell into my lap.

I was contacted by the German authorities in 1979 because they intended to prosecute Max Hans Peter Schmidt for war crimes. Three of us ex-prisoners were contacted – Bronek Jakubowicz, who was now calling himself Ben Jacobs and living in the United States, me and someone else whose identity I don't know. I presented the accusations you've read above and waited to be called. I never was. For ten years Schmidt had worked as a coal miner in the Rhineland, in the heartlands of Germany's Ruhr region, and lived under the false identity of Kapo Hans, the miner who he had shot at Tormalin. He must have kept in close contact with his family at Neuglasau because over the years he and Gerda produced three sons. I don't want to sound vindictive, but perhaps there was a vengeful God after all in the case of Max Schmidt; two of his boys died in accidents as teenagers – one drowned and the other was killed on a motorbike.

And it was a motorbike that probably saved Oberscharführer Schmidt from life imprisonment. On trial in Kiel before the High Court there he claimed he knew nothing about the killings on the death march because he had not been there at the time but had been ahead of the column on his bike arranging the next leg of the journey. Needless to say, there was no mention of Chaskele, the hangings at Fürstengrube, the massacre there which I believe he engineered or of the shooting of the Russian officer and Kapo Hans. Since I wasn't called to the court, I couldn't give any testimony under oath and various character witnesses from Neuglasau testified to what a fine fellow he was. Ostholstein had a reputation of being fiercely Nazi under the Third Reich and communities like that, insular and rural, don't shake off old ways quickly. Max Schmidt was a good man. He was a good father. What a tragedy about his sons. And it was all so long ago. You could just hear the old excuses being trotted out. But the depositions Jakubowicz and I had sent couldn't be ignored. There could be no question that men had died in large numbers on Oberscharführer Schmidt's watch and because of that, the High Court of Kiel gave him a ten-year probation sentence. Not bad for a man guilty of mass murder.

In the late 1980s, I was contacted by Dr Gerhard Hoch, an historian from Alveslohe, north of Hamburg. He was carrying out research into the Nazi period in his native Ostholstein and wanted my help. He had come across my name as a deponent in Max Schmidt's trial and was intrigued. Hoch himself had been brought up as a Nazi, had joined the Hitler Youth in the year of its creation and fought in the *Wehrmacht* during the war. It was his experiences after the war that changed him. He spent three years in England and became a Christian and with this new perspective went back to Germany determined to stamp out elements of anti-Semitism and bring war criminals to justice. The result of his research was a book, *Von Auschwitz Nach Holstein: Die Jüdischen Häftlinge von Fürstengrube* – From Auschwitz to Holstein: The Jewish Prisoners of Fürstengrube – which sadly is only available in German. It carries the photo of me taken in those weeks after liberation when I was living in his part of what once had been the Reich.

The other result was a television documentary made by *Norddeutscher Rundfunk* editor Bernd Janssen. I wasn't sure whether to take part in this or not. A television crew were asking me to return to my past, to the end of the death march with men being shot behind barns and the expectation that at any moment the SS might yet kill us. By the 1980s the Holocaust deniers were in full cry. They called themselves Revisionists, which in their case meant they intended to rubbish the truth of the past, especially the war years. So a few Jews died. A lot of people died between 1939 and 1945. Things like that happen in war. As for a systematic plan to carry out genocide, they said, where was the evidence? Of course hundreds of empty cans of Zyklon B are preserved in the museum in Auschwitz-Birkenau; Zyklon B was a disinfectant, used for de-lousing the camps. Rather than a murder weapon, the stuff was used to prevent typhus – it was designed to help us.

But I had survived all that. And more. There was something at the back of my mind, a sense that I had unfinished business in Neuglasau; a job not yet done. So I went, along with help from the 45 Aid Society that regularly supports Holocaust victims, and they sent along Barry Davis, a lecturer in History from Ealing College of Higher Education. The man was an expert on the Holocaust and spoke Yiddish so I felt at home even as I walked again the bleak roads of my memory.

April 1989 was not at all springlike. Hamburg was grey and cold and I was glad to get into the welcoming warmth of Gerhard Hoch's house. With us were three young German techies – the camera and sound crew – and we talked from our different viewpoints about the insanity that was the Third Reich. With us too was Moritz Koopman, a Jew from Amsterdam. He had joined our death march somewhere en route to Neustadt and he and I were going to tell our stories in front of the camera.

A Kind of Justice? A Kind of Peace?

On the quay at Lübeck, where I'd squatted all those years
before waiting to board the *Cap Arcona*, the wind blew
with a vengeance, playing havoc with the sound boom and
shaking the camera. I couldn't help shivering and hoped
the youngsters with us would assume it was the cold. I've
told and retold the story of the *Cap Arcona* many times,
but there, in the place where it had happened, it felt different.
Sleet began to drive into our faces but all I saw was the
grey sea mist and the burning, roaring hull. All I heard were
the screams of dying men and the snarl of aircraft. I was
glad to get away. Moritz had been one of the luckier ones;
as a Western Jew he was accepted onto the Red Cross buses
and for him the war was over.

On the third and final day of filming I stood again outside
that farm in Neuglasau, the home of Max Schmidt where
such bizarre events had happened. In front of an outbuilding
which I don't think was there in 1945 was a huge rectangular stone with a name carved on it – 'Max Schmidt'.
What sort of man has his name carved in four-inch-high
letters outside his home? It reminded me of that other, far
better known, symbol of the Third Reich, the dreadful,
mocking words over the gate at Auschwitz I – *Arbeit Macht
Frei*; Works Sets You Free.

I had been waiting for this moment for forty-four years,
the time I would come face to face with a mass murderer.
Would he, in a spirit of a new-found contrition and guilt,
fall at my feet, as I once had fallen at Dr Mengele's, and
beg forgiveness? Or would he put a bullet in my head for
old time's sake? In the event he took the coward's way out
and sent out his daughter-in-law, complete with dog. 'Herr
Schmidt,' she told us, 'is not at home.' Did I see the curtains

twitch in an upstairs window or was it just a trick of the light? She went back inside and the cameras rolled as I told the story of the death march and the role played in it by Oberscharführer Schmidt.

While filming we met a woman whose family had sheltered on this farm back in 1945 as they fled west from the Russians. I remembered her older sister and I asked her about the kind Miller family who had fed us those delicious schmaltzy potatoes and whose daughter Mendeler the shoemaker had married. Yes, she knew the Millers, but they had moved away long ago. Mendeler and his wife had emigrated to the United States.

Then we came face to face with the old Germany, the Germany of the Reich. A Germany that Germans like to pretend doesn't exist any more. The owner of a petrol station nearby told us he was a *Volksdeutscher* Pole. He was a boy of ten at the end of the war and, he assured us, there were no prisoners here then, nobody in a striped uniform. 'Why do you people,' he wanted to know, 'have to keep on returning to the same thing?'

I told him I was a Jew.

'Ah, you Jews,' he grunted as though I'd pushed a magic button, 'always in trouble, always making trouble . . . I'll tell you they always make trouble, they killed Christ . . .'

I was exhausted after those three days and barely remember the journey back home. I suppose I had done all I could in the context of Max Schmidt. Barry Davis was kind enough to say I'd come through once more and perhaps I had. But all I could remember were the graves of six concentration camp prisoners in Ahrensbök and the inscription carved there – '*Den Lebenden zur Mahnung*'; a reminder for future generations.

I wonder.

There was a curious postscript to all this. Towards the end of the 1990s I was contacted by Pastor Schwab, the Lutheran priest in charge of the Evangelical Church in Ahrensbök. Schwab had met Gerhard Hoch and he had given the pastor my address. One of his congregation was Max Schmidt and the pastor suggested that he and I might meet. Was this a move from Schmidt himself, an attempt at atonement? Or was the pastor, no doubt for all the best reasons, keen to get Schmidt to face his past? I told Schwab I would indeed meet the man on the condition that he write me a letter of apology first. He wrote this to me, in German:

Dear Herr Pivnik,

I learned from Herr Schwab that you wish to have contact with me. I am quite ready to answer anything for you that I can, so ask me. I greet you and remain friendly,

Max Schmidt

Like all historical documents, it raises more questions than it answers. The implication is that I had asked to see him, which wasn't actually true. I was certainly curious to know how he would answer the questions I could put to him: who tipped you off about the planned escape of the Russian officer from Fürstengrube? Why did you shoot Chaskele in the same camp? How can you possibly justify the hanging of Maurice, Leon and the others while you were *Kommandant*? And will you admit, which you did not in the court at Kiel, that you *were* directly responsible for everything that happened on the death march? As for the last line, I couldn't believe the gross hypocrisy of it. How generous of him to greet me and to remain friendly, rather as he had that day at the farm when he turned up with a shaved head and the stolen papers of a man he had shot. I call this my letter of apology but of course it is really nothing of the sort.

That letter was followed by another one from Pastor Schwab telling me that Schmidt had withdrawn his offer to meet on the advice of his lawyers and demanded that I return the letter. That I refused to do – it was addressed to me and that made it mine. And Oberscharführer Schmidt had taken enough from me in the brief months during which our lives were linked.

Max Hans Peter Schmidt died on holiday in Spain in 2001. Towards the end of his life he still held parties at the farm for his cronies of the old school and after enough schnapps they would remember and sing the old songs:

The trumpet blows its shrill and final blast!
Prepared for war and battle have we stood.
Soon Hitler's banners will move unchecked at last
The end of German slavery in our land!

I hope he'll forgive me if I don't join in.

15
Return to Eden

Nathan went back first. We were interviewed separately by University College London in the 1990s as people suddenly realised that Holocaust survivors were a vanishing breed. For years I had been making a living in the art business, buying, restoring and selling paintings. For a while I had my own gallery just off the Portobello Road, the Mecca of antique hunters in West London. Nathan married Jill in 1975 and around the house we shared – they were on the ground floor, I lived above – I built a garden wall with the old skills I'd learned in Fürstengrube. After the experience of so many survivors who had gone back in search of their past, I wasn't keen. Janek the *Kapo*, who had given me a hiding at the Schmidt farm, was murdered by local Poles when he tried to get his house back.

But Nathan went back. He did it with students from various West Midland universities in 1996. The trip was led by Stephen Smith, the founder and director of the Beth Shalom Centre in Laxton, Nottingham. The Centre is the only one in Britain dedicated to the Holocaust and beneath a pillar in its peaceful gardens lies a plot of earth taken from the six death camps of the Nazi regime – a little reminder of Auschwitz on the edge of Sherwood Forest. The party got to Bedzin early one morning and within minutes of getting off the coach they were surrounded by

Poles, all men, mostly young and mostly drunk. One of them exposed himself even though there were several women in the party. Another prodded Nathan in the chest and the mood got ugly. They demanded to know why 'you lot' had come back. There was no chance, they told him, he'd get his property back. 'Why don't you go back to Auschwitz where you belong?'

Bedzin in 1996 was still what it had become fifty-three years earlier when they liquidated the Kamionka; it was *Judenrein*, cleansed of Jews. There were two Jewish memorials and I think Nathan was pleased to see that neither of these, at least, had been desecrated. One marked the site of the Bedzin orphanage and records that 250 children from there had been deported to the gas chambers. The other was a concrete block with menorah on each side, marking the site of the Great Synagogue I had seen blazing when I was a boy of thirteen. Nathan felt touched when the young students in the party began to place stones on the cube, a mark of respect for Polish Jews by Gentiles from far away.

The party was a bit alarmed when Nathan said he wanted to visit the Rapaport school. After the welcoming committee in the coach park, they didn't quite know what to expect. He recognised the basic layout of the red-brick building where he and I had taken off our shoes to protect the polished floors years before. He dashed inside, leaving the rest of them standing in the bitter Bedzin cold for twenty minutes. Then he dashed out again, grinning from ear to ear.

'Come in!' he said. 'The children want to meet you.'

They were ushered into a classroom – the Rapaport

school is still a school for primary children – and everyone stood up as they entered. They sang a Polish song for the visitors and talked about their history project on the Jewish heritage of the town. They were delighted to have a 'real' Jew to talk to because none of them had ever met one. It was an uplifting experience in the end, but Nathan could not help thinking how soon these sweet little children would turn into the anti-Semitic yobs outside.

I have now been back twice. Why? I can't honestly say. It was a mixture of things really. Just as I *had* to know what happened to my family, so I *had* to see what had become of my home. Our group was led by a rabbi and we visited places I didn't know because they have become iconic in the history of Polish Jews – Warsaw, where the inmates of the ghetto rose up and fought a bitter, hopeless war of attrition against the SS; Kraków, where Oscar Schindler saved more than 1,100 Jews from the gas chambers. We went to Wodzislaw, the first time I had set foot in the Garden of Eden for sixty-six years. There are no Jews there now, not since the SS, like the Angel Jophiel, drove them out into the wilderness. The homes of my relatives, my aunt's mill, my shoemaker uncle's workshop have been gentrified and upgraded and are lived in by Gentile Poles.

I took a photograph of the old synagogue on a still snowy street that spring. The glass of its windows had gone and the roof had fallen in. The windows stared like sad, dark eyes and the plaster was cracked and peeling. The ground floor rooms had been used as a rubbish dump. That said it all. I had only ever seen Wodzislaw in high summer when everything was golden beneath a sky of unclouded blue. I shouldn't have gone back.

I shouldn't have gone back to Bedzin either, although I didn't experience the highs or the lows of Nathan's visit. Kazimerz's castle was still there, still a ruin more or less unchanged, except the price of admission had gone up! I wandered the streets with my party and I was surprised that I was remembering names I thought I'd forgotten. Many of the houses were still there, even if they were no longer Jewish. I could almost see my friends and neighbours smiling out of their windows, waving to me from their doors. The furniture factory at Feder's, next door to Welner's, the ironmongers, and the Wechselmans next door to that. The Jakubowics were oil merchants and then came the house of the Shanebergs and the Klingers. I remember that Lejbus Klinger was a passionate Zionist and he had four daughters and a son, an engineer. No doubt they all died in the camps.

I walked under the archway that led to our courtyard and stood again on the flat cobbles where I used to kick a ball around. Number 77 is Number 81 now, but it hadn't changed that much. I could almost see Nathan's bike leaning up against the wall and little Chana skipping with her friends. As I walked in, I felt numb. It was a feeling of such utter loss I can't describe it. Part of me saw my mother in the kitchen, making the *Shabbat* meal with Hendla and Ruchla-Lea. I may have smiled when I thought to myself: Father won't be home. He'll still be at the *stiebel* or locked in earnest conversation with the rabbi.

I had to shake myself clear of all that. There was no rabbi in Bedzin now, no *stiebel*, no synagogue. Someone took a photograph of me standing outside my home. The shadows of late afternoon are falling across the courtyard and you can't see the tears running down my cheeks. I fell ill on one of my visits and ended up in hospital, a newer version of the one Jews weren't allowed to use during the German occupation. I was delirious with pneumonia, part of the old chest weakness I'd had all my life. I remember saying to someone in our party, 'Get me home. I don't want to die here.' It would have been supremely romantic, I suppose: Szlamek Pivnik – the joiner, the builder, the tailor, the art dealer, the survivor – had gone home to die. But Bedzin wasn't my home any more. It was a place I'd dreamed about for so long. But it was empty now, with no heart, and the dream turned out, after all, to be a nightmare.

There was one uplifting moment about my return to Modzejowska Street. I heard them before I saw them, but in the narrow garret loft at the top of the houses in the courtyard I heard and then saw little grey birds, strutting, fluttering and cooing in their cages. Mr Rojecki's pigeons – or at least their descendants – were still there and had come home to roost.

Then we went back to Auschwitz. Auschwitz-Birkenau today is the most infamous of the Nazi death camps because it has been preserved for all time as a monument of man's inhumanity to man. The fences are no longer electrified and well-kept lawns have replaced the irregular surface of the Quarantine Block that I helped make back in those hopeless, desperate, terrible days. The place was full of visitors, mostly young, all of them fascinated. Some of them were schoolchildren from all over the world, carrying out history projects because the Nazis, I know, are big business in school curricula today. I visited parts of the camp I'd never been to before, with the glass cases of the belongings of the dead – the hair, the shoes, the prayer-shawls. I found the block I'd lived in when I worked on the Rampe and could even remember where my bunk had once stood.

But I didn't stay under a roof for long. The old terrible fear came back and I had to get out into the air. I stood again back on the Rampe where striped madmen swarmed around me in my imagination, whispering, 'Tell them you're eighteen. Tell them you're eighteen.' I looked around and where Israeli children were carrying the blue Star of David on their flags and singing their Israeli songs I could still see those other Jews, the Jews of my childhood, stumbling off the cattle-trucks, blinking in the sunshine or the snow. I could hear again the barking dogs, the snarl of the SS commands. And as I looked along the Rampe I saw an SS *Hauptscharführer* in shining boots and carrying doeskin gloves. He looked at me, smiled his gappy smile.

And he flicked his gloves to the right.

Notes on Sources

The central source for this book is Sam Pivnik himself. He has told his story over the years to family, friends and to various media interests but never before in such detail. Between 2007 and 2011, Sam gave a series of taped interviews to his friends Philip Appleby and Adrian Weale. Historian Mei Trow came on board latterly and ghosted the book for Sam.

In the tapes, Sam is reliving experiences that took place from the age of thirteen to twenty-two. He is now eighty-five. Inevitably, some of the details are now hazy in his mind and where this is the case the text of the book says so. Some details are probably too painful for Sam to confront directly. When he says 'I felt numb,' or 'The fear came back,' outsiders reading the book and even those who worked on it can only attempt to understand. The experience of the Holocaust was so agonising and so destructive that it is probably impossible for anyone to grasp it fully.

Lyn Smith, interviewing other survivors for the Imperial War Museum over the last few years, sums up the problem succinctly. 'Many camp survivors get confused about names, locations . . . and no wonder; it is only the emergence of the history, especially since the Eichmann trial in 1961, that there has been massive interest in the Holocaust and the full history and organisation has become known. These people [survivors] would have been in the midst of a chaotic, bewildering, confusing situation – designed as such by the Nazis.'

People of Sam's generation underwent no counselling after their appalling experiences. Today, there is a whole raft of psychological and psychiatric help available to survivors of traumatic events. In post-war Europe, neither the losers nor the winners wanted to know. Holocaust victims just had to get on with it, whichever country they ended up in.

Sam's memories expressed on tape have been verified where possible by multiple revisits by Philip Appleby, checking and double-checking on the events that Sam remembers. He was interviewed in 1989 by *Norddeutscher Rundfunk* for a German documentary and in 2012 he took part in a documentary on the sinking of the *Cap Arcona* for Channel Five. In common with a number of other Holocaust survivors, he was interviewed in 1992 by a research team from University College London.

The events that form Sam's experiences have been placed in context so that readers will appreciate what is happening. For instance, the invasion of Poland by the *Wehrmacht* in September 1939 was misunderstood by Polish adults at the time – they expected the arrival of British or French tanks – so how much was a lad who had just turned thirteen supposed to grasp? The context of the Holocaust has to be explained too, with its racial connotations, but always we come back to the events as Sam saw them, filtered through rumour and propaganda.

What Sam remembers of Bedzin is confirmed by the

available material on www.jewishvirtuallibrary.org, a series of articles, memoirs and essays by Jewish and Polish experts. His memories of Auschwitz-Birkenau can be verified by the vast literature on the camp that is available today, the most impressive of which are *Auschwitz: Nazi Death Camp* published by the Auschwitz-Birkenau State Museum and Douglas Selvage, 1996 (2nd Edition) and *Auschwitz: The Nazis and the Final Solution* by Laurence Rees published by BBC Books in 2005.

Sam's memories of the death march and especially the end of it can be cross-referenced with Dr Gerhard Hoch's *Von Auschwitz Nach Holstein: Die Jüdischen Häftlinge von Fürstengrube* written in 1998. His vivid recollection of the sinking of the *Cap Arcona* can be checked with reference to the official Royal Air Force material best encapsulated in *A Survey of Damaged Shipping in North Germany and Denmark* (1945) and verified today by the Air Historical Branch of the Ministry of Defence.

Further Reading

Avey, Denis with Broomby, Rob *The Man Who Broke into Auschwitz* (Hodder & Stoughton 2011)

Cesarani, David *The Final Solution* (Routledge 1994)

Dwork, Deborah *Children with a Star* (Yale University Press 1991)

Dwork, Deborah and van Pelt, Robert Jan *Holocaust: a History* (John Murray 2002)

Farmer, Alan *Anti-Semitism and the Holocaust* (Hodder & Stoughton 1998)

Garlinsky, Jozef *Poland in the Second World War* (Macmillan 1985)

Gilbert, Martin *The Righteous: The Unsung Heroes of the Holocaust* (Transworld 2002)

Goldhagen, Daniel Jonah *Hitler's Willing Executioners* (Abacus 1996)

Hart-Moxon, Kitty *Return to Auschwitz* (Beth Shalom Ltd 1997)

Hersh, Arek *A Detail of History* (Quill Press 2001)

Hoch, Gerhard *Von Auschwitz Nach Holstein: Die Jüdischen Häftlinge von Fürstengrube* (VSA-Verlag 1998)

Jacobs, Benjamin *The Dentist of Auschwitz* (University of Kentucky 1995)

Lagnado, Lucette and Cohn Dekel, Sheila *Children of the*

Flames: Mengele and the Twins of Auschwitz (Sidgwick & Jackson 1991)

Ligocka, Roma with von Finckenstein, Iris *The Girl in the Red Coat* (Hodder & Stoughton 2002)

Lucas, James *Last Days of the Reich* (Arms and Armour Press 1986)

Müller, Filip *Eyewitness Auschwitz: Three Years in the Gas Chambers* (Routledge & Kegan Paul 1979)

Piper, Franciszek and Swiebocka, Teresa (Eds) *Auschwitz: Nazi Death Camp* (Auschwitz-Birkenau State Museum 1996)

Rees, Laurence *Auschwitz: The Nazis and the Final Solution* (BBC Books 2005)

Shimen, Abramsky and Polansky, Antony *The Jews in Poland* (Basil Blackwell 1986)

Sobolewicz, Tadeusz *But I Survived* (Auschwitz-Birkenau State Museum 1998)

Todorov, Tzvetan *Facing the Extreme* (Weidenfeld & Nicolson 1999)

Whitworth, Wendy (Ed) *Survival* (Quill Press 2003)

Appendix

These lists (the original documents are in the Auschwitz Archives) show that I was registered as prisoner Pivnik, number 135913 at Auschwitz II-Birkenau on 6 August 1943.

They also demonstrate that I was admitted to the prisoner infirmary in the Quarantine Block on 27 December of the same year. Looking at this now, it is obvious I was moved from one hospital to another, but I was too ill at the time to know exactly where I was.

XVII

Lfde. Nº	Häftlings-Nº	Bemerkung	Lfde. Nº	Häftlings-Nº	Bemerkung
1084	141001		1112	140793	
85	161712		1113	A9042	
86	B13350		1114	B6950	
87	A4263		15	141117	
88	B6927		16	B13358	
89	A3388		17	B13359	
90	B6952		18	B13336	
91	B6892		19	141181	
92	B13530				
93	159631		20	B13346	
94	B6972		21	B6973	
95	B13606		22	B13256	
96	B13518		23	B13521	
97	176034		24	B5382	
98	B13310		25	B13519	
99	141104		26	141040	
1100	B7077		27	159664	
1101	113863		28	141245	
1102	174282		29	135913	
1103	B6917		30	140789	
1104	B13332		31	161584	
1105	B13340		32	176805	
1106	113694		33	140999	
1107	B13319		34	161711	
1108	140802		35	141150	
1109	140732		36	B7032	
1110	B13313		37	141019	
1111	B13317		38	141042	

(567/53)

Index

Index